I0759696

TO LEAVE A WARRIOR BEHIND

ALSO BY JON TATTRIE

NON-FICTION

Peace by Chocolate:
The Hadhad Family's Remarkable Journey from Syria to Canada

Daniel Paul: Mi'kmaw Elder

Redemption Songs:
How Bob Marley's Nova Scotia Song Lights the Way Past Racism

Cornwallis: The Violent Birth of Halifax

The Hermit of Africville: The Life of Eddie Carvery

FICTION

Limerence

Black Snow

TO LEAVE A WARRIOR BEHIND

THE LIFE AND STORIES OF CHARLES R. SAUNDERS, THE MAN WHO REWROTE FANTASY

JON TATTRIE

McCLELLAND & STEWART

Hardcover edition published 2026

Library and Archives Canada Cataloguing in Publication

Title: To leave a warrior behind : the life and stories of Charles R. Saunders, the man who rewrote fantasy / Jon Tattrie.
Names: Tattrie, Jon, author
Identifiers: Canadiana (print) 20250258374 | Canadiana (ebook) 20250260441 | ISBN 9780771004216 (hardcover) | ISBN 9780771004223 (EPUB)
Subjects: LCSH: Saunders, Charles R. (Charles Robert), 1946-2020. | LCSH: African American authors—Biography. | LCSH: African American journalists—Canada—Biography. | LCSH: African Americans—Canada—Biography. | LCSH: Fantasy fiction, American—History and criticism. | LCSH: Adventure stories, American—History and criticism. | LCSH: American fiction—African American authors—History and criticism. | LCGFT: Biographies.
Classification: LCC PS3569.A8 Z88 2026 | DDC 813/.54—dc23

Cover design by Andrew Roberts
Cover art: Imaro © James Gurney, BDSP, 2016
Typeset in Sabon by Sean Tai
Printed in Canada

McClelland & Stewart
A division of Penguin Random House Canada
320 Front Street West, Suite 1400
Toronto, Ontario, M5V 3B6, Canada
penguinrandomhouse.ca

1 2 3 4 5 29 28 27 26 25

To my wife, Giselle Melanson Tattrie.
Every book begins as a long conversation with you.

CONTENTS

INTRODUCTION

GRIOT OF SWORD AND SOUL: THE LEGACY OF CHARLES R. SAUNDERS

BY SHEREE RENÉE THOMAS

Charles R. Saunders, a luminary whose light continues to illuminate the genre of speculative fiction, has left an indelible mark on the literary world. His words, like stardust, scattered across the pages of his works, ignited imaginations and challenged perceptions. I first encountered Charles's work from the 1970s and '80s, discovering his fantasy short stories. These tales introduced me to a world of adventure, magic, and myth, where I first encountered the formidable figure of Dossouye, a warrior queen who defied societal expectations and blazed her own trail. Dossouye, an unusually independent and strong Black woman character in fantasy, was groundbreaking because she was inspired by the real-life female warriors of the King of Dahomey in West Africa. Charles's memorable creation was among the first such characters in sword and sorcery, appearing around the same time as powerful women in Octavia E. Butler's *Patternmaster* series (1976–84) and Samuel R. Delany's *Return to Nevèrÿon* series, which began with *Tales of Nevèrÿon* in September 1979. Like those in the pioneering works of Butler, Delany, and Jewelle Gomez (*The Gilda Stories*), Dossouye challenged stereotypes and inspired countless readers.

In 1998, I reached out to Charles, eager to reintroduce him to the literary world. At the time, many believed he had passed away, but I discovered that he was living in Nova Scotia, where he was highly respected for his journalism and creative nonfiction writing. His return to the literary scene was met with enthusiasm, and his inclusion in *Dark Matter: A Century of Speculative Fiction from the African Diaspora*, with his story "Gimmile's Songs," was a significant contribution to the volume and marked a wonderful renewal of Saunders's fiction writing career. He later contributed the original story "Yahimba's Choice" to *Dark Matter: Reading the Bones*, which made it clear that he had far more stories to tell us.

Charles is often credited with creating the sword and soul subgenre, a blend of fantasy, adventure, and historical fiction rooted in African myth, history, and culture. His iconic character, the swordsman and adventurer Dossouye, has captivated readers for decades. Dossouye, a complex and multifaceted character, embodies the spirit of adventure and the pursuit of justice. Her first story, "Agbewe's Sword," appeared in Jessica Amanda Salmonson's *Amazons!* in December 1979, an anthology that went on to win the 1980 World Fantasy Award. Dossouye later appeared in Marion Zimmer Bradley's *Sword and Sorceress* anthologies, two landmark publications that sought to increase the number and recognition of female heroes in sword and sorcery fiction. It's worth noting that Dossouye predates the Dora Milaje, the female warrior guard in the *Black Panther* comics created by writer Christopher Priest and artist Mark Texeira, who first appeared in 1998. This highlights Charles's pioneering role in creating strong Black female characters in speculative fiction, years before they gained mainstream recognition.

His influence extends far beyond his own work. Charles was a mentor to many, including author and publisher Milton Davis, who discovered his work in the first volume of *Dark Matter* and was inspired to pursue his own writing as a fantasy and science fiction author. Milton's company, MVmedia, published *Abengoni: First Calling* in 2014 and *Nyumbani Tales* in 2017. Charles also inspired author and publisher Uraeus to create Sword & Soul Media to publish *Dossouye,* the collected short stories featuring the iconic character, in 2008 and *Imaro: The Naama War* in 2009, and *Dossouye: The Dancers of Mulukau* in 2011. Charles's legacy continues to inspire new generations of writers, who draw upon his rich tapestry of myth and legend.

Charles was a kind, erudite, and generous writer, and I was honored to have had the opportunity to work with him. His insightful essays, such as "Why Black People Should Read (and Write) Science Fiction," which appeared in *Dark Matter* in 2000, were a testament to his intellectual depth and his commitment to fostering diversity in the genre. This essay revisited his earlier work, "Why Blacks Don't Read Science Fiction," first published in 1977 in the *Windhaven* fanzine, where he lamented the lack of representation and challenged prevailing assumptions about Black readers' interests. As he eloquently stated in an April 2008 Black Science Fiction Society blog post, "In the segregated fifties of the 'Golden Age,' Black science fiction readers would have learned that the stars were as closed to them as the lunch counter in a Birmingham Woolworth's. That was then; this is now."[1] He saw rare exceptions to that exclusion in the works of Leigh Brackett (Sim in her 1945 novelette "The Vanishing Venusians"), Ray Bradbury ("Way Up in the Middle of the Air," which captivated me as a young reader as well), L. Sprague de Camp (Percy Mjipa, the Kenyan interstellar colonial official in *The Tower of Zanid*), Mack Reynolds (who

---

1 "A Bit of History," https://blacksciencefictionsociety.com/profiles/blogs/2010448-BlogPost-3581.

"concocted a combination NAACP / Peace Corps in his 'El Hassan' books, *Black Man's Burden* and *Border, Breed, Nor Birth*"), and Arthur C. Clarke's last man standing in *Childhood's End*.

It was a privilege to include Charles's work in my first anthologies and to include W.E.B. Du Bois's "The Comet" and "Jesus Christ in Texas" in *Dark Matter*. Neither Charles nor I suspected that a third science fiction story, "The Princess Steel" by Du Bois, would be rediscovered later in the 1926 issue of the NAACP's *Crisis* magazine that Du Bois edited. I discussed the inclusion of the groundbreaking comet story with Charles, and he enthusiastically agreed, providing me with a copy from his personal collection that was an earlier edition of *Darkwater: Voices from Within the Veil*, which I had on my own shelf. This was a fitting tribute to Du Bois's legacy and a testament to the rich history of Black speculative fiction of which Charles was a part.

Charles R. Saunders was a pioneer of Black speculative fiction, whose work continues to inspire and amaze. His groundbreaking stories and insightful essays have left an enduring legacy, shaping the landscape of the genre, and paving the way for future generations of writers. He even broke ground in film, with his screenplay for the 1986 movie *Amazons*, based on his short story "Agbewe's Sword"; the movie poster was created by artist Boris Vallejo. Thanks to the efforts of his good friend Taaq Kirksey, who spearheaded a fundraising campaign embraced by Charles's devoted fans, a beautiful monument and tombstone now grace his final resting place in his hometown of Halifax, Nova Scotia. Driven by a deep admiration for Charles's work, Kirksey had moved his family to Los Angeles to champion a Hollywood adaptation prior to his friend's death. The monument, designed by the talented artist Mshindo Kuumba, features a striking depiction of Imaro, and was erected in 2021 as a testament to Charles's profound impact on the literary world and the enduring love he inspired in his friends and fans. It is comforting to know that one of Charles's most celebrated characters stands watch over him, forever protecting his brilliant creator.

As you delve into the pages of this lovingly written new biography of Charles by Jon Tattrie, you will discover the fascinating and humble man behind the myth, the writer who dared to dream and to create new worlds for you and for me. As you explore his life, his work, and his impact on the world of speculative fiction, I hope you will appreciate the extraordinary gift he has left us, which is the gift of his imagination, rooted in his love and appreciation for Africa and his connection to that diverse and ancient heritage. But most importantly, I hope you will join us, his many fans and supporters, and celebrate the enduring legacy of Charles R. Saunders, a visionary whose stories will continue to resonate and inspire for generations to come.

I often think about how thrilled Charles would be to see the explosion of talented African writers creating original and innovative science fiction and fantasy works today. In his own way, he helped to create more space for such publications, and I am sure he would have been a great supporter, adding his voice to the chorus of praise.

May the legacy live on!

1

THE CALL

The call to adventure came from a stranger in July 2020. It was a regular day in that plague year. Amid the mix of work emails came one from an address I didn't know, but with a subject line that immediately pulled me in: "Charles Saunders."

Hi Jon, I am hoping you might know or know about the writer, Charles Saunders, who lives in Dartmouth, the message opened.

Reading his name conjured up strong images of the towering newspaper editor I'd worked with a decade ago. Built like a heavyweight boxer, but he moved like a cat. A genius with words and a wealth of writing wisdom, Charles was the senior editor on the Halifax *Daily News* and had written an iconic column on Black issues. The *Daily News* was a scrappy newspaper that broke a few noses in our city. Politicians feared us and regular folks cheered us. I'd started working there as a night-shift copy editor in 2006. One colleague said working on the news rim was like doing your homework with friends late at night. We'd fall into a studious silence as we cleaned up the writing, checked the facts, and crafted the headlines, then burst into laughter when someone—occasionally Charles—made a pun too rude to publish, but too delightful not to share.

Often, as the laughter faded, one of us would look over to the centre of the rim, where Charles sat with his back to us, facing the harbour window, to ask him if we'd accidentally split an infinitive, only to find his empty chair spinning. He'd disappeared once more.

But Charles always popped up again to split the lips of the fat cats who ran the city with a blistering editorial that put their foolishness in plain English. He loved Canada, loved writing—and was well-loved by his adopted home. People would work with Charles for years before hearing a rumour that he hadn't always been a Canadian, that he'd started life elsewhere—in America, if you could believe it—but had moved north decades ago.

Charles had been a legend but, like all of us at the *Daily*, took a knock-out blow on February 11, 2008, when the fat cats got the last laugh. The world Charles and I shared blew apart that day, and it ended our work friendship. Our newspaper had been bought by a media chain, then sold, then sold again. We tried to ignore the latest new owners and their plans to "turn this ship around." We journalists dreaded to think what they meant by that. We were already sailing on open waters. Did they see an iceberg they wanted to hit?

Usually, the newest owners soon forgot about their little east coast tabloid. We liked it that way. But the people who bought us that last time didn't forget about us. They kept sending in smiling professionals in fine suits who talked about the future and how better days were ahead for our newspaper. We kept quiet. Our better days would begin as soon as they left.

But they didn't leave. Instead, a few months into the big turnaround, they ordered staff to gather on a Monday morning. We formed a scrum around the slick big-city suit they'd flown in from Montreal to teach us how to do our jobs. He'd promised us sunlit uplands but now stood before us with a frozen face. You can't BS a room full of journalists, so we stared at him coldly. He told us it was over. The latest new owners had pulled the plug. We were all fired. The newspaper was dead. It was about then that we noticed the grey-suited sympathetic smilers lurking in the corners of the newsroom. They told us lay-offs were hard, but they would educate us about our severance packages. And then they would escort us off the property. A pointless rage built up in the disbanded news corps. We were tempted to burn the place down. Instead, we gathered our notebooks and family photos and were escorted out. Somehow reporters from our rival newspaper, the stately *Chronicle Herald*, found out what was happening and their photographers shot a couple of us as we came down the front steps of our building one last time. It was humiliating—we couldn't even break the news of our own demise.

In the drunken bacchanalia that followed, many of our reporters, photographers, and editors left Halifax for jobs out west or in the States. We partied to celebrate their leaving. Others gave us a shiver up the spine when they took jobs on the Dark Side—working in public relations. We roasted them, got drunk, and hoped we wouldn't be next. Most of us moved on. A smaller group stayed alive as freelance journalists, or got casual work in other newsrooms. Journalism is a crazy career that seems mostly to want to leave you broke and disillusioned, but we preferred that to the life-draining success of a regular job. Getting paid looked a lot like selling out.

I thought back to those chaotic after-days. I'm sure Charles was invited to all the farewell parties, but I never saw him turn up, except once. It was a small, sober gathering of the remainders of the news rim. Those of us who had sat like friends doing their homework at night. It was the highest honour for our departing colleague, to have Charles celebrate him in flesh and blood. We didn't ask Charles what was next for him; we didn't ask that of ourselves in those days.

I'd stayed in the city, stayed in journalism, hanging on by my fingernails. Charles . . . what had happened to Charles? I could recall seeing him at least once in the decade since our newspaper shut, or maybe twice. I'd heard people mention his name more often, especially on the annual February Deathiversary we threw for our fallen newspaper. What was the last thing I'd heard about him?

And, come to think of it, why was this person writing to *me* about Charles? I couldn't imagine how someone I didn't know would know I knew Charles. I read on.

The last time I was in Halifax (a few years ago now), Charles marched me into a bookshop and insisted I buy The Hermit of Africville. *I was glad he did and I'm glad you wrote it. Thank you for doing that.*

I was absurdly pleased to receive Charles's praise second-hand. And I remembered that was one of the times I'd seen him after the newspaper closed—in Africville in 2010, for the launch of my biography of the legendary civil rights protester Eddie Carvery.

I turned back to the message.

A longtime friend, I haven't heard from Charles since early March, nor has another longtime friend who looks after his website. We would very much like to have assurance he is OK, the writer continued.

He is though a very private person and we seek to be very discreet in any inquiry, certainly not have attention drawn to him in any way. Do you by chance see or hear anything of Charles these days? And if perchance you are in touch with him, could you let him know we'd be glad to hear from him when it is convenient? Thank you.

I'm sorry to trouble you but these are strange times when friends everywhere are looking out for each other. Thank you, Jon. We would be very grateful for anything you might be able to tell us.

Because of the pandemic, even healthy young extroverts were spending twenty-four hours a day inside, and alone if they lived alone. Charles had always lived alone, as long as I had known him, and didn't seem like the kind of guy to post upbeat messages on social media, as he was locked down on the inside, too. I suspected he had mountains of books to keep him company, including a few he'd written himself. In truth, I was glad for the opportunity to barge into his life. Every time we gathered for the Deathiversary, my eyes kept tracking to the pub door, hoping to see it push open to reveal giant Charles, his dignified face surrounded by a lion's mane of hair and beard that seemed of one cloth. He was our Gandalf, pulling himself out of distant realms and returning to our mundane earth to join us for a drink and to treat us to his company. And like Gandalf, just when you thought he was gone forever this time, he'd turn up—in the flesh, or on paper. He hadn't appeared in my life for far too long. I decided on the spot I would appear in his.

Thanks for writing, I typed. *I have long admired Charles as a person and a writer and am honoured to hear he recommended my book to you. We worked together on a newspaper and I learned a lot from him.*

I have not heard anything from him recently. His Facebook page seems active, but I don't see any comments from Charles. I am quietly asking around. I agree with you that he is a very private man and I will try not to barge into his life, if he's merely wishing to be out of touch now. I will update you when I know more.

I signed off, sent it, and went back online. I wrote Charles a couple of messages through email and social media. I tried as many mutual friends as I could think of, mostly journalists from our days on the *Daily News*. The answers all sounded the same, like some coded message: *No, I haven't heard from Charles in a while, but I'm not worried because he often drops out for weeks or months*. My old colleague had turned into quite a recluse, I realized. Everyone thought it was just them. We all cherished Charles. He may only have lived across the harbour from most of us, but he could turn that water into a vast ocean, and even emails, travelling near the speed of light, could take months to reach him.

Charles didn't write back to me. I considered heading over to his house and knocking on his door. As soon as I thought that, "11 Primrose Street, Dartmouth" popped into my head. That was weird. Why did I know where Charles lived? I'd never been to his house. In fact I'd never heard of anyone going to his house. Maybe I'd driven him home one night after work? We edited the newspaper until midnight on days with late-breaking news—back when you actually had to stop the presses to get the drunk-driving politician on the front page—and sometimes the last bus had already gone. Maybe that was it. I had a sporty Toyota Yaris in those days. I smiled trying to envision Charles squeezing into the little hatchback but couldn't find the memory file. His three-storey apartment building sat just off a major road that connected my home to his home, and both of us to downtown Dartmouth, so I drove by it. No sign of him. No sign of anyone, really. Nova Scotia was under a state of emergency, and we had been ordered to "stay the blazes home," as our premier put it. Police had been handing out big fines to people caught walking in a park, or in an apartment building that wasn't their home. I nearly convinced myself to break all the Covid rules and knock on his door. But turning up on Charles like that, unannounced and nosy in the quiet of quarantine? That seemed wrong. As far as I knew, Charles was connected to the outside world online and by phone and was choosing not to respond to me or others. And I guess I worried that if I did barge in on Charles, he might vanish from my life altogether. I'd rather have him as a dear old friend I never saw than a former friend I bumped into. I drove home.

When all the Halifax connections turned up nothing, I went to work as a journalist. Searching his name took me to CharlesSaundersWriter.com, which redirected me to DifferentDrumming.com. The landing page proclaimed it to be the home of Charles R. Saunders, creator of sword and soul. The page showed a painting of a pensive man with an ancient look about him, balancing a spear on his shoulders as sunlight drifts into his cave. I was immediately struck by the message that accompanied it. "Welcome to my new Website and Blog, both of which I am calling *Things Fall Together.* This designation is a tribute to the title of the Nigerian author Chinua Achebe's classic novel, *Things Fall Apart.* And, indeed, things often do fall apart and shatter, as a look at any day's newspaper headlines will tell you. But sometimes, things fall together and connect, or perhaps interlock. I'm hoping that on this site, there will be some interlocking, even as things are bound to fall where they will."

Huh.

Charles wrote that his old website focused on the fantasy genre, which he'd been writing since the 1970s. That surprised me, but then I remembered a moment from my stint at the *Daily News*. I was working on my first novel, and one day Charles gave me a signed copy of *Imaro*. I could still picture the cover: a Black warrior wielding a blood-dipped sword, roaring triumphant over a mountain of men and lions. When I read it, I loved it, even though I didn't entirely know what to make of it, and I would later learn my white brain had missed half the story.

He warned his website would contain "shameless self-promotion ... is there really any other kind?" And he promised his new platform would host reviews and essays about fantasy writing, plus his thoughts about current affairs and "(gulp)" politics. "One of the most enjoyable aspects of my previous site was the interaction and feedback generated in the forum section. I would like that exchange of thoughts and opinions to continue," he wrote. "So please feel free to comment on what you read on this site. And let's hope that as the world progresses, things fall together and not apart."

His website and social media led to a web of friends, collaborators, and fans across Canada and the U.S. I tracked them down, and one by one the replies returned to me: *No, I haven't heard from Charles in a while, but that is no cause for concern. He does drop out.*

Those of us in Canada didn't know about his American fantasy publications, and I discovered that people in America knew little of his Canadian journalism. I kept digging. I pictured myself sitting down with Charles post-pandemic and telling him all I'd learned about him. I had so many questions. Why did dozens of people think they were his only friend in the world? As July turned into

August, and the virus turned every day into Covid the 19th, I got back to that original message that had started my journey into the extraordinary inner world of Charles R. Saunders. I answered the call to adventure with a no. No, I hadn't been able to reach Charles directly, but no, he wasn't in trouble. Everyone seemed to think he was fine, enduring the lockdown in his own way. One person had spoken to him in March and all had been well with him then. So we assumed all was well with him now. The writer thanked me, and we promised to stay in touch.

A few weeks passed before I heard from her again. She carried devastating news: Charles was dead. He'd been dead the whole time I was looking for him. He'd died alone. The grim tidings were drummed across North America, Europe, and beyond, proclaiming the news: He is dead. All of us were already stuck in the pandemic's cobweb of grief, and the brutal loss of our friend ripped hearts open. People wrote about a semi-mythical man who had created a fantasy world that freed them in reality. Nyumbani, his other-Africa, had become their home. We all swim on our inner oceans, studying the horizons for someone who sees us, and yearning to be seen. Charles saw people and, through his writing, they saw themselves. The effect was electric. I spoke to several of his friends and readers and prepared to write an obituary for CBC, Canada's national news organization and my employer. I realized a very strange thing: Few of the Americans had ever met Charles in person. Most had never heard his voice, nor seen him in motion. Only a few pixelated photos, letters and, later, emails. I knew he'd left America at some point, but I hadn't realized he'd stayed up north with us for the rest of his life. It seemed he'd only returned to America once in his fifty-year exile—for the funeral of his mother. I would later learn I was wrong about that, too.

I spoke to Milton Davis, Charles's publisher in later years, and to Taaq Kirksey, a young man determined to bring Imaro, the hero of Nyumbani and the king of Charles's writing heart, to the screen. Friends from the Halifax *Daily News* shared memories of Charles—and rare photos. I had the uncanny sense that I'd been drawn into the centre of a web that Charles had been carefully weaving for decades. People emailed me to tell me they'd gone to Lincoln University with Charles in the 1960s and were saddened to hear about his lonely death. I heard from people who knew him well in Ontario, when he'd first moved to Canada, and who had kept in touch with him over the years. And I heard from his fans around the world who wondered what we could do for his legacy. Nearly everyone thought they were the only person Charles kept in touch with, and many felt that burden heavily and did their best to keep an eye on Charles, often from a distance. David Woods, an artist with whom he'd helped found the Black Artists Network of Nova Scotia in the 1990s, lived near Charles and would drop by on occasion with an offer of work, or of friendship, or just to see how he was keeping. But Charles had in those last years retreated from outer life. He kept in touch via letters and online messages, but rarely in person.

I thought I was done with the Charles chapter of my life but bolted upright in my bed at three a.m. as if someone had yelled. *Where is the body?* I'd never buried anyone before. It always just . . . happened. An aunt would die and there would be a funeral and she would be buried. It seemed like something that occurred naturally. But Charles had died alone in May 2020. His death was made public in late August.

Where is his body?

What happened to poor people when they died alone in my province? Was he spellbound in some morgue? Abandoned in a pauper's grave? I tossed and turned. Where was his body? What would happen to Charles's legacy? To Imaro?

When the sun finally lanced its life-giving light through the red spruce and the white birch and into my bedroom, the call to adventure was clearer than crystals. This couldn't be the end of Charles R. Saunders. This couldn't be the end of Imaro. This time I said yes.

2

UNCLAIMED REMAINS

Troy Wiggins is the publisher of *FIYAH*, an American magazine that publishes speculative fiction by Black authors. I saw him post about Charles's death on social media and reached out to him for an interview. He agreed to take a call at his home in Memphis, Tennessee. He told me he had first read Charles's *Imaro* novels in the 2000s. "How I describe him is a genius Black man writing sword and sorcery fantasy set in Africa," he told me. "He's the father of sword and soul."

Troy, like Charles, grew up reading and rereading J.R.R. Tolkien and other fantasy classics. And just when he had totally escaped into those worlds, he ran face-first into the same nasty racism he was trying to escape in the real world. "I stopped reading science fiction and fantasy in high school because I was tired of not seeing Black people," he told me. "If Black people or Brown people showed up in them at all, we were the antagonist, or the comic relief, or the secondary characters who didn't contribute much to the story. Or we died."

And then he found *Imaro*. It changed his life from the first page. Black people were the antagonist, the comic relief, the secondary characters—and of course, the heroes, too. Everyone was Black. Troy never forgot how it felt to be seen in full dimensions.

"It was a world filled with people who could be my ancestors. I'm an African American male, and I remember feeling vividly the sensory information: how the air smelled, how the people looked, how they were very regal and how they were very human," he told me.

At the centre of Charles's epic other-African adventures was this powerful, vulnerable warrior named Imaro. Deep in his core, Imaro knows he's destined for great things, but nobody believes him. He comes to doubt himself. Troy told me he, too, had doubted himself. But feeling bold one day, he wrote a letter to Charles and included a short story. He'd always wanted to write sword and soul but hadn't known it existed until he found Charles. "He actually read my story and gave me comments. For a fanboy like me that was pretty amazing." And it was good advice. Troy's story included a clunky piece of technology that he loved, but it didn't quite work in the story's world. Charles suggested ways to make it work, which Troy tried to implement. And eventually, the story was published. Most of the messages Troy received praised exactly that section of the story as its strongest part. "He had the ability to see through what I was trying to do and give me advice on how to rework it to better serve my story, which is something that great editors do."

I talked to some of my colleagues at the *Daily News*, and a few who predated my time, whom I only knew by reputation. Editor Doug McKay hired Charles to work for the newspaper in the 1980s. "Charles was a big, kindly, very gentle man with a huge interest in boxing. And he was a gifted writer. We saw that in a small way in his weekly column at the *Daily News*," Doug told me from his home in Toronto. "He was covering Black Nova Scotia, in part, but he was also doing a remarkable job of explaining Black Nova Scotian life to predominantly white readers. He was doing in a way what Black Lives Matter has been doing this year in trying to explain the Black experience to white people."

I had noticed Charles's recent novels had been published by MVmedia, so I tracked down the publisher, Milton Davis, at his home in Fayetteville, Georgia. By day, he's a research and development chemist; by night, he writes and publishes Afrofuturism and other Black speculative fiction. He told me that when *Imaro* was first published, the hero was called the Black Conan, drawing comparisons to Robert E. Howard's legendary barbarian. "Most people would put Charles right up on the same level as Robert E. Howard, and there are some people who would argue his work was really above that. His prose was just amazing," he told me. Milton went on to say *The Naama War*, the fourth book in the *Imaro* series, was Charles's finest. "At this point you shouldn't even be comparing Charles with Robert E. Howard. It blew me away."

When I mentioned my years working beside Charles, Milton asked what he looked like, how he moved, and about the sound of his voice. Despite their deep partnership over many years, they never met. I shared my impressions of Charles in flesh and blood from the two years we'd spent on the night shift.

I heard a similar account from Taaq Kirksey, who considered Charles a mentor and a friend. Like Troy, he read *Imaro* in the 2000s and immediately knew his life had changed. He wrote to Charles. "I told him I will make it my life's work to translate your vision to the largest possible audience I can. Charles being Charles, he was agreeable to it," Taaq told me in a phone call from his home in Los Angeles. He'd just moved his young family from Brooklyn to L.A. expressly to work on the *Imaro* project. Taaq grew up devouring the speculative fiction classics—and having to stomach their often racist undertones. "You are expected to make a rough peace with the racial attitudes of the authors. Charles rectified that at the outset," he said. "Charles reminded me of a wizard. He worked a certain magic that allowed you to really see and feel and experience the sentiments his characters were feeling or struggling against."

He discovered Charles had an astonishing ability to create "lived-in" worlds where Imaro might slay a supernatural beast but then struggle to keep his marriage together or be a good father. "It was grown-up in a way I had never seen this kind of fiction be. It was clearly wrought from the mind of someone who had lived a full life, and it was a response both to things in Charles's own life that might have been missing, and things in the wider culture that were certainly missing. It's just beautiful."

His fantasy worlds were deeply rooted in the human experience, Taaq said. "Being a hero isn't always riding off into the sunset. Sometimes there are real sacrifices, even for saving the world. I've never seen anyone articulate that—and certainly not with a face of colour, a face that looks like mine." Making *Imaro* into a movie was hard work, and Taaq was soon reeling from rejection. For *Imaro*, but occasionally from Charles, too. "Charles could be so hermetic, so reclusive," he told me.

Taaq had never met his hero but resolved to change that in 2019. The movie was inching forward, and he had a cheque he wanted to personally deliver to Charles. "It was a triumph for me because I felt I was finally in a place where I could help him financially." He emailed him to say as much, but Charles didn't write back. Taaq couldn't figure out what to do. He only had a small window for a visit to the far east coast of Canada, so he hopped on a plane and hoped for the best. In the summer of 2019, he turned up unannounced at an address he had written on many envelopes: 11 Primrose Street, Dartmouth, Nova Scotia. "I practically had to break into the place. I get into the vestibule, rang the bell, no response. Management let me into the building, I knocked on his door, no response. I went around the side—thank God he was on the first floor—and banged on his window. No response," he said. He tried a few more times. Finally, the door slowly opened, revealing Charles himself. "We didn't say anything. We just smiled at each other and hugged." They spent the day together. It was a bit awkward, but they spoke and shared the space. That was more than enough for Taaq. He struggled to understand how Charles lived a secluded life of apparent poverty on the outside, and of unimaginable wealth and companionship on the inside. "Here was this guy who clearly had left this indelible mark, but I got the impression he didn't leave his house much," Taaq said to me. "And it begged the question for me, how is he doing all these things?" But Taaq had an answer to his own question. "He was a wizard."

I'd managed to gather some basic biographical information about Charles for the obituary I was writing for CBC, but huge chunks of his life were missing. From working with him, I knew his mother had died and he'd gone home for her funeral. I didn't know her name. Otherwise, his formative years were blank. On his website, Charles wrote that he'd been born in Elizabeth, Pennsylvania, in 1946, had studied at Lincoln University, and moved to Canada around 1970. That was all anybody seemed to know about his life before exile. I published what I had, frustrated that I knew so little. The obituary headline read: "The Extraordinary Inner World of Charles R. Saunders, father of Black sword and soul."

> *Those who knew Charles R. Saunders from the outside never would have guessed at the vast universes contained within him.*
>
> *A big, solid man with a lion's mane of beard and hair, he moved about his Dartmouth, N.S., neighbourhood like a cat, seemingly able to make his earthly frame disappear. One former colleague described Saunders as "the second-quietest journalist I've ever known." Another thought he was dealing with a wizard.*
>
> *Born in Elizabeth, Pa., in 1946, he earned a psychology degree from Lincoln University. In 1969, the U.S. draft summoned him*

to fight in Vietnam. Instead, he moved to Canada, living in Hamilton before settling in Ottawa for 15 years. In 1985, he moved to Nova Scotia, where he lived for the rest of his life.

He worked as a civil servant and teacher until 1989, when he launched a career in journalism. Saunders died in May at 73, though word of his passing was only made public this month.

The obituary was finished, but it was hard to feel satisfied. I kept thinking about what I didn't know. Chiefly, where was his body? A little research taught me that the Nova Scotia medical examiner investigates any "suspicious or unusual" deaths, including when someone dies "when in apparent good health, when unattended by a physician." That seemed to be what happened to Charles, so I found a number and called. The person who answered checked their records and confirmed that they had been called to 11 Primrose Street in May and had taken custody of the remains of Charles R. Saunders. He was placed in the central mortuary. The staff member told me about the competing pressures the medical examiner's office then faces: out of respect for the deceased, they want to bury the person as soon as possible; yet out of respect for the living, they want to allow as much time as possible to find someone before the state makes those decisions. Charles's time expired after three weeks, and they transferred custody of his remains to the Nova Scotia public trustee. When someone has been declared mentally incompetent, the public trustee takes legal control of their life and makes financial and health decisions for them. The same goes for children who find themselves alone in the world, and for missing people. And when someone dies in Nova Scotia and no one claims their remains, the public trustee takes control. I called their office.

"Hi, my name is Jon Tattrie, and I'm calling in what I think is an unusual situation," I said, and began to explain that situation. The person who took my call agreed, and promised to look into it.

I got the feeling people were trying to figure out what scam I could possibly be running with my strange quest to find my colleague's body. I got a call back a few days later. The public trustee told me that in 2020, about ten thousand people died in Nova Scotia. Charles was one of forty-two who died alone and were given the hideous designation of being "unclaimed remains." Nobody had come for his body. When that happens, the government gives the public trustee enough money for a plot, and for a burial, but not for a grave marker. In forty-one of the cases, the public trustee found someone to mourn the dead, even if they couldn't formally claim the remains. Only once were they unable to find a single person to grieve: the case of Charles R. Saunders. After three weeks of fruitless searching, they buried him. Where? She didn't know, but she did know the grave was not marked. I sat back, stunned.

Nova Scotia's a big place. How was I going to find his unmarked grave?

I figured someone must have physically buried him. I started calling funeral homes around Halifax and Dartmouth. I got lucky on my third or fourth try. The man who answered the phone agreed I was calling in an unusual situation. He didn't recognize Charles's name, but he did know how the system worked and what is supposed to happen to people who are declared unclaimed remains: A local graveyard gets paid to bury them. He had no idea which graveyard buried Charles, or where it put him. There is no public record of unmarked graves. He promised to look into it for me, and to my surprise called me back a few days later with a location: Dartmouth Memorial Gardens. I knew the place. Eleven years earlier, Halifax's Baha'i community had created an eternal resting place for its people in that cemetery and I had done a story on it. I had a clear memory of driving the highway leaving Dartmouth and stopping at a sprawling cemetery that stretched back into the woods. The Baha'i had selected a spot in the Garden of Serenity, and I'd joined them on a clear, sunny summer day in a green patch of tree-ringed paradise at the back of the big burying grounds. "Release yourself, O Nightingales of God, from the thorns and brambles of wretchedness and misery, and wing your flight to the rose-garden of unfading splendour," they had said by way of prayer.

On autopilot, I called the graveyard and asked them to check their records. After a long search, the cemetery staff called back and told me their records showed they had indeed buried a Charles Robert Saunders, born in 1946, in their graveyard in June 2020. His grave was not marked, but the woman I was talking to knew where it was. Would I like to see it?

A few days later, I drove away from my house, around the back of Halifax harbour, past Charles's apartment, and out of town to the cemetery. I parked near the office. I realized I didn't want to leave my car. I didn't, at the moment, want to find his unmarked grave. *What was I doing?* The whole world was locked down in terror in the first months of the worst pandemic anyone alive had experienced. The schools had been closed for months, work was drying up, money getting thin, and my wife and I, who had two young children, were struggling to keep from going under. Shouldn't I be with them?

I wondered again about Charles. His early years were a mystery. People who had known him for decades had no clue about his childhood, and when I asked about his father, they were genuinely perplexed. Nobody knew the man's name, or anything about him. It seemed as if Charles had fathered himself. Even people who adored his *Imaro* novels had not noticed that while Imaro's story is defined by his search for his unknown father, Charles had apparently never whispered a word about his own father to anyone. But he had a father. He had family. He had people to claim him. Shouldn't someone closer to Charles be the first to visit his grave?

But I was the only person who knew where he was buried. I took a deep breath, put on my mask, and stepped out of the car.

Jenny, the staff member I'd been talking to, greeted me at the front door and treated me like a grieving family member. She handed me a lot of paperwork. She seemed as confused and upset by the situation as I was. Jenny explained that they would look after Charles's grave forever, mowing the lawn and keeping the area clean. She gave me a map and circled a remote area in the back: Tranquility Garden, just down the hill from the Baha'i's Garden of Serenity. She wrote down a three-digit number and told me to look for it on a medallion on the ground. His grave would be a few feet to the right of it.

I thanked her and headed back outside. It had been two months since I first got the call to check in on Charles. Here I was, on the cusp of finding him, and I was at a literal dead end. I sat down in my car. The lot was empty. The streets were empty. I felt empty. I started my car and drove out of the lot, following the paved lane to the Mothers Against Drunk Driving memorial and parked my car off to the side. I wanted to walk the final steps. In my memory, it starts raining. The Garden of Serenity rises up on a hill, enclosing the Baha'i and others on a green height surrounded by boreal forest. A lane leads from the far side of that section through the trees and to the top of a grassy hill that cascades into the forest primeval. I checked the map and followed the paved lane to the bottom of the hill. There were no graves in this new section, just grass. Where should I stand? Were there other unmarked graves in front of me?

I shook off my nerves and stepped onto the field, staring at the ground. I knelt on the damp grass and searched for the small medallions, pressed into the ground, with the lot numbers stamped on them. They were hard to locate. I crawled along, scraping through the mud, until I found and cleared a medallion with the three digits that marked Charles's general lot. I stood and followed Jenny's instructions and stepped a few paces to the right. Everything just looked like grass, not graves. But then I noticed a rectangle of newer grass, not yet stitched into the rest of the lawn. Charles was a little taller than me. I compared myself to the sod and saw it was a fit. This was it, the final resting place of Charles Robert Saunders. It hit me like a punch to the temple and I dropped to my knees. I was the only person on earth who knew where Charles was buried. Even the name of his cemetery was not public knowledge. He was slipping into nothingness. I felt sick. I couldn't continue to live in Nova Scotia knowing his remains were being treated to such an indignity. I had to mark his grave, and I had to find someone to claim him.

I wrote a second story for CBC about the fate of people who die alone and unclaimed in Nova Scotia. The headline about a "literary lion buried in an unmarked grave" travelled far and wide, and I started getting emails from people who knew Charles and were deeply upset about his tragic end. One of them was Morris Fried, a retired man living in New Jersey. He told me he'd gone to Lincoln University with Charles and remembered him vividly. They were the top two students on campus and were friendly rivals from 1964 to 1968. I did the math—Charles would have been eighteen then, a new man on the cusp of the world. I found the university had a great online archive and I was able to read every edition of the campus newspaper from 1964 to 1968.

I video-called Morris. He was sad, but happy for the chance to talk about Charles. He told me he'd lost touch with Charles after graduating. In 1985, Morris was browsing in a U.S. bookstore when his eye stopped on a paperback missing its cover. The interior excerpt read, "Imaro was beginning his northward trek when he heard the singing." Morris was hooked and bought the book.

When he turned the page, he saw it was written by Charles R. Saunders. He wrote to the publisher, DAW Books, and asked them to forward his letter to the author. Charles wrote back, and so began a letter friendship that lasted until the end of Charles's life. Morris had saved all of Charles's letters. He mentioned a few other people they'd both known at Lincoln and sent me their graduating yearbook. He said Charles never returned to the U.S. for any Lincoln events over the years, but Morris had been in touch with many of their classmates to organize reunions. He gave me names, and the cities he'd last known them to live in. I tracked them down. A shape of Charles's formative years began to emerge from the mist of his past.

3

LINCOLN UNIVERSITY

Lincoln University sits amid the rolling farmland and tree-capped hills of southern Chester County, Pennsylvania, between Philadelphia and Baltimore, and about a five-hour drive away from Elizabeth. Lincoln was founded in 1854 as the Ashmun Institute and was America's first degree-granting college or university for Black Americans. It was named for Jehudi Ashmun, a white American who opposed racism and helped found Liberia, the new African state that was to be a homeland for freed Black Americans. Ashmun moved to Monrovia, the capital, to represent the U.S. in Liberia. Many of the first graduating class moved to Liberia to establish what they hoped would be a free colony for liberated slaves. Eleven years after the institute opened, U.S. president Abraham Lincoln was assassinated, and the college took his name.

Lincoln University has shaped generations of Black leaders: At one point, 20 per cent of Black doctors and 10 per cent of Black lawyers in America had studied at Lincoln. The graduating students became ambassadors, judges, mayors, and city managers. The university occupied a special place in America, especially among Black Americans, as a path to power and prosperity. In 1921, after white mobs killed, burned, and looted on the Black Wall Street of Tulsa, Oklahoma, President Warren Harding chose Lincoln as the site of his first major speech about the crime. He spoke about the need for healing and harmony and praised the Lincoln alumni who had recently fought in the Great War.

Much of this was beyond Charles in the early 1960s. He later said he was too "unsophisticated" to understand the importance of the March on Washington in August 1963, which happened when he was seventeen, or of the hundreds of thousands of people who walked to the Lincoln Memorial to hear Martin Luther King's "I Have a Dream" speech. But the killing of John F. Kennedy broke through that November, during his senior year in high school. "Shock is too mild a word to describe my reaction. I do remember an argument I had with a classmate who said that LBJ would make a better president than JFK. I almost got into a fight with him over that one," he later wrote.[2]

In the summer after Charles graduated from high school, President Lyndon Johnson passed the Civil Rights Act, a federal law prohibiting discrimination based on race, religion, sex, or national origin. Uprisings and riots had rocked Philadelphia and other U.S. cities that summer. White terrorists dressed in the white robes of the Ku Klux Klan had murdered three civil rights workers in Mississippi as they tried to register Black voters. It was against this backdrop that Charles began his post-secondary education.

We get our first glimpse of eighteen-year-old Charles as he stepped off the bus and onto the Lincoln campus in the late summer of 1964. He had short, slick hair and a bare chin. He was approaching his full height of six foot four but weighed only 135 pounds. At first glance, many assumed he came from a military family, though he never discussed it. To fellow freshman Joe Williams, who worked at the student union, the scrawny beanpole of a kid

---

2 Letter to Morris Fried, November 2013.

was clearly away from his family for the first time. "Charlie looked like a character from *Leave It to Beaver*. He dressed like a white boy, he talked like a white boy," Joe later said.[3] "He did not curse, he did not smoke, he did not drink. Charlie thought that sex was the mating of two amoebas and a splitting."

Joe always called him Charlie, though he doesn't remember how Charles introduced himself. Recalling the tall, lanky kid heading across campus, he's reminded of Big Bird bobbing down Sesame Street. Other people noticed Charlie, too, including some cruel upperclassman who detected a vulnerable outsider. One day that fall, Charlie lined up at the student union building to get his meal. The upper-class bullies pounced on him. "They would delight in making Charlie feel uncomfortable," Joe said.

The ringleader of those upperclassmen was a guy called Sonny, a slick dude with the process, or conk, hairdo popular among a certain set of young men that meant taking your naturally woolly black hair, bathing it in chemicals, and smoothing your locks into an Elvis Presley pompadour. People had heard Charles was from Norristown, a working-class community near Philadelphia. Sonny mocked Charlie's rough roots, flouting his own cred from the streets of Philadelphia. Sonny and his pals surrounded a nervous Charlie outside the student union and tormented him with lewd stories of sexual conquests, some of which might have even been true. Charles blushed, squirmed, and tried not to let the images into his mind. When it got too obscene, Charlie covered his mouth and ran for the bathroom, abandoning any thoughts of eating. Joe Williams noticed that Charlie stopped coming for food. He made him a sandwich and got a friend to deliver it. "The guy was just scared to come to meals back then."

---

3 Interview with the author, 2021.

Campus life at Lincoln marked the first time Charles had lived amid a Black majority. Black people ran the college. They taught, learned, and cared for the buildings and grounds. Black people were the bullies, the bullied, and the protectors. Lincoln had officially been welcoming female day students for a decade, but there were only a handful of women on campus in the fall of 1964. Mostly everyone was a young Black man—but there were exceptions. Charles soon met and befriended a militant white Jewish man named Morris Fried. Morris loved his "school full of weirdos," where he felt like he belonged for the first time in his life. He had actually been in Washington and heard with his own ears MLK speak of judging people by the content of their character, not the colour of their skin. He noticed that Charles didn't drink, and when someone passed him grass, he passed it along without a puff. As others had surmised, Charles seemed to pass on other pleasures, too.

"I don't believe in sex," Charles once told Morris.[4] "The human race is going to evolve away from sex." Charles elaborated on this brave new fantasy, where babies were grown cleanly, discreetly, in labs, not messily, noisily, in human bodies. "The future is asexual," he proclaimed. Morris was far left and thought Charles might share his beliefs, but Charles showed no interest in politics.

People were drawn to Charlie's individual way of life. "They'd heard Charlie was a thinker, the guy who set the curve in most of the classes he attended at Lincoln," Morris said. It seemed as though anytime he saw Charlie, his head would be buried in a book. Morris noticed the quiet freshman at most cultural events on campus. Charlie would slip in, find a seat to make himself invisible in, and sit rapt as guest lecturers flooded his young mind with new ideas. The campus celebrated a free-thinking vibe and a distrust of the

---

4 Morris Fried interview with the author, 2020.

status quo. Students contrasted the official truth with the informal "rabble," their word for what was really going on.

One of those talks was given by Sam Anderson of New York, a key member of the legendary Student Nonviolent Coordinating Committee, better known as SNCC or "snick." Anderson may have spoken about the African Liberation Support movement, a North American group fighting for African freedom. About one in five Lincoln students came from Africa, and it was at such talks that Charles first met African people. Anderson would a few years later co-found the Black Panther Party in Harlem. Another talk came from Charles V. Hamilton, who later cowrote *Black Power: The Politics of Liberation* with Black Panther Stokely Carmichael, later known as Kwame Ture. The book and the thinkers behind it popularized the idea of systemic racism and its antidote, Black Power, and wanted to confront the totality of anti-Black oppression in America. Charles later told a friend he was part of a Malcolm X group on campus, though he "kept it quiet." He may have helped bring X to campus for a speech. On Saturday mornings, a group of professors and students would pack into a big hall. Dr. Laurence Foster, or Dr. William T. Johnson, would talk to students about chemistry, racism, the meaning of life—everything was fair game. Bill Mathis, president of CORE (the Congress of Racial Equality), joined sometimes, and Carmichael turned up once in a while. Joe saw Charles at many of those sessions.

Malcolm X was murdered in February 1965, and that summer police and their dogs attacked hundreds of civil rights protesters marching from Selma to Montgomery. The voting act removed the literacy tests that had been used to prevent many Black people from participating in elections.

As his second year began in the fall of 1965, Charles roomed in the basement of a squat, square building called Amos Hall. It had been built as a red-brick bathhouse before being converted into a recreation centre, which gave it the enduring nickname of the Old Canteen, after the first-floor snack bar. Charles brought his belongings through the arched entrance and down to the basement, inside of the old bookstore.

He shared his room with fellow sophomore Joseph Bernard Ellois, whom everybody called J.B. It was a small campus, and they'd seen each other distantly but had never met. J.B. noticed that the short crop of hair Charles had arrived with had begun to sprout into an Afro.[5] He knew Charlie as a tall, quiet, scholarly student. They lived in one big room with a bed on each side and a small desk area in the middle. The two nineteen-year-olds shared a bathroom and shower with the other residents of the basement.

Charles spent little time in his room. He didn't tell J.B. what he did with his days, but people most often spotted him in class, or studying in the library. J.B. was usually home and ready for bed by the time Charles slipped into the room around eight or nine p.m. Charles would nod a short greeting and go straight to sleep. J.B. was a quiet, studious person, too, and their friendship was slow to bloom. He learned little about Charles's family, though Charles did occasionally mention his mother, and J.B. would meet her at graduation. J.B. knew nothing about Charles's high school, or father, or if he had brothers or sisters.

One night, J.B. watched Charles slide home at the end of the day, sit down at his desk, and write an entire academic paper, complete with footnotes, straight out of his head. He never consulted his research material. He'd read everything in the library and retained it in his iron-clad mind. J.B. was blown away. He spent more time in the room than Charles, and one evening, he noticed that Charles had left one of his big notebooks on the desk. It was

---

5 Joseph Bernard Ellois interview with the author, 2021.

open. He expected to see lecture notes but was surprised to find it was filled with wild pencil drawings of exaggerated figures, crazy situations, and occasional abstractions.

"Oh, you're an artist," he said to Charles.

"Well, I like to draw stuff," Charles answered. He said he didn't consider himself an artist, though. Charles opened up and they talked about the thoughts behind his illustrations.

"You have an interesting mind, my friend," J.B. told Charles that evening. "So, are these drawings like a kind of therapy for you?"

"Yeah, maybe. In a way," Charles answered. "It's just what I think about."

"You should show some of your psychology professors some of your work," J.B. half-joked. "I bet they'll have an interesting take on it."

Charles took him up on the idea and soon showed them to a professor he was keen to impress. She was a woman who had just gotten her Ph.D. and, at twenty-seven, was not much older than her students. When Charles got home that night, J.B. could see the showing hadn't gone well. Charles told him she'd been appalled by his drawings.

Women were a rare sight on campus, but starting in 1964, female students were allowed to live at Lincoln. About a dozen women pioneered amid hundreds of young men. More women joined them in 1965, and the university converted the Guest House, which had boarded visiting women, into the first female dorm. The university made sure all students knew the "progressive" rules governing the co-ed campus. On designated weekends, male and female students were permitted to visit the opposite sex in their rooms, under strict guidelines: They had to sign in, and the doors had to remain open all the time. J.B. laughed at how those rules were followed: "Open" became "ajar," and the tiny crack of light making the door open was often offset by a heavy barricade on the other side, so you'd need a gang of men to push into the room.

Charles often told his university friends that he didn't believe in sex, and most of them never saw him date anyone. He was either leading them on, or he had begun dividing his life into separate compartments. Only his roommate—and a few women—knew the truth. J.B. noticed one particular young woman who would sign into the Old Canteen and walk down the stairs to their shared room. This tall, curvy, beautiful woman always brought a Bible on her visits to Charles. J.B. learned to make himself scarce. He remembers her dating Charles for a semester, and a few other women came calling after her. They were, according to J.B., drawn to Charles's outrageous intelligence. They'd soon be drawn to his courage, too.

During Charles's second year, the KKK had been on a cross-country recruitment blitz, inviting white people to pull on the robes and burn crosses. In 1965, an article in the *Lincolnian* campus newspaper warned that the KKK was planning to march in force across the college grounds. Dozens of students patrolled the woods and campus border night and day. Others dragged heavy cement benches to roadways to act as barricades, stockpiling rocks and bricks. A scout spotted several KKK members entering a white-run restaurant across the street from the campus. Later reports said the thugs threatened the owner with violence if he didn't join the KKK. It's not clear what he did. But the KKK evidently saw the fortified campus and didn't set foot on it. Joe Williams was with the students on guard. So was Charles. "Some things you don't know about a guy's heart until you actually see it," Joe later said.

On another dramatic day, Joe passed the library and saw Charles talking to the librarian, Mrs. Goldye Johnson, who was frantic. Joe looked way up to a fourth-floor window and saw a fellow student hanging precariously out of the building. His body stuck out over the ledge and he seemed poised to jump. Mrs. Johnson told Joe and Charlie the young man was thinking about ending his life, and they needed to save him. "Go talk him back in," she urged the two of them. The friends raced up the stairs to the fourth floor. They found the young man hanging out the window—but with a fire rope tied around his waist and to the bed. He was just having some fun with Mrs. Johnson. "Hell, he isn't going nowhere. He'd have to bring the bed out," Joe told her.

Joe saw Charles a lot in their second year, because Joe lived near the library. Often, he'd see Charles and Morris, head-to-head, deep in conversation. They were widely acclaimed as the smartest students on campus, and the only question was which one would end up on top. Charles, always open-minded, learned a lot about Black history and Black activism from his Jewish friend. "Morris could exist on campus because he was a brilliant guy," Joe said. "Morris probably could cite more Black history than you could shake a stick at. He probably read everything there ever was."

Around that time Charles met Ron Welburn, who was the editor of the *Lincolnian*. Ron was older and had started a semester before Charlie arrived. He was a confident athlete, a leader, and a well-known writer on campus. As a poet, Ron was developing the form and voice that would carry him through a long, distinguished career. Ron enjoyed the quiet of the rural college, but he suffered from jazz fever, from which he found relief only by leaving campus and heading to the Birdland Jazz Club in New York City.

Ron had noticed Charles on campus prior to meeting him. He understood Charles to be a withdrawn, self-conscious person whose innocence could be startling.[6] Charles was curious about the newspaper and offered to help edit it. Despite their differences in temperament, they developed a mutual respect. At the Alpha Phi Alpha fraternity, Charles found an outlet for his growing sociability. His fraternity held a strong and treasured reputation for respectful

---

6 Ron Welburn interview with the author, 2021.

behaviour and academic excellence, while the others focused more on having fun. Nobody knows quite what went on during his Hell Week at the fraternity, but it seemed to break his shell and let a new Charlie emerge. Ron published a photo of Charles in the next edition of the newspaper—perhaps the first public photo of the author. Charles towers over two shorter fraternity members. The photo caption reads: "The tall and short of fraternity life." It was the type of groan-inducing pun Charles loved, and he may well have written it.

Ron loved language and could rattle off Lincoln's literary alumni: Melvin B. Tolson, class of 1923; Langston Hughes, class of 1929; Ray Patterson, class of 1951; and Larry Neal, class of 1961. Lincoln invited these great writers to campus, and the students often gathered to discuss poetry. But Ron never saw Charles there. He seemed to have little interest in literary writing or poetry, preferring comics and speculative fiction. Ron and Charlie had some rudimentary talks about writing, but both were heading in such different directions they might as well have spoken a different language. Charlie was fascinated by fiction, especially fantasy and sci fi, but those art forms were not celebrated at Lincoln, nor many other places. The *Lincolnian* often published poetry, but there was no section for fiction, and certainly not fantasy.

Charles was trying new things. Drawings, at first, but the *Lincolnian* already had a regular cartoon. It was called *Little Man on Campus* and featured a dim-witted white teenager struggling to get educated. Charles had an idea for a new cartoon, and it would be the first character he created and shared with an audience. His hero was a young Black man cracking wise at the absurdity of life. Charles and his friends had a word for just such a young man: a splib. They used it in place of the n-word that some other young Black men preferred. "I remember when I was in my early twenties, still in the States, a bunch of us started using the word 'splib.' I don't know where it came from, but it was in use for several years," Charles later wrote.[7] He named his comic hero Super Splib. Decades later, Joe would still remember a cartoon Charles drew where Super Splib met Superman. Superman wants to prove he's the most super dude on the page, so he eagerly shows off his strength. It culminates in Superman hoisting twenty women into the air, his whole body straining under the weight. He looks to Super Splib for approval. Super Splib watches the whole show with a detached attitude, right up to the last panel, where he calmly tells Superman that he can elevate the same number of women—and he needs only one appendage to do it.

Joe howled with laughter when Charles shared it with him. The punch line hit, and how often do you see a young Black kid getting the better of the greatest white man ever, Superman himself? When he stopped laughing, Joe wondered at how looks can be concealing. He remembered seeing Charlie in first year, tormented by lewd stories out front of the student union. From that mind had come this creation? "Charlie used his unique talents to make us aware of the avant-garde rationale of his cosmic character, and has treated his readers and followers to limitless literary adventures," Joe later said.

But the outside world was beginning to intrude on the educational sanctuary. American forces had been in Vietnam since 1954 to support the U.S.-friendly South against the Communist North. In March 1965, President Johnson deployed combat troops to the country. By June, 82,000 American warriors were fighting in Vietnam. Military leaders called for 175,000 more soldiers to reinforce the failing South Vietnamese army. The far-off violence slouched toward campus. Midway through his university degree, Charles began to realize it was coming for him.

---

7 Letter to Charles de Lint, 1987.

4

AN UNHOLY TRAGEDY

One of Charles's classmates at Lincoln University was hiding a secret. He was an older student who went by the name Donald Martin Lambright, and he was captivated by the revolution in Black consciousness. A photo later published in a newspaper shows him wearing his hair short and bushy and sporting a moustache. He was associated with a militant Black group that wanted to reclaim five Southern states and declare them independent Black republics. Family said he roamed the country, looking for a way to attack the racism that was strangling his life. He had been denied a haircut due to his skin colour and ejected from a laundromat for the same racist reasons. He joined the U.S. Air Force and did two tours of Vietnam in his four-year career. He was discharged in 1961 and later enrolled at Lincoln in the hopes he could learn a way to fight racism, perhaps as a writer or journalist. He attended Black Power events on campus and sometimes spoke at them. He wrote for the *Lincolnian*. Charles was not close with him but did see him on campus.

Donald's secret was that his father, Lincoln Perry, was a famous actor who went by the name Stepin Fetchit. Perry was the child of parents from the Caribbean who immigrated to the United States in the 1890s. Their son was born in Florida in 1902 and named after a slew of U.S. presidents: Lincoln Theodore Monroe Andrew Perry. He ran away from home at twelve to join a carnival as a singer and tap dancer. By twenty, he was working as a vaudeville artist in a travelling show. One account of the origins of his stage name was that he won big on a racehorse named Step and Fetch It. He used the name originally as part of a two-man act, Step and Fetch It, but later took it solo as Stepin Fetchit. In the 1920s, he turned his attention to movies and developed his persona as "the Laziest Man in the World." He stole the show in films like *In Old Kentucky* (1927) and *Hearts in Dixie* (1929), the second being one of the first mostly Black movies ever made. He had a cameo role on *The Little Rascals* in the 1930s, en route to becoming one of the most famous Black people in America. He was the first Black actor to earn a million dollars. In all, he acted in about forty-four films, earning up to $2 million over his career. A typical joke appeared on *The Little Rascals*, where he is asked to read a letter—and then asked if he can read at all. He says of course he can read; he learned at night school. "So I can't read it until night," Fetchit continues, handing the letter to a kid to read to him and ensuring the child's ears are plugged with cotton so the boy can't hear its saucy contents.

Perry had two sons, though he was not a presence in either's life. He was violent toward both of their mothers, and both boys were raised away from him. Donald's mother sued Perry for child support. This came as he boasted about a lavish lifestyle. "Anything money could buy, I had. I had 14 Chinese servants and all kinds of cars," Perry said at one point. "I showed people just because I had a million dollars, the world wouldn't come to an end."

But by the 1960s, his comedy routine was wearing thin. In 1970, he sued Bill Cosby, of all people, for defaming him in a film about Black history; Cosby had called Perry a "lazy, stupid, crap shooter, chicken-stealing idiot." Perry lost the lawsuit, as the judge ruled Cosby was talking about Stepin Fetchit, not Perry himself. The NAACP also criticized his work (decades later they changed course and gave him an Image Award to go with his star on the

Hollywood Walk of Fame). "The name Stepin Fetchit came to be the ultimate term for negative racism stereotypes. Nobody wanted anything to do with Lincoln Perry and he was devastated by that," wrote Champ Clark in his biography, *Shuffling to Ignominy: The Tragedy of Stepin Fetchit*.

Other Black thinkers said those who dismissed Perry as an "Uncle Tom," shaming Black people to please whites, had missed the entire point of his character. He was a trickster, they argued, and he depicted one of the great Black American folk heroes. "The lazy man character that he played was based on something that had come from slavery," his biographer Mel Watkins wrote in *Stepin Fetchit: The Life and Times of Lincoln Perry*. "It was called 'Putting on Old Massa'—break the tools, break the hoe, do anything to postpone the work that was to be done. Blacks understood it perfectly and laughed heartily at it."

Perry always defended his work as positive for Black Americans, especially the many Black stars who later drove down the road he paved. "Just because Charlie Chaplin played a tramp doesn't make tramps out of all Englishmen, and because Dean Martin drinks, that doesn't make drunks out of all Italians," he said in a 1968 interview. "I was only playing a character, and that character did a lot of good.

"I became the first Negro entertainer to become a millionaire. All the things that Bill Cosby and Sidney Poitier have done wouldn't have been possible. I set up the thrones for them to come and sit on."

But when his second son, Donald, set foot on Lincoln's campus in the mid-1960s, he claimed no father. He used his stepfather's last name and never spoke of Perry. He did not know the man growing up, and apparently only met him once, around the time he went to Lincoln University. Donald was becoming a Black Power militant at the same time his father was defending his very different approach to being Black. Accounts differ on the end of his academic life: Some say Donald graduated with a political science degree, others say he withdrew in 1967 without graduating. By 1969, he was sleeping with a rifle because he felt he needed "protection from whites," according to an uncle. On Easter weekend in 1969, he went for a drive with his wife, Annette, on the Pennsylvania Turnpike. He cradled a rifle in his arms and began shooting around ten a.m. The war vet carried an M 1 .30-calibre semi-automatic rifle and a .30-calibre Marlin carbine, guns used by U.S. troops in Vietnam. Witnesses reported him slowly weaving from lane to lane, firing into other cars. Occasionally he pulled over and fired from the roadside. He shot a white man in the face, killing him, and the man's wife died in the resulting crash. They had been going to visit their older son at university. Their younger son was in the car and was left traumatized and badly hurt. Donald shot a third person, who later died. As police scrambled to stop him, he pulled over and murdered Annette and killed himself. He'd killed four people and wounded seventeen more. The headline the next day read, "Pike Killer Felt Violence Only Radical Answer."

"A burning sense of racial frustration is blamed for launching Donald Martin Lambright, 31, into an orgy of death and terror along the Pennsylvania Turnpike," the newspaper account began.[8] State police called him a Black militant. His uncle opined that Donald "thought shooting might be a necessary tactic, sometimes. It is an unholy tragedy that a brilliant young man could be so frustrated by his life in the United States that he could only see achieving success through destruction," he told reporters.

The newspaper wrote that he had been "born, as he died, in the spotlight." The only two public reports on his life came first in a celebrity column when he was born to the famous actor, and three decades later when he died in a killing spree. "He was dissatisfied

8 *Lebanon Daily News*, April 7 1969.

and quite anxious to involve himself in 'Black Power' liberation activities," the uncle said. "Donald thought he had the answers to a lot of problems. And he felt the only way some of them could be resolved would be through violent action." Lincoln Perry, then sick with cancer, had no answers. "I can't understand it; he was such a cool, calm and intelligent boy."

Charles would reflect on Donald's life and death for many years, fascinated by the tragic tale of a warrior with no father who sought answers in violence.

The violence of the Vietnam War grew to dominate the futures of those on campus. Hundreds of thousands of young American men were being sent to the war; 16,899 would die in 1968. The *Lincolnian* published an editorial called "Vietnam and the College Student." "Students feel that the United States should not draft a student to fight and possibly die for an undeclared war after he has spent four years of his life in order to gain a better education and future," the editorial began. "His future has been disrupted for a seemingly worthless cause."

Some graduated but then squandered that education with a pointless death in the jungle. The editorial portrayed these dead soldiers as lost lawyers, teachers, and technicians. "The Black student is made to go out and fight a war in another nation while he has a war to fight at home, a war on the ghetto and open housing. This is the war in which the Black student should be engaged. The United States should clean up the trouble in its own backyard before trying to clean up someone else's. The Black student says, 'My fight is not in Viet Nam but at home.'"

Ron, the *Lincolnian* editor, knew of three classmates who fought in Vietnam: one died, one returned "a basket case," and the third seemed fine. Many of the young men at Lincoln had fathers who had fought in the Second World War and so had inherited a tradition of service. But nobody remembers any passion for the Vietnam War on campus. Lincoln University seemed to share that attitude, as it regularly invited anti-war speakers to mandatory assemblies, and often those speakers provided detailed plans of how to avoid getting drafted. Ron, for example, needed a knee operation, and that caused him to fail the physical. The rumour was that some people were drafted right out of their college studies, deferral or no deferral. Ron remembers a fear that someone would knock on your door, and you wouldn't be able to find the paperwork proving you were a student. "In the middle of the night, Uncle Sam shows up. 'Okay, boy, get your gear, you're coming with us,'" he said.

Morris Fried objected to the war from the start. He saw no moral justification for dying—or killing—in a war that made no sense. Morris knew he'd likely get called up shortly after graduating from Lincoln. He created as many requests for deferment as he could dream up. Some were far-fetched, but luck helped, and when his requests were rejected, he appealed. He'd read an article saying that in the early years of the war, the draft board made a point of snatching up anyone who seemed reluctant. But then they got feedback from the military commanders, and it turned out people who didn't want to fight made lousy soldiers, and they were often more trouble than they were worth.

"On campus, particularly those I ran with, the attitude was generally anti-government and opposed to anything the government was doing, and anti-war was just a part of that," Morris later said. "How could we fight for 'democracy' abroad when Black people in the South weren't allowed to vote?"

J.B. had a friend who, on the night before his physical, spent hours doing exercises designed to drive up his blood pressure. He had high blood pressure already and was on medication to control it. He stopped taking the medication. He went in cool as a cucumber, so there was a shocked reaction from the draft board when they saw his blood pressure. "Oh my God," they told his friend. "You need immediate medical attention." They declared him unfit for service and sent him to a doctor, who prescribed the medication he was already taking. Every time he was called up again, he'd drive up his blood pressure and stop taking his medication. He avoided being drafted.

Morris never heard Charles express any opinion about the war. J.B. remembers Charles being dead set against it and never intending to let himself become an American warrior. Charles was taking in the world around him, seeking a pathway that appealed to him. As a supporter of Malcolm X, he considered joining the Nation of Islam, but he didn't believe white people were the devil, or in Black supremacy, or that Black people should separate from white people. "I thought they were nuts," he later wrote. And he wasn't a fan of the Nation of Islam's most famous convert, Muhammad Ali. To a young Charles, Ali seemed like "a clown, an embarrassment, a disgrace."

"You know how it was in the early 1960s—bourgeois Negroes were trying to be 'respectable' and would cringe whenever a Black person 'acted the fool' in public, and supposedly made us all look bad," he later wrote to Morris. "I remember when [Ali] spoke at Lincoln in 1968, during our last semester. The chapel was packed; you were there too, I assume. I remember him beginning almost every sentence with: 'The Honorable Elijah Muhammad teaches us . . .'"[9]

Shortly after that visit, Martin Luther King was assassinated. The administration sent all the students home. "They were afraid the Black students were going to kill the white students on campus.

---

9 Letter to Fried, June 10, 2016.

The thought never crossed my mind at the time," Charles wrote later.[10] "I do remember the aftermath, when Jackson Burnside said that to him, the death of some freshman in the Newark riot was more important than the death of King. I'm going to write about all that one of these days. The premise probably will be, what might have happened if they *hadn't* sent us home . . ."

In his senior year, he attended a play set in a Southern U.S. town where all the Black people had vanished, and the white people struggled to survive without them. What really caught his eye and imagination was the all-Black cast, including some actors donning "whiteface" to play the white people. In an America where Black people seemed to be a problem to be killed or sent home, the play flipped the situation and showed Black people as the glue holding a town together.

On the nearly all-Black campus of Lincoln, these events coalesced into a new creative idea bubbling deep in his soul. But little of that can be seen in his outer work at the time. He was published as a writer for the first time in the May 1966 edition of the *Lincolnian*. On page 4, the paper ran a regular Poet's Corner. The poets were comparing dawn to smoke from a million cigarettes, or decrying a pale person's "livid phonyism and barrels of unlike." Charles's piece is short, and strange. It's likely his only published attempt at poetry, or perhaps a poetic short story. It was called "Cacophony in Color," and it has never appeared outside of that newspaper. Here it is in its entirety:

> *The interior of the chamber resembled a vacuum, an empty, intent blackness which can only be the product of nothingness.*

---

10 Letter to Fried, July 20, 1988.

Into this vast void lanced spear-like rays of white light, which, as they gradually softened and diffused throughout the chamber, seemed to be striving to eliminate the blackness.

As the conflict continued, the whiteness seemed to lose its glare, and finally to merge with the tenacious blackness, creating a peaceful gray which eventually pervaded the limits of the chamber.

Abruptly the grayness disappeared. In its place shone a bright bluish radiance. Then, equally abruptly, four human figures materialized: two male, two female, two Black, two white. They were naked; this attenuated their contrasting hues. As they stumbled about trying to reorient themselves to this new environ, they seemed to be walking on nothing—no ground, no floor, no sidewalk, or street, nothing tangible. Thus, they seemed suspended in nothingness.

The initial astonishment at this sudden transportation had stripped the humans' minds of all but their basic childhood conditioning. Part of this condition was a mutual feeling of animosity between the contrasting couples. With this animosity at the fore of their minds, the couples warily approached each other, muscles tensed in readiness for combat.

As they sprang at each other and grappled, white man with black man, white woman with black woman, the entire chamber suddenly became ruby black, a profound blackness caused by the absence of the faintest glimmer of light. Just as abruptly, rays of blinding whiteness strove to take possession of the chamber. The the conflict they were within and, as the external blackness and whiteness merged into a placidly neutral gray, so the battling couples merged into a grayness, distinguishable from the surrounding gray only in its turbulence.

When the blue light replaced the greyness, the couples had vanished.

That typo, "The the," in the second-last sentence, no doubt drew a sigh from Charles.

The *Lincolnian* gave him his start, but it was a bit stuffy for his changing persona. It was the official newspaper of life on campus, published by the university, and it often left out the "rabble," which is what Lincoln students called the frank truth of their experiences. Charles found a better home at the *Axiom*, the campus literary magazine. Students published it. They wrote it, laid it out, mimeographed it, and stapled the editions together. His Super Splib cartoons were published in the *Axiom*.

By March 1967, in his third year, Charles had become such a notable person on campus that he earned his first profile. A *Lincolnian* reporter named Nathaniel Ellis devoted that edition's Junior Interview to a feature on Charles Saunders, under the headline "A Quiet Man Speaks Out." "We only know the quiet men on campus by reputation. One such quiet man has begun to speak out in order to let us know him. Charles Saunders, a junior, has felt the need to withdraw from his solitude and express himself as a Lincoln Man interested in Lincoln's future," Ellis begins.

He tells readers Charles is part of the student government, belongs to a fraternity, and is a perpetual Dean's List student for his studies in psychology. Charles talks about Lincoln going through a transitional period from a smaller, male campus, close to faculty, to a bigger, co-ed campus, more distant from faculty. "There can be no sudden switch from the Lincoln of the past to the Lincoln of the future," he says.

Charles makes it clear he speaks to the university president about a wide range of campus issues. About the coed campus he says, "It was thought that it was unhealthy for men to be at Lincoln in an almost totally isolated situation," hiding who exactly thought that.

He mentions that coeds can only hang out in dorms or the student union and suggests the faculty "aren't facing reality" when thinking about how the campus is integrating. He wants longer "open house" hours when people can visit each other's rooms—no doubt keeping that door ajar. He says students have grown apathetic, as seen in the "collapse" of student government and the decline of demonstrations. "To most students, it seems that rallies and demonstrations are an end unto themselves," he says. "The issue which precipitated the rally is a bad word, secondary to the rally itself."

The last question Ellis asks is about Charles's plans after graduating. "My immediate plans are attending graduate school at the University of Pennsylvania and eventually to become a clinical psychologist," Charles answers. At the time, graduate school would have kept him out of the war draft.

Lincoln had changed him, and he found himself growing distant from his roots. "My family consisted of bourgeois Negroes and I was just like them until I woke up in 1967. From that point on, damn near everything I did appalled them," he later wrote.[11]

When the class of 1968 graduated in the spring, Morris ended up in first place. Charles took second. The 1968 edition of the *Lion*, the campus yearbook, was dedicated to the theme "Identity in an Era of Transition," and showed two hands clasped in solidarity. The editorial reflected on how, between 1964 and 1968, Lincoln had become "a changing campus in a changing world." The 1968 class graduated 239 men and five women, but the overall campus population now included two hundred women amid one thousand men. Charles

11 Letter to Morris Fried, October 2009.

edited the yearbook, and a photo shows him at the newspaper with Ron, Joe, and an editor named Cynthia Amis. Charles wears glasses and appears to be focused on a looming deadline.

For each student, the yearbook published an official photo and name, plus a "rabble" photo and nickname. The official entry for Charles R. Saunders records his hometown as Norristown, Pa., and his major as psychology. The photo shows a clean-shaven young man with a light mustache, his short hair slicked down and combed back neatly over his ears. He wears a black suit, white shirt, and black tie. It may be a high school photo and certainly wasn't taken in 1968. Charles was voted "most studious," while Joe was "most industrious," and Ron was named "class writer." Morris won "most radical." Charles signed Ron's yearbook, mentioning the name of one of Ron's comic characters: "Long Live Purves!! Keep on pushing and writing.—Charlie"

On the next page come the rabble photos and identities. Charles "Snake" Saunders stands tall and skinny and dapperly dressed in a warm coat and too-short pants that expose his socks. His right hand rests on his hip and his left hand holds a notebook over a trash can in front of the Old Canteen. The caption reads: "Snake Charlie went through so many changes during his four years that it is difficult to find the real him. Intellectually inclined, he could always be depended upon for deep rabble, out of which sometimes came useful ideas. We will always remember his 'metamorphosis.'"

J.B. Ellois remembered Charles heading next to Purdue University in Indiana for graduate school. Many students went to graduate schools at least in part as grounds for exemption from the draft. But the Military Selective Service Act of 1967 had made it much harder to get an exemption, especially for graduate students. Charles may have felt himself growing more vulnerable. In 1969, President Richard Nixon introduced the national lottery draft, which was to be televised. It meant men could only be drafted during one year, and if they did not get drafted, they were safe. Each day of the year was given a randomly drawn number between 1 and 366 (February 29 was included), and if you were born on that day, that was your number. The lower your number, the higher your chances of being forced to fight. On December 1, 1969, the U.S. televised the first lottery draft—Charles's draft. Charles drew 15 and would have been deployed in 1970 had he stayed in America.

Purdue University records show him spending the first and second semester of the 1968–69 year studying at the university, but he did not graduate. J.B. Elois wasn't close with his former roommate, but a mutual friend at Purdue reconnected the two of them and they exchanged letters. J.B. didn't want to fight in the Vietnam War either and went straight from Lincoln in May to graduate school at Rutgers in June. J.B. still got a letter from the draft board that September, telling him it was time to report for duty. While J.B. was in basic training, Charles was ordered to report for duty. Around the same time, Charles went to a Purdue campus talk from Dick Gregory, a famous Black comic who cracked jokes about racial injustice, bigotry, and the Vietnam War. Gregory offered some draft-dodging advice at the expense of the son of Dean Rusk, the secretary of state driving the war. His son had managed to avoid the draft. "So Gregory said, 'Handcuff yourself to Dean Rusk's son, and say, Whatever's wrong with him is wrong with me,'" Charles later wrote.[12] Charles shook hands with Gregory.

The blueprint was to go to Canada *before* you got drafted. The draft board had little power to reach you then, and you'd hang out in Canada until the war was over, and hopefully your odd status would blow over. You weren't breaking any laws. You were just . . . in Canada. But Charles seemed determined to make a point. He

12 Letter to Morris Fried, November 2016.

did not do strange exercises to agitate his blood pressure, or find lame excuses to fail the physical. He didn't plead that he was a student and should get a deferment. He seems to have waited until he was drafted and required to turn up for a physical. And then he did not attend the physical. That maneuver turned Charles's situation into a criminal offence. Rumours had him slipping back and forth across the Canadian border, like Super Splib outwitting the man again. Charles himself would later compare his departure to the two times he ran away from home as a child. "I guess coming to Canada to avoid the draft was the ultimate instance of running away from home. This time, I was successful. Fortunately, this time the cops didn't take me back."[13]

By the time J.B. got to advanced infantry training, Charles's letters bore Canadian stamps. J.B.'s drill sergeant was deeply suspicious of those letters. J.B. told his old roommate that he'd accepted the draft out of a sense of obligation, and because he was sure his parents would kill him if he dodged it. His father had served in the Second World War, and he expected his son to continue the military tradition. J.B. knew he could never tell his father he was going to Canada. It would have devastated his father and broken the bond between father and son. Charles didn't explain his decisions.

"I don't feel I have enough training to go to Vietnam," J.B. told Charles at one point. He re-upped to get MOS, or military occupation specialty, which would require specialized training. His goal was "delay, delay, delay." He hoped either the war would end before he was deployed, or he'd actually learn enough to survive the jungle. "Wait a minute, I've been in the military six months, and now you're going to ship me off to war? And just hand me a weapon and say, 'Go get 'em?'" J.B. wondered.

---

13 Letter to Janet LeRoy, April 19, 2019.

Eventually, they did. He spent a year in Vietnam. Charles wrote to him there, at least two letters in twelve months. J.B. went into military intelligence and found a relatively safe part of the war zone. He wasn't going into the jungle every day but to the top of a mountain. He engaged in covert electronic intelligence. He survived and returned home but lost touch with Charles.

Charles had called the war a "sword of Damocles" hanging over the heads of his generation. "Some people in my family were mad as hell at me for hauling ass to Canada after I got drafted, although I was never formally disowned by the men in the older generation, all of whom had served in one branch or other of the segregated armed forces during World War II," Charles later wrote.[14] "They all came to realize that the Vietnam War was nothing like World War II, and draft-dodgers like me weren't so wrong-headed after all. Yet I never felt so vindicated as I did when former defense secretary Robert McNamara, one of the architects of the war, spent the last years of his life going on a *mea culpa* tour, tearfully apologizing for his part in the prolongation of a conflict that never should have happened in the first place."

In September 1969, Charles crossed the U.S. border into Canada and did not return. He was running from a war, and from demons that clawed at his heart. They followed him into Canada. So did a warrior.

---

14 Letter to Morris Fried, September 2016.

5

A WARRIOR AHEAD

Imaro was born in Canada, though Charles was pregnant with him when he left America. "I can't remember the exact, 'eureka' moment, but sometime in 1970, the Imaro character emerged from the depths of my subconsciousness, and his story demanded to be told," Charles later wrote.[15] "I became seriously interested in African history and culture," Charles explained in an interview.[16] "Before that, I was an avid reader of fantasy and science fiction. And I had always done well at 'school-type' writing: term papers, essays, compositions. For a while, these three interests seemed to occupy separate compartments of my mind. And then the walls of those compartments suddenly disappeared, and I decided to start writing African fantasy."

We can trace Imaro's roots back to Charles's earliest reading. Tarzan was the first fictional character to capture his imagination. He devoured movies and comic books showing the Herculean hero pounding his chest, swinging on vines through the trees with Jane clinging to his back. Tarzan had no father, no mother; only himself, alone in Africa. Tarzan had grown up to be a fierce warrior who feared nothing. Young Charles loved it.

---

15 Introduction to *Imaro*, Night Shade edition, 2006.

16 Unpublished transcript of interview with Jeffrey M. Elliot.

Tarzan may seem like a primeval myth, but he's a modern creation. The white warrior emerged from the mind of the white writer Edgar Rice Burroughs in the early twentieth century. Much of Burroughs's white audience was hungry to read about Africa, which to them was a dimly known place that seemed half-fantastical. An edition of 1914's *Tarzan of the Apes*, the first novel, shows a green jungle with vines and tall, thin trees. In the foreground is a mighty elephant wielding sharp tusks. Riding the beast is the powerful Tarzan. He wears a loincloth and throws both arms up in primal triumph. His left hand grips a knife and his right a spear.

"I am Tarzan," are his first recorded words. We learn Tarzan means "White Skin." "I am a great killer. Let all respect Tarzan of the Apes. There be none among you as mighty as Tarzan. Let his enemies beware."

He's eighteen before he encounters other humans: a group of Black villagers fleeing white raiders and looking for a new homeland. Tarzan feels his homeland is being invaded, and hates these people for their "bestial brutishness." They rebuild their village near Tarzan's turf. Too near. Tarzan flies through the treetops and stops over one man.

"Tarzan looked with wonder upon the strange creature beneath him—so like him in form and yet so different in face and colour. His books had portrayed the *negro,* but how different had been the dull, dead print to this sleek thing of ebony, pulsing with life," Burroughs writes. "He could kill him at his leisure."

Tarzan throws a vine down from the treetops and catches the man unaware, then hauls him up until he's dangling, feet kicking. Tarzan stabs the man in the heart. He studies the dead man closely, marvelling at his teeth and tattoos. He decides to eat him but changes his mind. Tarzan instead goes to the man's village. "Tarzan of the Apes was no sentimentalist. He knew nothing of the brotherhood of man," we learn. "Few were his primitive pleasures, but the greatest of these was to hunt and kill."

Burroughs tells us Tarzan laughs happily while killing, which is part of "being a man," often for the fun of "inflicting suffering and death." He creeps into the village and steals weapons and food. Tarzan terrorizes the villagers, inventing the noose so he can lynch Black people. "So the Burroughs books weren't all that 'escapist,' because the racism in the Tarzan books made me uncomfortable even as I enjoyed the scope of the author's imagination. At that time, though, I never thought about writing in the genre myself," Charles said.[17] He saw hope in one Tarzan title. "*Brothers Of The Spear* was beautifully drawn by an artist named Russ Manning, and it showed Blacks and whites as equals. That made a deep impression on me, but it was only later that it influenced my work."

An idea for a new hero started to flicker in his young mind. "Imaro is the man I always wished would come bursting out of the Hollywood jungle to beat the hell out of Tarzan! When I was a kid, I would watch Tarzan movies and hope that Jim Brown or Sonny Liston would jump up and kick Johnny Weissmuller's ass off the screen," Charles said. "Him, his chimpanzee, and his Indian elephants. I always used to wonder what the hell Indian elephants were doing in Africa, anyway."

He looked for a better semblance of Africa in fantasy writing but was disappointed. "Most fantasy and other fiction that uses African settings is written from a viewpoint that sees little or nothing of value in the people and cultures of Africa," he wrote.[18] "It's as though the evolution of African fantasy stopped with Edgar Rice

---

17 Elliot interview.

18 Elliot interview.

Burroughs's *Tarzan and the Ant Men*, and after that there was nothing left to say."

He found something very different in 1952's *Star Man's Son—2250 A.D.* by Andre Norton. "I read my first SF book when I was about twelve years old. That would have been in 1958. It was about a post-nuclear-holocaust Earth in which mutations ran rampant. The hero had a mutated Siamese cat that was the size of a cougar. That's what really turned me on to the genre," he wrote later.[19]

Andre Norton's birth name was Alice Mary Norton, but she used a male pen name, thinking boys might object to a female author. The central character is a young white man named Fors, but I suspect it was another person who made such a lasting impression on Charles: a "dark hunter" named Arskane. "His wide-shouldered, muscular bronze body was bare to the waist and at least five shades darker as to skin tint than the most deeply tanned of the Eyrie men. The hair on his round skull was black and tightly curled. He had strongly marked features with a wide-lipped mouth and flat cheekbones," Norton writes.

Arskane, we learn, descended from "flying men," likely a coded reference to the famous Tuskegee Airmen, African American pilots who fought in the Second World War. Arskane tells Fors his tribe today is under attack again and scouts are seeking new lands where they won't be harassed. His mission is to find good land suitable for farming for his people. He drums his news to the other scouts, and the message is drummed home to his people.

The dark hunter is wise, intelligent, strong, and gentle. At one point, he even figures out how to drive a truck to crash out of a trap and free himself and his friend. Fors begs him to come back to Eyrie with him, but Arskane declines. "This is a world in which hate lives

---

19 Email interview with Amy Harlib, circa 2000.

yet," he says. "Let me tell you of my own people; this is a story of the old, old days. The flying men who founded my tribe were born with dark skin—and so they had in their day endured much from those born of fairer races. We are a people of peace but there is an ancient hurt behind us and sometimes it stirs in our memories to poison with bitterness. So now we have hardened our hearts and we stand for ourselves if the need be."

Fors is ashamed and angry. Why should skin determine brotherhood?

"Brother, my people believe that all the actions in this life have behind them some guiding power. And it seems to me that we two were brought to this place so that we might meet thus. And from our meeting perhaps there will be born something stronger and lighter that we have not known before," Arskane replies. Fors vows to follow Arskane wherever he goes. Charles loved the "heady brew of magic and mayhem, horror and heroism, warfare and wizards."

But he was a teenager before he discovered the writer who would change his life. "Influence Numero Uno is Robert E. Howard. After all, he created the sub-genre in which I do most of my work. I've been told I do action and battle scenes well, and I would attribute that to Howard's influence," he said. "Around 1966 or so, Lancer Books reissued Robert E. Howard's Conan stories, with those breathtaking Frank Frazetta covers. Once I started reading those books, I was hooked! Of course, I still read the hard- and New Wave SF. But fantasy appealed to something deeper in me—the soul of the storyteller, perhaps. It was when I discovered fantasy that I also discovered that I wanted to be a storyteller—a *griot*."

Conan was born in a small, stifling room in a sagebrush town in central Texas, to a man hunched over a manual Underwood No. 5 cast-iron typewriter, as David C. Smith puts it in *Robert E. Howard: A Literary Biography*. The man writes poetry. Wild adventures. Historical yarns. Comical disasters. He bangs the keys and worlds tumble out. "There was no one like him anywhere, certainly not in the small Texas town where he lived. He was unique and he was alone," Smith writes. "Because when one is alone and lives close to the earth, one must fight to live."

Smith also writes fantasy and adventure fiction. He and Charles connected through the letter pages of fantasy zines in the 1970s, and while they never met in person, they forged a strong bond. Smith says it began as a professional exchange between two rising writers trading tips. "We wound up sharing a true friendship via our letters," he told me.[20] They were both American men born in the postwar baby boom and grew up in a similar country, though Smith is white. Both earned some success in the 1970s and 1980s but saw their fortunes sag as the market changed away from their "masculine fantasy fiction." Smith stopped writing for decades before returning to the field, but he and Charles remained letter-writing friends throughout.

"Our friendship actually deepened as we discussed more personal matters in our letters, such as the deaths of our mothers. When Charles hit low spots—writer's block—I shared with him some techniques I'd used to get back into the groove," he says. Smith supported the civil rights movement in the 1960s, but his friend revealed to him what it truly meant. "I was naive in many ways," he says, especially about the racism Charles found and faced in the fantasy world. "I was really behind the curve on that one, thinking that racism must not have been the issue. But of course it was, even a kind of 'soft' racism by white fantasy enthusiasts. He truly opened my eyes."

Smith wrote in Howard's shadow too, though he also drew inspiration from H.P. Lovecraft and Tony Goodstone. "I wanted to write stories with that pulp feel—energetic popular fiction. I even

20 Interview with the author, 2021.

bought a circa-1925 Rand cast-iron typewriter and used that for years, as if I were writing fifty years earlier!" he says. He moved onto weightier subjects with his trilogy *The Fall of the First World*. Both he and Charles fell short of their goal of making a full-time living writing fiction, but they helped each other appreciate what writing added to their lives.

When Smith wrote his biography of Howard, he asked Charles to help him understand the racism present in some of his work. "The sheer power of Howard's prose captivated me to the point where I was willing to ignore the stone in my shoe and snap up and devour every new book I could find with his name on it. However, the mid-60s was also a time of ferment and explosion in the Black community, with a surge of pride in African heritage. I found myself beset with a severe case of cognitive dissonance," Charles wrote. "I resolved that conflict by writing my own Africentric sword-and-sorcery tales."[21]

Howard set all of Conan's stories in an alternative, pre-historic Europe, in the Hyborian Age. He gives places half-familiar names: the Pictish Wilderness, Argos, Cimmeria, and Kush. It was historical fiction for a fictional history. Howard's grand style of writing, sprinkled with archaic words like *thews*, adds to the otherworldliness. Decades later, author Fritz Leiber would coin the term "sword and sorcery" to describe this new genre. Howard's extraordinarily prolific career stopped when, besieged by depression and desperate thoughts, he ended his life at thirty.

"Howard's work received more attention after his death than it ever did during his short lifetime," Charles once said in an interview. "Paperbacks that were either Conan or in the tradition of Conan became ubiquitous in bookstores and newsstands. I was in

---

21 Quoted in *Robert E. Howard: A Literary Biography* by David C. Smith.

my late teens and early twenties when this publishing phenomenon occurred, and I was hooked from the get-go. I read all the sword and sorcery I could get my hands on. And my visits to the authors' imaginary worlds were enjoyable—for the most part."[22]

He called it his "dilemma."[23] He cited two Howard short stories in particular: "The Vale of Lost Women" and "Shadows in Zamboula," which he described as "typical anti-Black hysterics . . . reading them is like having a front-row seat at a Ku Klux Klan rally. In their depiction of Blacks as savages, cannibals and slaves, these stories deserve a place of dishonour beside Edgar Rice Burroughs in the lowly annals of racist literature."[24] But he loved fantasy writing and wasn't willing to leave. "I began to realize that in the SF and fantasy genre, Blacks were, with only few exceptions, either left out or depicted in racist and stereotypic ways. I had a choice: I could either stop reading SF and fantasy, or try to do something about my dissatisfaction with it by writing my own stories and trying to get them published. I chose the latter course. I was crazy enough to think I could break into what was essentially a white genre—at the time, I didn't know Chip Delany was Black, even though I'd read, and enjoyed, his work. That fact wasn't exactly advertised back then." (Charles would later gift a copy of *Imaro* to Samuel Delaney, signing it to "The Master!") Charles loved *The Lord of the Rings* and gave J.R.R. Tolkien faint praise for constructing a world "wherein Blacks are absent." "There is really nothing wrong with that. Who needs Black Hobbits? Seriously, the point is that it is better to be ignored than maligned."[25]

---

22 Elliot interview.

23 Introduction to *Griots: A Sword and Soul Anthology*, 2011.

24 "Die, Black Dog!," *Toadstool Wine*, 1975.

25 "Die, Black Dog!"

Smith studied Howard's life in depth and knew Charles for decades. "I see them as both being highly sensitive and very aware of the circumstances around them. They were both big guys, both loved boxing, both were extremely intelligent, both had the knack of weaving masculine adventure stories of great imagination with backgrounds suggested by the historical record. They lived their lives sincerely. Each was authentic, genuine. I wish both of them had led less turbulent lives and gained more recognition for their fiction, even when they were alive, as successful as both seemed to be. But it takes time for greatness to be recognized. Recognition of his work will continue to grow and grow and grow."

Charles read Cheikh Anta Diop's 1974 nonfiction book *The African Origin of Civilization*, which makes a strong case for Black people as the first founders of culture. Diop points to extensive evidence that "the ancient Egyptians were Negroes. The moral fruit of their civilization is to be counted among the assets of the Black world." After exploring the evidence of many African civilizations that thrived before the sixteenth century, Diop calls for someone to write a unified history of humanity, starting in Africa. "The history of humanity could be quite lucid. We still have enough documents left to write a clear history of man. The West today is fully aware of this, but it lacks the intellectual and moral courage required, and this is why textbooks are deliberately muddled. It then devolves on us Africans to rewrite the entire history of mankind for our own edification and that of others."

Charles also read *The Lost Cities of Africa* by Basil Davidson. Published in 1959, it was one of the first white-written books to take seriously the ancient history of Africa. Davidson challenged the white-championed idea that Africa had no history. "Africans, on this view, had never evolved civilizations of their own; if they possessed a history, it could scarcely be worth the telling," he writes in the introduction. In this distorted worldview, Africans lived in primitive chaos until Europeans arrived and began civilizing the wild tribes. This was the view of Tarzan, and Davidson rejected it.

"The peopling of continental Africa over the past fifteen hundred years or so was seldom or never with the peoples who are known today," he wrote. "For the most part they were peoples who have slipped from memory or remain there only in the guise of legendary ancestors, marvellous men with shining eyes and unbreakable courage who opened unknown country long ago for those who should follow and come after. Their heroes were the Feinn and Beowulf of the modern peoples of Africa; and even now the echoes of their pioneering still wonderfully linger."

Charles felt a bold idea rising in his soul: What would happen if he crossed sword and sorcery with the marvellous men with shining eyes—in Africa? That creative spark thrilled him. "Damn right! That proverbial one percent of inspiration is what motivates me to squeeze out the 99 per cent perspiration that accompanies all creativity. Without inspiration, I'd just as soon keep my pores dry, thank you," he said in an interview.[26]

"I realized that this non-stereotypical Africa of history and legend was just as valid a setting for fantasy stories as was the ancient and medieval Europe that served as the common default setting for everything from *Conan* to *Lord of the Rings*," he said. "A character came into my head then: Imaro, a Black man who could stand alongside mythical warrior-heroes like Beowulf and Hercules, as well as fictional characters such as Conan and Kull."

His third major nonfiction influence was W.E.B. Du Bois's *The World and Africa*. Published in the aftermath of the Second World War, it contains Du Bois's brilliant account of the rise of anti-Black racism and the idea of white supremacy that culminated in the Nazi

---

26 Elliot interview.

killing factories. "There was no Nazi atrocity, concentration camps, wholesale maiming and murder, defilement of women, or ghastly blasphemy of childhood, which the Christian civilization of Europe had not long been practicing against colored folk in all parts of the world in the name of and for the defence of a Superior Race born to rule the world," he writes.

Du Bois traces virulent anti-Black racism to its origin. "Nothing which has happened to man in modern times has been more significant than the buying and selling of human beings out of Africa and into America from 1441 to 1870," he writes. Du Bois argues that once white people started growing wealthy off the stolen labour of abducted Africans and their children, they created anti-Black racism to justify the project. How awful would a race of people have to be to merit such treatment? Racist white people found out by creating a fantasy world in which all Black people were morally inferior, craven and cruel. Through this Tarzan lens, Black or brown people are only the bad guys, the comic relief, or the weak secondary characters who die.

Charles cited these three core books as his main sources: Diop, Davidson, and Du Bois. "Of course, there have been other books since then—scores, if not hundreds. But those are the foundation stones."[27]

Imaro was raised among the Kitoko clan in the territory of the Ilyassai people on the Tamburure in Nyumbani. Charles drew on the real-world Maasai people of eastern Africa, whose traditional territory stretches from Kenya to Tanzania. Imaro's Tamburure looks much like the Serengeti grasslands. Imaro, too, lived on a vast

27 Elliot interview.

savanna amid lions, cheetahs, hyenas, rhinoceroses, and elephants. Nyumbani elephants. His people are proud warriors, free nomads who cherish their cattle above nearly all other life. A central ritual for the Ilyassai is the *olmaiyo.* "This is something I picked up obscurely in a novel about the Maasai. I don't know whether it's true or not. But in the novel that I read, a person who fails in his test against a lion is ostracized. As far as a specific Days of Shame, that was my own invention. But there is ostracism (among the Maasai). What the exact ceremony is, I'm not sure," he once said.[28]

Charles described the name Imaro as one of the "hidden meanings" he embedded in his work. "The name 'Imaro' was derived from the Swahili word for strong," he said.[29] He doesn't specify the Swahili word, and a direct translation of English's *strong* yields Swahili's *nguvu.* However, the Swahili word *imara* means solid, stable, steadfast, sturdy, and strengthened. Imara is used as a first name, typically for girls. Charles likely turned the *a* to an *o* to get the male name Imaro. "Swahili is a fairly dominant language in the eastern region, and that's where Imaro is born, raised, and has his initial adventures. So I used Swahili there," Charles explained.[30] "I've done some stories set on the west coast of Nyumbani, and for that I've used Hausa as my base language, mainly because that's the only West African language I've been able to find a textbook or teach-yourself book for. There's also Yoruba. I've got a book on that, so I kind of mix Hausa and Yoruba in the west. In the middle, I have a book which has some words of Mali, which is a north-central African nation, and when I start writing about South Nyumbani I'm going to have to get hold of some linguistic sources for Zulu

28 Interview in Polar Borealis, late 1980s, republished in 2020.

29 Elliot interview.

30 Interview in Polar Borealis, late 1980s, republished in 2020.

and Xosa. In modern Africa it would be ludicrous to try to use Swahili as a base language for a whole continent, so I use linguistic diversity in my fantasy version as well."

Imaro is an exile, and perhaps that's why Charles needed to leave the United States for his own exile in Canada before the warrior emerged. When Imaro finally breaks with his Ilyassai people and leaves the Tamburure, "he shunned all spoor of humans," we learn.[31] "Fear was not the cause of his avoidance of man. For Imaro, solitude meant freedom. He had no desire for contact with others of his kind." But just a few lines later, things shift. "Though he never would have admitted it aloud, the dearth of human companionship was beginning to fray his nerves. Yet he had *chosen* exile . . ."

Charles, too, hesitated at the edge of his great literary adventure. "For a while there, I wondered what the hell I was getting into," he said in an interview.[32] "I felt like a basement-workshop putterer suddenly confronted with the task of building a house. At that time, writing fiction suddenly seemed a dauntingly formidable proposition. Now, it's only moderately petrifying."

In the summer of 1972, he wrote an eighty-four-page novella about Imaro and submitted it for publication. He never heard back. He turned to small-press fanzines, where people like him gathered in paper and ink to read and write. Some of his favourite titles were *Space and Time*, *The Diversifier*, *Weirdbook*, *Fantasy Crossroads*, *Fantasy and Terror* and *Spoor Anthology*. Some lived only for a few editions, while others published for decades. Charles read them, wrote letters to the editors, and responded to other fan letters. The passable boundary between fantasy fan and author creates a strong bond between the groups. Charles loved that reader-focused style

31 *Imaro*, 1981.

32 Elliot interview.

of writing, where authors would try something out in a zine, absorb the feedback from fans, and write a better story the next time.

He built a community of fantasy writers: Galad Elflandsson, Gordon Derry, and Charles de Lint were at the centre. "We're kindred spirits waging a struggle against a hostile world," Charles wrote. "It's a tough battle. One can go it alone, but as the Norse used to say, 'Bare is the back without a brother behind it.'"

Elflandsson moved to Ottawa in 1978 to join the band of brothers in person. He had a place on Church Street, and the writers regularly met in his kitchen. "We'd compare bits and pieces of what we were doing . . . struggling to do, actually, because at that time de Lint had been at the game for years and wrote with what was, to me, a maddening facility," Elflandsson later said.[33] "I don't think we were actively 'jealous,' but trying to keep up with him was impossible. We'd take a week on one paragraph; he'd be halfway through his next novel. Needless to say, the rest of us were still learning."

Charles Saunders struggled to write anything at all. Days, then weeks, would pass without him adding a word to the count. Unable to connect to his creativity, he tried to connect to a cute young lady he'd noticed on the edge of his writers' group. A friend set him up on a date with Shell Madden. Shell rolled her eyes at the way her friend put them together. "She rather bluntly told me that as I had at one time dated a 'Black' man, I shouldn't see any problems in dating Charles . . . I'm still miffed at her attitude, it was incredibly rude and insensitive, but that was her way," she later said.[34]

She'd noticed Charles at one of the writing meetings, even though he was outshone by the gregarious de Lint. They went on a few dates. "Charles was a very nice man, quiet, and polite, with a

33 Interview with the author, 2023.

34 Interview with the author, 2023.

quiet sense of humour, a great smile, and a glint of the demon in his eyes when he was about to do or say something a little 'out of character'... and Charles was very aware of the character he had built for himself," she recalled.

He told her he'd come to Canada to avoid the draft, which didn't bother her. She was struck by the contrast of the big man with a teddy bear heart. The two went on walking dates, as both were too broke for dinners or movies. "So we spent time talking about everything and anything," Shell says. "During those walks, I recognized how insecure he was; his speech was littered by references to 'being a Black man,' things about the teasing he took back home because of how light his skin was, and any number of things that were to my way of thinking very American. I kept trying to explain that Canadians had a different spin on things."

Charles called her most evenings. She realized this mysterious writer was not actually writing. "I didn't know any writers at the time, and was afraid he'd never get back to his typewriter. I asked him about his writing each day, but he would put me off with other topics. Finally I told him outright that I had no intention of being the person responsible for an aspiring writer falling by the wayside."

Shell asked him how many words an active writer could produce in a day. He gave her a big number. She asked him what he was averaging. He admitted his daily tally was closer to zero. Shell put her foot down: He couldn't call her until he'd written five hundred words. "The next day, when he called, I ask how the writing was going; he told me he hadn't made it to five hundred words, so I said, 'Go back to it. You can call me later.'"

He did. And he did it again the next day. His calls came later in the evenings, and he told her he'd been lifted into his fantasy world and written more than one thousand words one day, and then two thousand. Charles started sitting down earlier in the day to plan out the stories, write new passages, revise existing ones, and work on character outlines. In the end, the budding romance didn't blossom, but the writing habit took root.

Elflandsson read the early Imaro stories. He saw them as a way of Charles "becoming by proxy the heroic figure he never dreamt he could become." He saw his friend constantly struggling to maintain his self-esteem long enough to get the words on the page. But once Charles established the daily habit of writing, he saw its power. Nothing thrilled Charles as much as a good day at the typewriter. "He was shy, self-conscious about almost everything about himself. Imaro gave his soul street cred. Every chapter served to legitimize Charles as a valuable (if mostly non-participating) member of the human race," Elflandsson later said. "Out of all of us in Ottawa, Charles is the one who should be celebrated the most because his was the rockiest road, his accomplishments made all the more impressive because of it. When he got past his terror of the world . . . his sense of being an outsider . . . he was a kind, generous, and very lovable human being."

Charles became president of the Small Press Writers and Artists Organization in November 1978 and launched a newsletter to connect the members. In his "acceptance speech," published in the newsletter, he joked that his winning strategy was "not withdrawing my name from the list of nominees." Membership was five dollars to join and then two dollars per year. In return, he hoped to connect the writers with each other, help them find the small presses, and ultimately get people published. They would create writing prizes, too, to encourage each other.

His dear friend Gene Day took the role of vice-president. Gene was touched by the title and vowed to help the SPWAO writers any way he could. "If you are being ripped off, hassled by editors or publishers, or simply need some advice or help, feel free to call or write anytime," he wrote, adding his phone number. "If you feel, of course, that you have been having problems with me at *Dark Fantasy*, then you had better drop Charles a line and he will kick me for you. I would no doubt deserve it."

Stephanie Stearns came on as treasurer and secretary. "I'm sure many of you voted for me because it is a traditionally female position, but others among you have been yelled at by me already and you know this job happens to require a good yeller on occasion," she wrote. "Charles Saunders has always been an innovative writer and I'm sure he will bring these same talents to his presidency. Gene Day is obviously a hard worker and will make his contribution to our team as vigorous as his other work has been."

Charles and his crew printed off seventy-seven copies of the newsletter and mailed them all over North America. Day and Saunders were in Ontario, but Stearns lived in Denver, Colorado. The membership list shows addresses from New York to California and many places in between. Most of the Canadians are in Ontario, with the exception of John Bell in Nova Scotia. Bell would stay closely connected to Charles from 1978 until 1986. They both wrote for Day's *Dark Fantasy* and, as small-press editors—Charles created *Dragonbane* and Bell created *Borealis*—they published each other's works.

In the spring 1979 edition of *Borealis*, Bell writes that "probably the chief reason that Ottawa has emerged as the fantasy capital of Canada is the presence in that city of Charles Saunders." Charles contributed an essay called "Farmer of the Apes" on the American author Philip José Farmer and his "astonishing range" of creative output. Part of that range included *Tarzan Alive*, a fictional biography of Charles's nemesis. In Farmer's parallel world, Tarzan's "real" father is revealed to be not Lord Greystoke but Jack the Ripper. The essay gives readers a reminder that Charles had loved Tarzan at first, and still did in many ways.

Bell was then working in Nova Scotia, at the Dalhousie University Archives. Work brought him to the National Archives in Ottawa in 1978. For Bell, the best part of the trip was finally meeting Saunders, de Lint, Elflandsson, and Derry. When Bell moved to Ottawa in 1982, he joined the group, then known as the Ottawa Fantasists.

"Despite the description of Ottawa as a lacklustre city and the world's coldest capital after Ulan Bator, the city is not lacking in elements of fantasy," author John Robert Colombo wrote about the group.[35] "The city is home to a school of youngish fantasy writers who meet at the House of Speculative Fiction, 101 Fourth Avenue, a bookstore opened in 1979 that specializes in the literature of the fantastic, managed by the writer Galad Elflandsson, which features work by Charles R. Saunders, Charles de Lint, Gordon Derevanchuk, and bibliographer John Bell. No other city has such a concentration of new writers who specialize in High Fantasy."

Their homebase bookstore sold new and used paperbacks, hardcovers, and speciality-press science fiction and fantasy books. Visitors reported a taciturn proprietor who sat at the back, reading. A photo shows the four Fantasists standing in front of a wall of books. Bell would interview Charles Saunders for the academic journal *Black American Literature Forum*, a Quebec sci fi magazine called *Solaris*, and a Nova Scotia newspaper once Charles had moved east.

Charles found his own small-press home when he read the October 1973 edition of a zine called *Vampirella.* It contained a review of another zine called *Dark Fantasy*, published by Gene Day in Gananoque, Ontario. Charles ordered the zine and loved it. He decided to send Gene his first Imaro story but ran into a hitch: Canada Post was on strike. So he typed up the short story and delivered a copy in person, which is how he first met Day. "At the time Gene was sharing a house and studio with Gus (Augustine) Funnell, who later had a couple of books published by Laser," Charles said

---

35 *Canadian Literary Landmarks*, by John Robert Colombo.

in an interview.[36] "I sat down in Gus's office—he had a really huge collection of Fantastic, F & SF, and Penthouse—and I kind of leafed through his collection while Gene was reading the stories. Gene said, 'I'm finished.' So, I went up the stairs, sort of like heading off to the electric chair, and Gene just raved over them. He thought they were great and he even took the longer one."

The story was printed in *Dark Fantasy* four months later. Charles's first published Imaro story was called "M'ji Ya Wazimu," or "The City of Madness," in *Dark Fantasy*, edition five, in 1974. It gives us our first glimpse of the mighty warrior.

What's it like when Imaro attacks you in battle? Charles turned to a surprising source for his mythical hero: Jim Brown, the legendary fullback for the NFL's Cleveland Browns in the 1950s and '60s. Fullbacks play offence and line up behind the quarterback. They are some of the biggest offensive players on the field and typically catch short passes or power-run for a few yards at a time. They aren't favoured in the modern NFL, but they were stars in the 1950s and '60s. On runs, the quarterback hands them the ball and they charge upfield, trying to avoid the other team's defensive players. But when Jim Brown saw someone running to tackle him, he would not sidestep to avoid the confrontation. Something in his soul commanded him to meet the attacker in a head-on collision. "I thought a lot about Jim Brown when I created Imaro. Brown would run straight at tacklers, daring them to hit him. Imaro has something of that spirit."

How about if you attack Imaro? For this, Charles watched Mean Joe Greene, a defensive tackle for football's Pittsburgh Steelers in

36 Borealis SF 2, late 1980s.

the 1970s and core of their famous Steel Curtain defence. DTs are the biggest defenders on the field and start at the line of scrimmage. Their sheer bulk can stop the offence as the ball-carriers crash into the wall of flesh. The 1970s Steelers won four Super Bowls with their crushing defence. Most teams scored about twenty points a game in those days; the Steelers over one stretch only allowed three points per game. Joe Greene exemplified their approach. He didn't hope ball-carriers ran into him; he assaulted them and smashed them to the ground. Mean Joe Greene wasn't playing; he was out to hurt people. Greene also starred in a famous Super Bowl commercial for Coca-Cola that showed a gentler side, especially to children who looked up to him.

Imaro, too, forbids himself from stepping backward. In the story "Slaves of the Giant-Kings," he is drugged and abducted. His captors bind his arms tight to his side, so when he lunges to his feet, he loses balance and falls full-length on the ground, to the laughter of his tormenters. He regains his feet and looks up: He has to, for the man before him is more than seven feet tall. His demeanor and the reaction of others make it clear he is in charge—he is one of the Giant-Kings. All but the Giant-King angle their heads oddly. A guard realizes Imaro's neck has not reached the ritualistic angle of subordination, so he grabs the warrior's woolly matt of hair and yanks his head back.

"Imaro stiffened his neck muscles into a column of iron. The raging Kahutu pulled harder, but Imaro's head did not move. Then, with the guardsman straining futilely against rigid thews, Imaro suddenly snapped his head backward, smashing his skull full into the face of the startled Kahutu. Howling in pain, the guardsman dropped to his knees," we read. Imaro takes a beating for it, but the Giant-King recognizes him as "a lion." "We have tamed lions before . . ." he says.

What if you get in close enough for hand-to-hand combat with Imaro? You poor thing. Climb into the ring with Sonny Liston, the devastating heavyweight boxing champion of the world, to find out. Charles, a lifelong boxing fan, once wrote that when Liston hit people, they reacted like they'd been shot with a gun. Foes staggered away, a stunned look on their faces, before crashing to the ground. Boxing fans say Liston knocked out heavyweight champ Floyd Patterson just by looking at him. When they first fought in 1962, Liston's record was 33–1, with twenty-three knockouts. Patterson had more knockouts and was the reigning champ, but he looked like he was going to his own execution as he entered the ring. When they faced off, Patterson stared at his shoes while Liston glared at him. In the first round, Liston hit him with an uppercut that stiffened Patterson's legs, then clubbed him with heavy punches that crumbled him to the canvas. In the footage, Liston looks like a construction worker taking a sledgehammer to a wall. He destroys the champ without emotion. Liston would later lose to Muhammad Ali, but Charles never forgot his prime. "I remember seeing a picture of Liston lifting the back end of a pickup truck. That made an impression on me that outlasted the picture of him looking up from the canvas at a sneering Ali," Charles wrote. "I've always liked Ali; but there's nothing of him in Imaro, strangely enough."

Imaro grows up hunting and slaying animals from boyhood. He's fourteen when he kills his first human. It is utterly unlike Tarzan's first blood. The story is told in "Turkhana Knives." Imaro is tending his *ngombe*, his cow, when Kanoko, his great rival among the Ilyassai, drives the animal off, forcing Imaro to chase after her. Imaro calls her Kulu, which means "friend," and "thinking sorrowfully of the pain his friend was enduring, Imaro inadvertently allowed the resulting hatred for Kanoko to seethe like a fire-coal in his mind. Momentarily, he lost his *kufahuma*—the attunement of his senses, the melding of all his faculties into one, making his awareness at one with the Tamburure." *Kufahuma* is Swahili for "to know," and it's one of Imaro's superior weapons. He is abducted by a patrol from the rival Turkhana people, famed for their wrist-knives. Imaro ends up bound and prepared for a sacrifice. The band is led by an *n'tu-mchawi*, a magic man like the *oibonoks* of Imaro's own people. But this man, N'tu-mwaa, wants to kill Kulu, kill a lion, and kill an Ilyassai warrior—and eat all three hearts. "I—a man apart from all others. I, who will become all three," the dangerous man tells Imaro. He eats the lion heart, eats Kulu's heart, and begins to shapeshift into a beast. "He tossed his horned, maned head. Beast-madness shone in his eyes. He waved the dagger he had removed from his neck. It still dripped with the blood of Ngatun and Kulu," we read.

"With one hand, Imaro caught the Turkhana's arm, just above the wrist-knife. And he dragged N'tu-mwaa to his knees. For all the horror of his altered appearance, the Turkhana had not completed his conjuring. He was still only N'tu-mwaa, and even maddened as he was, he could not match Imaro's strength. He looked upon the features of the not-Ilyassai. Those features had twisted into a terrifying mask of vengeance and hatred. For a moment, the derangement that drove N'tu-mwaa subsided. And he knew, then, that he faced his doom." Imaro crushes his hand, takes his knife, and stabs him between the dangling remains of the hearts of Kulu and of Ngatun, piercing the magic man's own heart. "For a reason he could not name, Imaro leaned over N'tu-mwaa to hear his dying words. The lion-eyes were dimming, but the Turkhana's voice was still clear. 'I . . . cannot die now . . . ,' he rasped. 'I still have to *show* them . . . I am better than they . . . I am better, even though *they* say I am not.'"

Imaro watches him die. There is no joy in the fourteen-year-old warrior. "Imaro shook his head angrily, as if to rid himself of the inexplicable sense of . . . *kinship* . . . he felt with his dead foe."

Charles described his own mind as a "gumbo" stew, into which he cooked everything he read, saw, and learned about the world, and rebirthed it in Nyumbani. Nearly every fantastical line is underwritten by our real world. The Turkana live in northern Kenya and were feared for their deadly wrist knives, exactly as depicted in his writing.

Imaro is a super-athlete who would be a star in football or boxing. But he doesn't play games because he's born in Nyumbani, where the fights are real and to the death. Brace yourself: Here comes Imaro.

"M'ji Ya Wazimu," the first story Charles ever wrote about Imaro, begins on a hot day in an isolated stretch of woodland. The trees are tall but spaced apart, joining in a tight canopy overhead, mellowing the bright sun Jua into a green-gold glow. Two people enter a clearing: a man and his woman captive. They pause, then run out. Later, a new man enters the space, smelling of "blood, steel and hatred." Bright flocks of birds scatter to the canopy and long-tailed monkeys sprint from treetop to treetop, fleeing the danger below.

"The warrior was a fearsome sight. His umber-coloured skin glistened sweat-slick through garments that hung in skimpy tatters from his massive frame. Crimson-crusted wounds scored his skin like glyphs inscribed by demons. Dried blood matted his woolly black hair. His face was hardened into an implacable mask of hatred. Unrequited vengeance burned like a torch in his eyes, yet beneath the lamina of that emotion lay a core of grief so bitter it threatened to consume him entirely," Charles writes in words that echo Andre Norton's talk of an "ancient hurt behind us and sometimes it stirs in our memories to poison with bitterness."

Imaro longs for the open Tamburure grassland of his home. There, he was unparalleled, and could track even the slightest scent.

Here, in the woodlands, filled with strange smells, he is at a disadvantage. Imaro's blood races in murderous joy when he hears voices. One yelps in pain, while the others laugh. Imaro peers through the foliage and sees three big men and one small person—an adult the size of a boy, with skin the colour of cocoa. A pygmy, Imaro surmises. The three tormenters are strange to his eyes, clad in leather armour and rusty metal. "But it was their complexion that made them so anomalous. Their skin was as pale as the belly of a fish, in sharp contrast to the black of their hair, which hung in strange, snakelike locks beneath their helmets. The white men were torturing the pygmy." As Imaro watches, a memory hits hard: "He was a child again. It was the day after his mother had departed the dwellings of the Ilyassai, leaving him behind. 'I will not cry,' Imaro had told himself grimly, fearfully, on that long-ago day. 'I will not cry.'"

Roaring, Imaro hits the clearing like a shock wave. The ferocity of his attack stuns the three bullies, and he beheads his first foe with one slice. Blood spurts out of the stump of the white man's neck and his body topples forward. Imaro stabs the stomach of a second tormenter, ripping it out with a shower of blood. The third man attacks Imaro, but Imaro blocks him, sending his enemy's sword clattering to the ground. Imaro thrusts his sword into the helpless man's heart. Imaro pulls his weapon out and wipes the blood off on the corpse's clothing. Imaro turns to the smaller man, who is terrified. Imaro is spattered in blood. His lips are pulled back, showing a snarl of teeth. His obsidian eyes burn with a hatred bordering on insanity.

The pygmy speaks first. "*Yambo*," he says. "*Yambo*," grunts Imaro. Hello, spoken in Kiswa, the root tongue of east coast lands. The small man introduces himself as Pomphis. "My name is Imaro," the warrior says.

Charles would later comment on the instant bond we see between man-child Imaro and child-man Pomphis. "Imaro, an orphan without an acknowledged father, is raised in a society that places little value on orphans without acknowledged fathers. Pomphis is a pygmy whose life is spent far from his natural environment," he said.[37] "So I'd say people who have to deal with alienation and rejection are the ones I'm most likely to write about."

He once revealed an unexpected inspiration for Pomphis, in particular in that opening scene, where Pomphis thinks, *I'd better say something quick before he decides to kill me, too!* "When I wrote that line, it seemed as though Richard Pryor were saying it. Every culture has its Trickster, the one who totally floors custom and convention and gets away with it. Anansi the Spider is the Trickster of West African culture. Puck is the Trickster of the Europeans. Pryor is the Trickster of modern North America. He utterly destroys conventional mores, and people pay to see him do it. Now, I didn't exactly model Pomphis the character in the mold of Richard Pryor, but there's a bit of Pryor in Pomphis's sense of humour. And Pomphis is a bit of a Trickster."

Pomphis gives Imaro a history lesson. One thousand rains ago, white men from Atlan, the island continent in the Western Ocean, invaded Nyumbani. They worshiped demons called the Mashataan, but the people of Nyumbani fought back with the help of their gods, the Cloud Striders. Locals called the intruders Mizungus, which means "those without mercy." (In our world, the Bantu word *mzungu* means wanderer, or spirit, or white skin, and is widely used to refer to foreigners.) The unholy Atlans devastated the west coast kingdoms of Nyumbani, capturing thousands of people and transporting them in ships bound for Atlan. The Atlans made a home in Nyumbani and stole its wealth. The Mashataan had long ago lost a war to the Cloud Striders and used the Atlans to get revenge. "In

37 Elliot interview.

Atlan, they had sown a malignant suggestion in the minds of the people of the sea-girt continent: a belief that the people of Nyumbani were subhuman, fit only for slavery, or sacrifice on the altars." Sorcery swirled around the Nyumbani's minds, preventing them from connecting to their own gods, the Cloud Striders. "Courage was the only weapon the people of Nyumbani had, and all too often, it wasn't enough," Charles writes. For one hundred rains, the white people assaulted western and central Nyumbani, before the ancient kingdom of Cush in the far north found effective tactics to fight back. "The sons and daughters of Nyumbani drove the Atlanteans back into the sea, slaughtering thousands in the process, even as the Cloud Striders defeated the Mashataan on their cosmic battlefield." All traces of the white invaders were destroyed in the Scouring, but legend persisted for hundreds of rains that some of them still lived in a stone city called M'ji Ya Wazimu. The City of Madness.

The two people Imaro pursues are now captives in that citadel of insanity, Pomphis tells him. Imaro swallows the history bitterly. "He was glad he had slain the three in the clearing, and he looked forward to killing more of them after Jua's setting."

Imaro's people have no legends of these invaders. He tells Pomphis he is . . . *was* of the Ilyassai, the Lion-Slayers. A nomadic tribe of warrior-herders who roam the plain called Tamburure. Pomphis tells him the Mizungus never reached his people. But, the worldly pygmy notes, Imaro does not look like Ilyassai people typically do. Is he of mixed ancestry? Imaro glowers and strikes fresh terror into his new friend's heart. "'I don't want to talk about it,' Imaro finally said, spitting out the words as if they were poisonous.

"'This man is in deep pain,' Pomphis suddenly realized. 'He has been in pain all his life.'"

As that first Imaro tale ends, Pomphis confides in the warrior that he has been sent by the ruler of Cush on a secret mission: "Seek the one who was forsaken . . . seek the mightiest warrior of all . . ."

"I need to know who you really are, Imaro," Pomphis says.

"So do I."

Charles's first Imaro story was an instant hit with readers. Gene Day greenlit more Imaro stories, and Charles got to work. *Dark Fantasy* was a rather obscure Canadian zine that paid writers with free copies, but Charles had read that Lin Carter, an influential editor with the prestigious New York–based speculative fiction publisher DAW Books, was looking for fantasy with new settings. With L. Sprague de Camp, Carter had played a critical role in bringing Robert Howard's Conan stories back into print and popularity in the 1960s—the exact stories that turned Charles into a fantasy writer. Charles sent him a copy of the story and nine months later Carter asked to reprint it. It's the kind of break writers dream of: A powerful person spots your first short story, sees your immense talent, and calls you up to the big leagues. In 1975, Carter published "The City of Madness" in DAW's *The Year's Best Fantasy Stories*. Carter tended to focus on established writers, but he saw Charles's talent and knew he could thrive on the national stage. Imaro was the cover boy when *Dark Fantasy* published the next story, in 1977. "The return of IMARO—thrilling Sword & Sorcery by C.R. Saunders," the front page promises.

"Our cover marks the first time that IMARO has ever appeared on the cover of a magazine," the interior copy reveals. In fact, it's the very first image of Imaro, and was created by Gene Day and Paul Lambo. Charles is listed as a consulting editor. Imaro grips a sword in his right hand and a severed head in his left. He's rippling with muscles and glaring at the viewer, his sullen face framed by an Afro. Also in that edition was a previously unpublished story from Tevis Clyde Smith, a long-time collaborator with Robert Howard. Charles follows Smith with the last story of that edition, entitled "Horror in the Black Hills." Charles had found his mission. "For a long time, I felt that I was alone in what I was doing . . . kind of like a voice howling in the wilderness, only to hear Tarzan howl back."

Charles was once asked how much of himself was in Imaro. "Not much. Maybe 10 per cent. No, not even that. My personal experiences are not the stuff on which fantasy is made. Some readers of Imaro think there's a lot of me in the character. One went so far as to call the novel my 'auto-fantasy-biography.' All I can say to that is whoever thinks that has a better imagination than I have. Imaro is a long way from being autobiographical, and I'm certainly no prototype for a barbarian hero," he said.[38] "Since Imaro was created from my imagination rather than someone else's, I suppose there's a little of my personality in him. But only a small fraction. Imaro is not my 'alter ego.' I don't sit around fantasizing about being Imaro. If I did the kinds of things he does, I'd be liable to get arrested."

Yet through the gumbo, his personal experiences were exactly the kind of stuff that was producing his new style of fantasy. Many people were writing Conan pastiche at the time, churning out repetitive novels with Conan covers to sell at the five-and-dime. Charles did not do that. The difference he was creating between his work and much of fantasy was not just the surface difference of setting it in Africa instead of Europe, and among Black people instead of white. Charles was discovering that the more time he spent thinking about Imaro, the more he learned about the warrior's inner world. And the more he wanted to know. Who were Imaro's mother and father? What child could have fathered such a man? Charles wanted to explore this Black warrior he had created to kick Tarzan's ass. But Tarzan was about to kick back.

---

38 Elliot interview.

6

TARZAN'S REVENGE

Charles's publishing career began like a fantasy but collapsed into a nightmare. Charles would later say that it took "about 100 megatons of nagging from my friends"[39] to push him to try writing a full-length novel. He knew he could write short stories and a novella. Writing always came easy, but the creative work of fiction could be brutal. Many a fighter has heavy hands, but no heart, and quits the first time someone hits back. Charles, for a time, worried he was the writing equivalent. His doubt was rooted in his secret: He'd already written a novel, though not about Imaro. "It was about Imaro's mother, Katisa, and what happened to her before she was forced to abandon Imaro," he said. "It took me almost a year and a half to write that thing. The finished product was piss-poor, but at least it was a learning experience. I never did try to market it."

That led him to stick to short stories, which was the default setting for sword and sorcery anyway. "Every time I tried to get started on a novel, I'd get sidetracked by a short story idea. I had come to think of myself as a short story writer. Writing a novel seemed akin to trying to fit a size-six foot into a size-12 shoe. Well, I *wear* size-12s, so make that a size-18 shoe."[40]

---

39 Elliot interview.

40 Elliot interview.

He wrote to his friend David Smith for advice. Smith, too, had started in short stories, including ones Charles published in *Dragonbane*. "How were you able to make the jump from short stories to novels? Like, I am going to do an Imaro novel some day, but I am a slow writer to begin with, and I'm afraid that in the year to two years it would take to write the bloody thing, the short story markets would dry up. It seems that for every new zine like *Dragonbane* that pops up, three of them go under," Charles wrote in April 1978.

He added that he typed with one finger, and the thought of handwriting a sixty-thousand-word novel, then pecking it out letter by letter, gave him "the shudders." He joked he hoped Imaro would learn to type for him. "At 32 years old, I realize that the only way I will ever make anything of myself will be through writing. I suppose I'm fortunate in that I have no family obligations. I don't have any driving career ambitions, either. It's just that I can't seem to develop the all-encompassing drive that it takes to attempt to write professionally," he said.[41] "I write obsessionally, as I feel that my African fantasy is a distinct contribution to the genre. That many other people think so, too, is one of the things that keeps me going. So I'll always keep writing, as long as I have stories to tell, and there are people who want to listen to them."

The other path was bleak. Charles knew well that his idol, Robert E. Howard, had ended his own life at thirty. In June 1936, Howard's mother was dying and it seemed he could not envision a life worth living without her. He shot himself. His father found him, and found in his typewriter a page with the final words Howard ever wrote, quoted from the poem "The House of Caesar," by Viola Garvin: "All fled, all done, so lift me on the pyre; The feast

---

41 Elliot interview.

is over and the lamps expire." Suicide seemed at times a natural predator to Charles, and when in 1978 he learned that his friend and fan David Madison had killed himself, he was devastated. Charles called him one of his "best friends in fandom." The two men had been writing to each other for three years, and Charles clearly hoped it would continue. Charles had published his friend in *Dragonbane* and thought he was poised for a breakthrough, before his demons overwhelmed him. "I don't know what drove David to suicide. He never gave me an indication that he was considering it. And I now have an inkling of the way Howard's contemporaries must have felt 40 years ago," he wrote.

Charles turned to writing for balm. He'd published several Imaro stories and one of them had been republished by DAW. Writing a novel seemed the clear next step, but Charles balked. In August 1978, he walked into the Royal York hotel in Toronto as a fan at the thirty-first World Science Fiction Convention. Also attending was Donald A. Wollheim, the founder of DAW Books and source of its name. Wollheim recognized Charles and introduced himself. Charles tried to capitalize on the moment by urging Wollheim to hire him to edit an anthology of fantasy writing. The publisher was not interested in that idea. "Don encouraged me to write an Imaro novel. Hell, I guess I'd better get to it, then. At least I know he'll look at it when I'm finished; indeed, he's interested in seeing me do a good job," Charles said. "In fact, that topic monopolized the entire conversation I had with him. I was reeling in astonishment, let me tell you. Here was a major publisher actually soliciting a novel from me!"[42]

Few writers get such an invitation, and it provided Charles a surge of energy and confidence. For the next two years, he toiled to

---

42 Elliot interview.

blend existing Imaro short stories into a "fix-up" novel. "Since then, I've been told by some that such a massive rewrite is actually harder than doing a novel from scratch. At the time, I didn't know that."

He updated friends when he passed twenty thousand words, and then thirty thousand, as if he were ice-picking his way up Mount Everest. He announced he'd reached the summit in a letter to his writing buddy Charles de Lint dated August 25, 1980: "Are you ready for the news? I HAVE FINISHED THE IMARO NOVEL!!!! Whooaahh . . . Don't go out and celebrate yet. This is just the first draft, written in long hand. I've got to write (I mean type) the submission draft. But I don't have to tell you that the most difficult thing is getting it all down on paper the first time. I actually look forward to doing the next draft. So far, I'm satisfied with the cobbling job I've done, but that could be just relief. No—I think I've got something here. Now, if only Don Wollheim at DAW agrees . . ."

Imaro had not learned to type. It took Charles two months to do the job. The finished novel was about seventy-seven thousand words. He submitted it and began the anxious wait for news of his fate as an author. He got his answer on a Friday the 13th in February 1981. He shared the news in a letter to a friend. "DON WOLLHEIM HAS ACCEPTED THE IMARO NOVEL!!!!!" he proclaimed in an all-caps explosion of joy to his friend David C. Smith. "I'm feeling no pain now. I mean, I'm as high as I'm going to get without the use of artificial stimulants." He got a $2,500 advance, which he planned to use against his debts. Charles consciously followed the blueprint created by Howard, who had turned Conan short stories into the only novel he wrote, *Conan the Conqueror*. Charles devoured African history, folklore, and anthropology.

"I took real historical places and transmuted them into places on a parallel Earth in which magic works and African societies developed in different ways. As I look back, I see that I may have emulated Howard a little too much," he wrote later of his first novel.[43] "Everything I absorb goes into a constantly simmering gumbo in my imagination and, when I write, I dip a ladle into that gumbo, and I'm always surprised at what comes out. It's usually a 'what-if,' as in 'what if the Zulus and Maasai were neighbours?' or 'what if the *chemosit*, a mythical monster of Mali, were real?' or 'what if an African group had domesticated the Cape buffalo and used it for warfare?'"

And what if Imaro lived in full novels, a whole series of them, instead of the quick-hit short stories? The result was *Imaro*, a blend of five reworked short stories: "Turkhana Knives," "The Place of Stones," "Slaves of the Giant-Kings," "Horror in the Black Hills," and "The City of Madness."

At the head of these comes a new piece of writing, the first chapter in Imaro's own life, and we glimpse the depths that would take Saunders beyond Howard. The novel opens not with swords or sorcery but with sorrow. In a prologue later called "I Leave a Warrior Behind," we begin with a prophecy: "Among them will come a Child of Wonder and they will know him not." In Howard's Conan stories, we rarely sense any struggle within the Cimmerian as he rises from outlaw to king. We never see a hurt child driving the mighty barbarian. With Imaro, it's often all we can see.

"A warm rain misted down on a small boy staring motionless in the tall, yellow grass. Although he enjoyed the sensation of rain on his skin, the boy's expression remained solemn—too solemn for a child who had seen only five rains wash through the Tamburure."

His mother stands with him, a "tall, slender woman with iron in her backbone and fire in her eyes." She's dressed to travel long distances and armed with a spear. "The woman's mahogany-brown skin reflected a sheen of beaded raindrops."

---

43 Interview with Amy Harlib, circa 2000.

It's Imaro fifth birthday. His mother, Katisa, brings him to the centre of their village and a collection of waiting elders. This is her family—her father, grandfather, mother, grandmother, aunts and uncles and nieces and nephews. We learn she was forced into a marriage but fled rather than wed. She stayed away for three years, then returned—carrying a child in her arms. She says nothing of his origins. She exposes a twisted man of her tribe—the man she was supposed to marry, the *oibonok*, or shaman, named Chitendu—as a traitor. Her people looked upon her child of no father with disgust. Katisa had shamed herself, and her people, by siring a child with an unknown outsider. The Ilyassai punishment for that crime is death. But Katisa made a deal with her people: She would raise Imaro for the first five years, as was custom, and then she'd hand custody of him to her tribe for his long warrior training, the *mafundishu-ya-muran*. And then she would choose not death but exile. Because she had saved them from Chitendu, her people accepted her proposal.

"She looked at her son. Already his body was hard and powerful beyond its years. She had seen to that. She had told him what was to come. He had accepted it with sullen stoicism," Charles writes. "Slowly, Imaro turned. He tilted his head upward to meet his mother's gaze. As always, Katisa interposed a barrier of lovelessness like a shield between herself and the son she had always known she must leave."

Imaro sees a flicker of emotion deep in her eyes. Mother and son hold hands. "We will keep our word. Now, keep yours. Go," the village leader tells her. She drops her son's hand. It's a devastating moment. Imaro trembles. "Katisa betrayed no reaction. Ignoring the silent onlookers, she turned to Imaro. She gazed at him long and intently, striving to convey a message beyond words, beyond touching; an expression of love held painfully in abeyance," we read. "Finally, at the very moment Imaro feared he would lose control and fling himself tearfully into his mother's arms, she spoke, as much to the gathered Ilyassai as to him. 'I go . . . But I leave a warrior behind.' " She strides off, not once looking back at her people. Or her son. Imaro watches her walk into the world beyond everything he's known. An old man hits him in the head and knocks the boy to the ground. Imaro feels tears forming in his eyes—for the last time. "We'll soon learn what kind of 'warrior' that woman left behind. Follow me, son-of-no father," the old man sneers. "Why, why, why couldn't you take me with you?" Imaro asks his mother in his heart. Outwardly, he sets his face in stone. "*The weapon was in the crucible*."

This first edition of the first novel ends quite differently from the modern versions. The DAW version concludes with this moment from the "The City of Madness": Imaro, a woman called Tanisha, and Pomphis sit happily together, eating around a fire. Tanisha is Imaro's partner, the woman he rescued from the City of Madness. Imaro has learned from Pomphis that his life is part of a bigger story, and they will set out for Cush to find answers. Chewing on the meat, they retell the stories they've just lived. Pomphis relates the curse word he used to get the Mizungus so angry. He told them their god "eats giraffe shit." Pomphis chuckles. Tanisha giggles. Then they hear a "whooping burst of mirth that exploded from Imaro's mouth, followed by another, and then another still. Losing his hold on Tanisha, Imaro guffawed louder still, holding his sides and slowly sitting down. There was a look of baffled wonder in his eyes as he continued to send loud, raucous peals of laughter skyward. Tanisha and Pomphis exchanged a glance. 'By Aspelta's claws,' the Bambuti half-whispered. 'I don't believe this man has ever laughed before.' He was right. Once again, the forging was true . . ."

DAW loved *Imaro* and scheduled it for publication in 1981. Charles was "walking on clouds" when he saw his name on the famous yellow spine of a DAW title in the advance reading copy.

The blurb does its best to lure in readers: "Imaro was his name—Imaro of the Ilyassai, Imaro the outcast, Imaro the legendary hero of the jungle continent. This is the epic, action-packed novel of how Imaro achieved manhood, won his rights among the people, and began his long march against the fantastic and unearthly terrors of that alternate-Africa known as Nyumbani."

Charles later described it as an origin and coming-of-age story: "In maturity, Imaro is a sullen, anti-social person, basically an outcast. The first novel depicts how he came to be that way. Imaro is a super-warrior, but he has problems. Those problems stem from a childhood spent among people who don't much like him. So, he doesn't much like himself, either. He has to overcome this self-rejection, and the first novel shows how he begins to acquire some self-esteem. At first, he does it by kicking the shit out of anything that threatens him. That's not enough, though. He has to learn that he's got to start caring about other people so he can care about himself. His discovery of that truth is the essence of the novel. Imaro wades through a lot of blood while seeking his identity. There is a psychological level beneath all the gore, though."[44]

Charles used his degree and his decade-plus of teaching psychology to portray the inner life of this warrior but never forgot his main job was to write exciting fantasy stories. "I don't sit at my desk and wonder about the Freudian significance of a sword fight, or how Imaro seems to be more into punishment than positive reinforcement," he once said.[45]

DAW positioned *Imaro* as the last of a legendary trifecta: "Imaro's saga will be compared with that of Conan and of Tarzan and of the heroes of history and legend and will rise above them for

---

44 Elliot interview.

45 Elliot interview.

authenticity, for vivid conception, and for gripping reading." DAW saw something special in Imaro, and in Charles. It hired veteran speculative fiction artist Ken Kelly to create the cover image. Against a dim backdrop of trees, two figures battle. The man holds a knife and is twisting his muscular frame against the pale monster, a fantastic animal with fangs and claws, which grips Imaro in its right arm. It's Isikukumadevu, the monster Imaro faces in "Horror in the Black Hills," the same one whose head he holds on the *Dark Fantasy* cover. But this image showed a different man. "When I saw the proof of the cover they intended to put on it, I came crashing back down to Earth," Charles said in a later interview.[46] "The cover copy included the phrase: 'The Epic Novel of a Black Tarzan,' and the cover artist, Ken Kelly, depicted Imaro as Tarzan with a suntan. Of course, I was outraged. Imaro was created to be an antidote to Tarzan, not a clone."

While authors have full control over the words that make up a novel, the physical book belongs entirely to the publisher. They generally consult the author about the cover and back copy, as they did with Charles, but they don't have to listen. And they didn't listen to him. "Anyone who knows about my work would realize that what I write is fantasy in an African setting. Not the Tarzan-type African setting, but something based on study of real African history, culture, and folklore. My heroic character, Imaro, has always been (in my mind at least) an alternative to the Tarzans of the world," Charles wrote.[47] "I didn't care much for that, to put it mildly. DAW said they thought that blurb would help attract readers' attention. It attracted attention all right—the attention of lawyers for Edgar Rice Burroughs, Inc. They had spotted some of DAW's advance

---

46 Harlib interview.

47 Letter to *New Canadian Fandom*, 1981.

publicity for IMARO, which included a proof of the cover. And ERB, Inc., threatened to sue DAW if IMARO were released with the 'Black Tarzan' designation on the cover! Rather than fight the matter in court, DAW decided to postpone release of IMARO until the new covers are printed minus the 'Black Tarzan' thing. Don Wollheim told me the delay would be 'about a month.' So Canadians won't be seeing IMARO until February at best. Hopefully, it has been released in the U.S. now, but I haven't heard anything yet."

The American edition finally came out in November 1981. It's a pocket-sized paperback with a green-and-white cover, titled *Imaro: The Epic Novel of a Jungle Hero*. The novel is dedicated to "the greatest mother in the world—mine!" Bookstores had already picked their fall choices, and *Imaro* was too late to get a push. DAW had loved the Imaro stories in part because they featured a Black warrior, but the "Black Tarzan" line was the only section of the exterior of the book that had identified him as a Black person. So when that line was removed, readers were left with a white-looking hero on the cover of a book set in an alternate Africa. And the title tells us he is a jungle hero, only for us to find him at home on the savannah. People had to pick up the novel and start reading to learn that Katisa has "mahogany-brown skin" and further still to glimpse Imaro's umber tones.

The book flopped. The late release killed the buzz, and not enough bookstores ordered copies to sell. DAW was already losing money on the series, but Charles was under contract for two more Imaro novels. From 1981 to 1983, he repurposed more Imaro short stories into *Imaro II: The Quest for Cush*, which was billed as "a whole new flavour of heroic fantasy." This cover features a Black Imaro, closer to the original image on the *Dark Fantasy* cover. Imaro stands before a rocky mountain range and a distant waterfall, towering over Pomphis and Tanisha. Imaro's dark brown skin bulges with muscles. "I loved the covers of the second two books, which were done by Jim Gurney," Charles later said.[48] The *Quest for Cush* ties together the stories "In Mwenni," "In Bana-Gui," "On the Bahari Mashiriki," and "In Cush."

"In this novel, Imaro is ready to discover the rest of Nyumbani. But the rest of Nyumbani might not be ready to discover Imaro," goes the blurb. The second novel follows the trio on their journey to Cush, a powerful and ancient northern Nyumbani kingdom modelled on our world's Kush, which comprises parts of Egypt, Ethiopia, and Sudan. Every step is met with increasing resistance as Imaro fights through a sea of monsters to get answers in Cush. Who is he? Who is his father? What became of his mother? What is his destiny? It's a great read, but it sold even fewer copies than the first. Bookstores didn't stock it, and the first Imaro had vanished from shelves, leaving readers with the unappealing prospect of starting the series on book two.

Charles got to work on the third installment, *Imaro: The Trail of Bohu*, his first novel written from scratch. The first two Imaro novels skillfully stitched together short stories published in fanzines, telling a powerful story of Imaro's early years, but they bear the marks of the sword and sorcery genre, with a rising-and-falling structure and a focus on exterior adventure. In his first true novel, Charles could plan out the entire structure and weave the story together with greater finesse. He also decided to start with a slower pace, much like he did with the added prologue to the first novel. For the contents of *The Trail of Bohu*, Charles must have turned to Diop's *African Origin of Civilization*, which details the ancient world of Kush, including the idea that the Judeo-Christian cosmology comes from Africa, as the wandering tribe later called the Jews encountered Egyptian religion, including a branch that worshiped

---

48 Harlib interview, circa 2000.

only Aten, the sun god. The theory holds that the Jews embraced the One God as their own. Diop cites fragments of ancient Egyptian texts that tell us: "In the beginning there was uncreated, chaotic matter, in perpetual disorder (*Bohu*); Breath (*Rouah*) hung over Chaos. The union of those two principles was called *Chephets*, Desire, which is at the origin of all creation." Imaro's greatest enemy, whom we meet in this novel, is named for the African concept of the chaotic disorder that came before creation. And the critical balance of power between Nyumbani and the spirit world is called *chephet*.

The Trail of Bohu introduces us to a different side of Imaro. After a supernatural prologue, Charles begins the novel with a tour of Meroe, a "city of iron" in western Cush. It sits next to the Gwaridi-Milimas Mountains, which never run out of ferrous ore. Lore has it that the city's first building was an iron-smelter's hut. "That single hut spawned a sprawling giant, with smoke from thousands of forges darkening the sky, and ancient slag heaps rising from the ground like offspring of the Gwaridi-Milimas," Charles writes in the leisurely first chapter. We learn about Meroe's important role in the Cushite kingdom, and how its forges have grown famous for the weapons they produce. "The steel of Meroe never shattered." Eventually, on page 13, we wander over to Shauf-i-Fayim, or the Section of Swords. We find Imaro "toiling at his newly acquired trade." The one-time warrior now makes weapons for others to wield. His mind is distracted and he commits a rare mistake in the forging. He's twenty-five rains old now, and has lived in Meroe for five years. These long years of starting a family are covered in a few lines of backstory. Imaro married Tanisha. They had a child, a boy named Kilewo, who is five rains when the novel opens. Imaro, who had no father to shape his idea of fatherhood, must figure it out on his own. He decides fatherhood means giving up his wandering life for a settled one. It means giving up his independence to take a paycheque. He is offered a position in the army, but Tanisha does not want him risking his life. He gets a job making swords in a forge run by another man. "Imaro remembered the day he began his own warrior-training," Charles writes. "The day marked the beginning of a long, painful journey to manhood for Imaro. It was a journey he was determined that Kilewo would not duplicate. Kilewo knew who his father was."

But he experiences a deep desire to return to war, to destroy his Naaman enemies, and to find his mother, and his father. "Lately, his feelings of unease had intensified. It was not the direct warning that his *kufahuma*, his attunement to the dangers of the wilderness, would have given him. This was more vague; a foreboding that his time of peace and inaction was about to come to an end."

He and Tanisha have grown distant. He won't tell her about his sorrows, and she can't bear his misery. She likes their cushy life in Cush. She has had enough adventuring. When Imaro suggests it's time to train Kilewo as a warrior, she almost laughs in disbelief. "Do you really want him to suffer, as you did?" They argue about it. Kilewo bursts into the room and Imaro lifts him high into the air. He cradles the boy in "arms capable of bending iron." In all his wild Howardian adventures, Conan never once hugs a child. But Imaro is not Conan; he is a human, and now a father. Tanisha sends Kilewo out of the room so she can talk frankly to his dad. "You are gone from me, Imaro. I don't know how, or why, but you are not with me anymore. You are here . . . but you are gone," she says. Imaro storms out and goes to work. It's a scene that takes us far from the escapism of fantasy writing.

Later, Pomphis visits the forge. Tanisha and Kilewo didn't show up for the boy's reading and writing lessons, he tells Imaro. He went to find them, but the house was silent and locked. Imaro tears out the door and races to his home. His kicks the door into pieces. He finds fresh blood splattered across the interior. And bodies, "butchered to the point where they were hardly recognizable as human." Two headless bodies, a woman and a child. Imaro is undone. *Weep and moan, Imaro, weep and moan,* he hears in his head. He knows that voice: It's Bohu, the Bringer of Sorrow. Bohu has killed his family. He has scarcely understood this when the authorities race in after him. Finding him amid the ruins of his annihilated family, they arrest him for murder. He charges at them and escapes the guards and their lions. He runs on, fleeing Cush, and goes hunting for Bohu. Imaro wants only revenge but begins to sense that somehow his own war with Bohu is entangled with the fate of all of Nyumbani. He chases the monster down an unravelling continent. The third novel ends with Imaro on the cusp of his destiny. Bohu lives. The final confrontation would come in the fourth novel.

But the fourth novel never came. *The Trail of Bohu* was stillborn. Few stores stocked it, and fewer bothered to order copies of the first two installments to entice people into the series. Nobody wanted to start a trilogy with book three. Charles knew the "writing was on the wall" but began writing the fourth Imaro novel and even outlined "part of a fifth" before he got the devastating news. In 1985, DAW Books told him it was killing the series. "None of the books made back their advance, and sales steadily declined with each novel. Other publishers didn't want to touch what they perceived to be a failed series of books," he said later.[49] "This pretty well put me into a funk. Maybe the time wasn't right for Afrocentric fantasy, I thought. Maybe my books didn't reach the right audience. Or, maybe they just weren't all that good."

Charles took it personally, but the entire sword and sorcery book industry was buckling by the mid-1980s. In *Flame and Crimson: A History of Sword-and-Sorcery,* author Brian Murphy contends that in the U.S., the yuppie ambiance of the 1980s weakened readers' appetite for barbarian tales. The motiveless malignity of sword

49 Harlib interview.

and sorcery didn't appeal to readers as much as quest fantasy did, as popularized by authors such as Terry Brooks. You can see the change in Arnold Schwarzenegger's 1982 movie *Conan the Barbarian*, which added a boyhood scene showing his family massacred to inspire the barbarian to seek revenge. Conan now has a quest that guides the story, unlike most sword and sorcery, which simply lets the adventures unfold in an old-fashioned, episodic way. "Blasted and reviled by the critics, groaning under a glut of poor Conan knock-offs, and unable to compete with elven princesses and epic quests, the sword-and-sorcery bubble burst, and the entire apparatus began falling to earth in the early to mid-1980s," Murphy writes. "Several authors were dragged down in its wake. Charles Saunders, for example, had just come onto the scene with the mass-market publication of *Imaro*."

Thrown out of his dreamed-of fantasy world, Charles was driven into the hard reality of life in Canada.

7

ALONE TOGETHER

A dozen of us gathered on what was for me a cold winter's day in January 2021. Milton Davis, Charles's great friend and publisher of some of his most important late-career fiction, had called us together. The sense of duty was overwhelming. The event captured the best and worst of pandemic video meetings. The best, in that we were gathered in California, Georgia, Colorado, Washington, Ontario and Nova Scotia. The worst, in that we were separated in those same places, all of us alone, all of us together for Charles.

I flipped through a preserved copy of the Halifax *Daily News*, and the ink smeared on my fingers. I laughed. In our days of print newspapers, we'd always had ink on our hands. The front-page headline read, "Sex Workers Can't Turn to the Cops—Prostitutes Say They're Afraid to Report Beatings, Rape." The edition was dated November 26, 2007, just a few months before the paper closed. I'd saved a copy because that was the first time I had a story published on the front page. I'd dug it out of my office closet to show it on the Zoom memorial. I wanted Charles's friends to see the newspaper where he'd worked for twenty years. I turned to the editorial pages, which were his domain. The editorial—unsigned, but written by Charles—concerns the then-new problem of drivers distracted by cellphones causing crashes. It's only a few hundred words, but Charles manages to lay out the entire case and conclude that drivers should be banned from using a phone while driving. Nova Scotia would pass such a law the next year. The letters to the editor, which Charles curated from the dozens or hundreds sent to the newspaper each day, mostly focus on a terrible incident at the Vancouver airport where a distraught and agitated Polish man was stunned by police and later died. Some letters call for better care for people with mental illnesses, others blame the police for a failed response, and others offer support for police officers caught in a winless situation, trying to protect citizens and themselves. The cartoon for the day shows a police officer at a press conference, saying: "Look, Tasers don't kill people . . . policemen kill people. Wait a second, that didn't come out right." I imagine that got a grim chuckle out of Charles.

On the call, Taaq Kirksey's camera flickered on and I saw him in the now-familiar spare room / office in his family's new home in Los Angeles. Last time we spoke, his young daughter had joined the call. It was a joy to see his joy in her. Milton sat in front of a bookshelf, a framing I'd grown familiar with as I watched his social media streams about the latest in Afrofuturism—his own writing, books he published at MVmedia, or other stories that caught his interest. Janet LeRoy joined us from a crowded back office stuffed with books and boxes. It was my first time meeting her. She'd worked with Charles in Ontario in the 1970s. Dale Armelin couldn't get his camera working but joined us on audio from Denver, Colorado. All of us knew Charles in one way or another—all of us but one. He was introduced as Neil Genzlinger, from the obituary desk of the *New York Times*. Did anyone mind if he joined? Taaq asked. No one did.

Charles had been dead for eight months and still lay unclaimed in an unmarked grave. We had launched an online fundraiser a few months earlier, and had pulled in a shocking $17,000 in the first twenty-four hours, from more than two hundred donations. I shut it down in a bit of a panic, as the flow was increasing beyond what we'd need to mark his grave. Some of the donations came with messages. One person had met Charles through International Pen Friends and struck up a seventeen-year correspondence. Another wrote simply, "Black writing matters. Black writers matter." Others remembered his short stories from the 1970s, or the DAW *Imaro* editions of the 1980s. Some had interviewed him. Illustrator Charles Fetherolf shared that his first illustration job had been to create the cover of Charles's novel *Damballa.*[50] "I was thrilled because I knew who he was and knew of his work," he wrote. I recognized many of the names from Nova Scotia: people who'd worked with him on the *Daily News*, or knew him through the Writers' Federation of Nova Scotia, or the Black Artists Network of Nova Scotia. Many were fans of his long-running column, and his books of nonfiction. "Charles's writing meant a lot to me. He deserves to be honoured, remembered and found," one person wrote.

Through emails, the small group of us who had raised the money tried to figure out what to do with it. One early idea had been to repatriate Charles and bury him next to his mother, but we soon realized that would be a difficult and perhaps impossible task. And Charles had chosen to live, and to die, in Nova Scotia. After I found his grave and shared photos of it with the group, we realized he was in a good place, and switched our focus to creating a fitting memorial to him there, where he fell. The staff at the graveyard told me only flat stones were permitted in that section of the cemetery. That didn't sit right with Dale, who had exchanged letters with Charles for decades and knew him well. He felt certain that we needed a standing memorial to Charles. I went back to the graveyard staff; they told me memorial standing stones were permitted on the perimeter of the yard. And it just so happened that the space for

50 Fetherolf created the cover for *Damballa*, and Clayton Hinkle did the inner illustrations.

such markers nearest to Charles's grave was vacant. We reserved it. I brought Paul Bacon, Charles's long-time fan and colleague from the *Daily News*, out to Charles's grave. Portia Clark, my colleague at CBC and a long-time friend of Charles's, also visited.

We decided to create two tombstones: a flat gravestone for Charles and a standing stone for Imaro. We selected a bronze marker with a granite base. The flat black surface had room for six or seven words. We started with the easy ones: "Charles R. Saunders, 1946–2020. Journalist and Author" came quickly. But African American? African Canadian? African Nova Scotian? Africadian? Nyumbani? He had worn all of those identities. We settled on "Black Journalist and Author." We were able to have his face etched into the bronze, too—and Portia came up with the excellent idea of adding a Black Power raised fist.

For the standing stone, we selected a craggy boulder with a smooth black face. The Americans came through with the concept for it: Could we get Imaro etched into stone, along with perhaps a quote and a tribute to Charles? The words came first. In the Night Shade edition of *Imaro*, Charles opens the book with a quote: "I leave a warrior behind." The full quote comes just a few pages into the novel, in that scene where his mother abandons him to her people: "Finally, at the very moment Imaro feared he would lose control and fling himself tearfully into his mother's arms, she spoke, as much to the gathered Kitoko clan as to him. 'I go . . . but I leave a warrior behind.'"

I ran the idea by the group. Everyone loved it. In real life, Charles adored his mother and remained a faithful son until she died. It seemed fitting to have Imaro's mother's words to him on the monument. Friends and colleagues who worked closely with Charles on his last books worked on the tribute. "Imaro, created by Charles R. Saunders, father of sword and soul. Rest In Power."

The image proved more difficult. Which Imaro? The DAW version, the one that proclaimed Imaro to be "the epic novel of a jungle hero," was my first suggestion. Milton objected. So did Uraeus, a writer and illustrator who had worked with Charles on the definitive editions of the Imaro series. Charles never liked that cover, they told us, as it looked more like a tanned Tarzan than a Black African. That was news to me at the time. The Night Shade Imaro had him standing astride the slain lion at the moment of his betrayal. It was hard to see how we could extract Imaro from that cover image without ruining it.

With time running out to claim the monument spot, I hastily suggested we go with the Imaro from the Night Shade edition of the *Quest for Cush*. Imaro stands, brooding, muscles rippling, left hand resting on his sword hilt, as he glares out at the reader. It was a clear image of Imaro, and it would fit on the monument. Charles's American friends saved me from making a huge mistake. Taaq conferred with Milton and Uraeus and got back to me. "Milton and I strongly think that one of Mshindo Kuumba's images from Charles's self-published works would be Charles's definitive preference for his headstone," Taaq told me. "The current image comes from the Night Shade run which, ending in the series being dropped as it was, was a tremendous personal blow to Charles that Milton and I remember vividly."

Taaq told me that the self-published editions were the first for which Charles actually got to decide the covers. We picked the image Charles had been working on in the last months of his life, a cover for a new edition of the first *Imaro*. But we couldn't crop Imaro out from Tanisha's embrace without maiming both of them. Uraeus connected me to Kuumba, a New York-based artist who specializes in Afrofuturism and who had created the new Imaro design. His website quotes him saying, "Africa being so central in civilizing the world, I found it peculiar that a strong positive image of Africa and indigenous populations is largely absent from contemporary media. In my youth, I recognized this and wanted to build a career addressing this discrepancy." We told him about our idea for the Imaro stone and he stayed up late, re-creating the Imaro image from scratch, designed to fit perfectly on the stone. Uraeus, who had laid out and designed the self-published editions, created and designed the lettering on the grave marker. We placed our order just before Christmas.

We got some bad news around then, too. Paul had taken on the task of finding out what had happened to Charles's possessions after he died. He learned that a real estate group had bought 11 Primrose Street in March 2020. When Paul visited Charle's former home, he spoke to a plumber, who told him the new owners had been doing a major renovation, and many of the residents had had to move out while the work was done. That may have been what led workers to find Charles's remains that May.

The new owners had only more bad news. Charles's next of kin, added in the 1998 lease, was Charlene Burrell—his mother. The number no longer worked, and no one could find anyone to claim Charles, so the real estate company held on to his belongings for two months. Legally, they only had to do it for one month. But by July, with police, the public trustee and the medical examiner drawing blanks on people to claim his remains, his possessions were thrown out. Whatever unshared projects he was working on were lost. So we met for the bleak Zoom funeral with mixed feelings. His legacy seemed to be slipping from our fingers.

Milton cleared his throat and began speaking. "Charles gave us that fictional hero that looked like us and existed in a world based on our origins. He did it without using the 'struggle' narrative that traditional publishers seem to require from Black authors. Imaro's struggles and triumphs were personal, not 'racial,' which for me was a breath of fresh air," he said.

Taaq struggled to compose himself when Milton asked him to say a few words. He told us about first meeting Charles through *Imaro*, and his amazement at how his fan letter to Charles led to a creative partnership to bring *Imaro* to the screen. Taaq told us about that visit to Nova Scotia in 2019, the year before Charles's death. "I had always been afraid that his living situation was suboptimal," Taaq said, "and when I got up there to see him, those fears were validated. My instinct told me he didn't have much time.

"For Tarzan to be the king of mythical Africa, it's an utter slap in the face to a young Black child who is looking for a place in his imagination where he can be indomitable, where he can be the king or the queen."

Dale spoke up, his faceless panel somehow the perfect way to represent his extraordinary friendship with Charles. Dale told us how he had come to love sword and sorcery as a young man, and been captured by Robert E. Howard's Conan stories. As a Black man, he, too, was disturbed by the racism ensorcelled in those worlds. When he read a revised Howard story in a comic book in the 1970s, he'd written a letter to the publishers praising them for excising the racist sections. Charles saw the same Conan story, and saw Dale's letter, and wrote to him. That first letter led to many others, and a lifelong friendship. Dale told us that as a young Black man at a nearly all-white Catholic high school, he'd "become an Uncle Tom." It was only in the long, patient, letter-conversations with Charles that he saw that, and saw the path back to freedom. "What Charles did was he gave me back my Blackness," he said quietly.

Dale and Charles never met in flesh and blood but forged their bond through paper and ink in endless letters exchanged over decades. That was what first led Dale to worry for Charles: No more letters arrived. It had happened before. In 2019, Dale grew so worried about a dearth of letters that he called the Halifax police and asked them to do a wellness check on Charles. Dale knew Charles deeply, yet he didn't know a single person in Canada who might know Charles. The police stopped by and found Charles well that time. Charles wrote to Dale, telling him he'd fallen and been in hospital but was alive and recovering. Dale worried again in May 2020, and placed another call to the police. They stopped by 11 Primrose Street on about May 2, and found Charles alive and enduring the lockdown. In late August, someone within Halifax police seems to have learned of Charles's death, or perhaps discovered it when they performed a second wellness check, and called Dale in Colorado—because that was the only name they had connected to Charles. Dale told Taaq, who shared the news on social media, which led to my finding out.

Janet LeRoy told us about seeing Charles teaching when she was a student at Carleton University in Ontario in the early 1970s. She glimpsed him through a doorway to a classroom as she passed in the hall. His great stature, Afro and dashiki top made a strong impression on her. "He looked like he'd stepped off the TV show *The Mod Squad*," she said. She graduated and found work at Algonquin College and was delighted to discover that Charles was now also working there. They struck up a friendship that would last the rest of his life. "He was a giant of a man, but he had such a tender, quiet voice," she said. "We could talk about the deepest, darkest moments in our lives, and Charles would find a way to say something that would make us both chuckle."

I was up next. I'd been asked to speak about his life in Halifax, and his work on the *Daily News*. I held up my copy of the newspaper and showed them the editorial page. "He was so quiet," I said. "He would never draw attention to himself. But you noticed him.

You could just tell there was a depth to him, a richness, that you don't find in many other people."

I told them how up here, in Canada, Charles was revered as a great journalist and groundbreaking author of nonfiction books. He was one of the very first Nova Scotian authors I'd noticed as a teenager, and long before I met him, he had started to create a cognitive leap in my own mind that I, too, could be a writer in Nova Scotia.

Nearly an hour had passed. Nobody wanted to end the memorial, but the video call was getting ready to cut us off. We spoke together for a few more minutes. I told them I hoped the gravestone and Imaro stone would arrive later in the winter, and that we wanted to hold a graveside service in May, if pandemic restrictions permitted. We began the awkward business of ending the video call and our screens went dark, leaving each of us alone again.

Neil's long obituary for Charles appeared in the *New York Times* on January 21, 2021. "On Jan. 16, about a dozen people from across the United States and Canada held a Zoom memorial for a man whose remains have been lying in an unmarked grave in Nova Scotia since last spring," it began. "He was Charles R. Saunders, and his lonely death in May belied his status as a foundational figure in a literary genre known as sword and soul. Some 40 years ago, Mr. Saunders reimagined the white worlds of Tarzan and Conan with Black heroes and African mythologies in books that spoke especially to Black fans eager for more fictional champions with whom they could identify."

The article was printed under the headline, "A Black Literary Trailblazer's Solitary Death: Charles Saunders, 73. His speculative fiction was built on Black heroes and African themes. He died alone and unrecognized, but friends are trying to make amends."

The story's top photo was a selfie Taaq had taken on his visit. He and Charles stand together, faces nearly touching, with matching mild, self-conscious smiles. Further down is a photo from his late Halifax days—a snapshot taken after the death of the *Daily News*, when the rim gathered for one last night. I'm standing right next to him, smiling.

Taaq was working on telling Imaro's story in film or TV. Milton and Uraeus were working on new editions of his books. As the video funeral ended, I wondered—could I tell Charles's story in a biography?

As a journalist, I'll cover whatever story is happening on any given day. But books are different. I'm an objective reporter but a subjective author. I won't write a book that doesn't come from my heart. The obvious first problem for me was that Charles was Black and had written a groundbreaking series about Black heroes, and I, his white reader, missed that entirely on my first reading of *Imaro*. It wasn't until Taaq, Milton, and Troy spoke to me that I began to realize my old colleague hadn't been writing novels just for fun, but in a cypher that was clear to Black readers and opaque to others. I didn't know much about fantasy, either.

But I'd always felt a heart connection to Charles in life. We were both journalist-authors, both enjoyed editing, and we were both eager outsiders learning about African Nova Scotia culture and history. I decided to start reading to see if the seed of an idea would bloom when watered with such words. I ordered and read *Tarzan of the Apes*, *The Complete Chronicles of Conan*, *Star Man's Son*, *The Lost Cities of Africa, The African Origins of Civilization, The World and Africa* and *Robert E. Howard: A Literary Biography* to get started. I also ordered and read every single book Charles had published. That took some digging. I also managed to track down the 1977 *Dark Fantasy* edition that put Imaro on the cover. To broaden my horizons, I read several Octavia Butler books (she has the best aliens I've ever met), Samuel R. "Chip" Delany, the *Lord of the Rings* trilogy, and a few biographies of J.R.R. Tolkien. I read contemporary Black speculative fiction novels including the beautiful *Skin of the Sea*, in which Natasha Bowen fuses mermaids, the slave trade, and ancient African traditions; *Brown Girl in the Ring* and other books by Nalo Hopkinson; and Andre Fenton's supernatural African Nova Scotian novel *Annaka.*

I never forgot the sight of Charles at the launch of *The Hermit of Africville*, and the fact that I got pulled into his story because he had marched a friend into a bookstore to buy my book. Charles always encouraged writers (including me) during his lifetime, and this sense of posthumous blessing gave me courage. And then I began receiving letters from Charles. His old friend from Lincoln University, Morris Fried, had saved every letter and card Charles sent him over thirty-five years. Twice a week, Morris scanned a letter into his computer and emailed it to me. Steadily, Charles began telling me about his life. The first letter came from the summer of 1985, and Charles showed me the beginnings of a new chapter he was writing for himself in Halifax. The letters continued, one for every few months in his lifetime, right up until his death.

Charles wrote 137 letters to Morris, his oldest friend in the world. From the time they first met as students at Lincoln University, their friendship remained intact until the end, spanning fifty-six years. Morris saw him turn from an eighteen-year-old freshman named Charlie to a seventy-three-year-old wizard called Charles R. Saunders. Nobody else outside of family knew him for the entire duration of that period. On the rare weeks when Morris was unable to send letters, I found myself worrying about how Charles was doing. It was an extraordinary view of one of the dozens of long-term correspondences Charles lovingly cultivated. Morris is unique in that he was friends with Charles in flesh and blood in America, and friends with him in paper and ink for the duration of his exile in Canada.

Charles had up to forty correspondents over his life, though that number had dropped to perhaps a dozen in his last years. Janet LeRoy became a close friend of Charles's when he taught in Ontario, and she treasured their friendship in letters after he moved to Nova Scotia. While Charles and Morris write about Canadian and American politics, old Lincoln friends, and the ups and downs of long lives, Charles and Janet speak more heart-to-heart. She curated her collection and agreed to share some of his most beautiful letters with me.

And the most astounding thing happened one day while I was writing at my desk. I saw two legs swish past my basement window and the doorbell rang. I jogged up the stairs and opened the door to find a heavily taped moving box on my front steps. I tried to pick it up but discovered its weight and dragged it over the threshold. I sliced it open with a knife and gasped: Inside was the complete collection of Charles's correspondence with Charles de Lint, the iconic Canadian fantasy writer whose long and successful career started in Ontario, in the 1970s, when he was a member of the Ottawa Fantasists along with his beloved friend, Charles R. Saunders. The first letter is from 1977, and for decades, the Charleses discussed writing, shared tips on character formation, read each other's work and gave hard-hitting feedback. I'd been talking to de Lint for a while, hoping to get his thoughts on Charles. But he was dealing with a difficult personal matter at the time and was unable to speak in depth with me. Instead, he gathered up every note he'd ever gotten from Charles and gifted them to me.

I unpacked the treasure chest and sat on my office floor piling Charles's papers around me, imposing a chronological order on the dozens of letters and photocopied columns. I found an unpublished forty-two-page transcript of an interview Charles did with Jeffrey M. Elliot in the early 1980s, offering a wealth of information about his formative years as a writer. I found an invitation to Charles's wedding, and many Christmas cards. I saw that when Charles sent letters, he decorated the envelopes with stickers or clippings he thought would amuse or engage the recipient. I found unpublished manuscripts. I had met my mentors, and I prepared to cross the threshold into Charles R. Saunders's extraordinary world.

8

SNAKE THOUGHTS

While Imaro's identity solidified inside of Charles, his own external identity as a new Canadian was being shaped by his response to his adopted home. There are rumours of Charles crossing the Canadian border several times in 1968 and 1969, perhaps preparing a landing ground for himself. He moved to Hamilton, Ontario, in 1969, a three-hour drive from the U.S. border. I didn't know how he'd got there, or why he chose Hamilton. I did learn he married a white woman named Margaret within a year of his arrival. It's not clear how they met, or if she was Canadian or American. In 1970 they travelled to Montreal, Quebec, for a weekend away. That fall, the October Crisis shook Canada. The FLQ, a terrorist group that wanted Quebec to separate from Canada, kidnapped and killed a Quebec politician and abducted a British official. The federal government invoked the War Measures Act—the first peacetime application of martial law in Canada. "The radical right-wing mayor of Vancouver at the time threatened to use provisions of that act to deport the 'draft dodgers,' 'hippies' and other 'American riffraff' who were infesting his country," Charles wrote to a friend.[51] "My thought was, 'Oh, shit. What if this idea spreads across the country?'"

---

51 Letter to Janet LeRoy, circa 2018.

It didn't. The crisis was controlled, and further disaster averted.

Charles moved to Ottawa around fall 1971. The people of his new homeland made some strange impressions on him. In Ottawa, Canada's capital city, a white guy started hanging around him and talking in a cringey impression of Black slang. Charles kept an open mind. "Eventually, I learned that he was being sincere; he genuinely admired Black people, and his use of idiom was an expression of that admiration. And we became great friends. He was kind of like my 'white soul brother,'" Charles wrote.[52]

In 1973 or 1974, Charles's old editor and friend at Lincoln University, Ron Welburn, visited him in Canada and gives us our first eyewitness of a changed Charles. In the yearbook they'd worked on together, they wrote about "Snake Charlie" and his many permutations, concluding, "We will always remember his 'metamorphosis.'" Charles had truly left the cocoon in Canada. The tall, skinny, quiet kid with "white hair" had transformed into a huge, hulking man with an Afro and beard. Ron thought he looked like a young lion and he barely recognized him. Ron was further flummoxed when Charles introduced him to his wife, Margaret. Ron chatted to her briefly but learned little about her.

Charles and Ron walked to a restaurant; Ron observed his friend. He remembered how as a teenager on campus, Charlie seemed to try and shrink to the point of invisibility. But in Canada, he appeared determined to take up his space. He powered along with his chin up. He was no Big Bird bobbing these days. Ron watched in amazement as his friend stepped out onto the road, in front of cars, as though the metal would bounce off him like he was Super Splib. He thought it was something of a lesson in Canadian cultural deference to pedestrians, but mostly he saw a new Charles

52 Letter to Janet LeRoy, June 4, 2017.

R. Saunders muscling his way into the world. They parted on good terms but soon lost touch.

Charles worked as a sessional lecturer at Carleton University and at Algonquin College. Friends and colleagues knew he was American and suspected he was avoiding the draft but learned little else. Few heard him speak of his family and none ever heard him discuss his father. Some friends had the impression he didn't know his father, or perhaps even know who the man was.

We get a second memorable early impression of Charles in Canada in the 1970s. He was teaching a sociology class to a cohort of early-childhood education students at Carleton University. Every student was white and female. He tried to lecture, but the class chattered away with Monday morning gossip. A tall Black man with an Afro and dashiki shirt, he seemed unable to raise his voice to control the classroom. He was twenty-five, barely older than the students. "It just happened," he told a friend. "I reached forward, picked the desk up off the floor by a few inches, and released it. It sounded like a gunshot!"

He didn't expect it to be that loud, but he kept his face implacable as every student jumped out of her seat. He started teaching. The next week was proof of psychologist B.F. Skinner's theory of operant conditioning: The students had quickly learned that when Professor Saunders was in the room, you'd better keep your eyes on him. He started the class with no angry or outraged students, no chatter, just silent, smiling, alert young pupils. He quickly became known as the gentle giant, a big man on campus, but a quiet one. Students would surround him at his desk at the end of the class to ask questions and share ideas.

He taught social sciences in a program called Man and His Environment. The universities provided work, but not a job, meaning he was constantly switched in and out, given new courses, or shelved for a term. Charles persisted and created Algonquin College's first course on racism. He introduced the Chitling test to his white students. It was designed to jolt students out of ideas they didn't even notice they had, like the notion that IQ tests impartially measure true intelligence. Yet the Chitling test reveals how much of what "neutral" IQ tests measure is not "general knowledge" but culturally specific knowledge. It's sort of a brown eyes, blue eyes experiment for the mind.

"Nobody was teaching that at the time. But Charles was," Janet LeRoy later said.[53] "Through his eyes, it was much easier to understand how minority groups of people had been put down through education, through health."

Charles blew his students' minds one morning by observing that Black people can struggle to tell white people apart. A young white woman was bewildered. "But you guys all have dark skin, curly hair, and dark eyes. We've got different coloured hair and eyes. So who looks alike?" she challenged him. "It all depends on what you're looking at," he answered. "Whites look first at hair and eye colour, because that's what's most different among them. Blacks look at things like skin shade, degree of straightness of hair, nose width, and lip shape, because that's what's most different among us. It's the point of reference that determines who 'all looks alike.'"

He later told the story to a friend. "I don't know if she was all that convinced. But when I describe white people in words, I find that I have to change my reference points to keep them all from looking alike. One thing for sure, though—you're not gonna see any 'snow white bosoms' in *my* fiction!"[54] In his writing, people show skin that is ebony, midnight, cocoa, umber, and cinnamon.

---

53 Interview with the author, 2021.

54 Letter to Charles de Lint, November 7, 1987.

Their hair is woolly, or kinky, or shorn, or matted, or long and braided. Noses have clear, individual contours, and lips are full or everted. He struggled to differentiate white characters beyond comparing their pale skin to the shade of a fish's underbelly.

He was perhaps the only Black professor on campus, and his expansive mind appealed to the young students. People joined the program so they could take classes with Professor Saunders. A few had heard about his fledging fiction career and wanted to talk about that part of his life. He was inspired by their interest, and kept writing. He arranged his course so that the design became a teaching element. He knew that psychologists had found that when people have choices, they tend to do better. So he gave students modules to select from, and then asked them if that ability to choose had motivated them to work harder. He created several pathways to the perfect score of 100, and provided an option to take a different path to improve the final grade. That taught them mental flexibility and resiliency. If there is only one path to success, and failure is not fixable, people lose hope. But if there are many ways to win, and mistakes can be overcome, people press on.

He told a few friends about his Imaro stories. Janet LeRoy, his university colleague, became a fantasy fan because of them. Janet found a good position at the college and settled into a long career. She and her husband would fight over who got to read the newest story Charles had mailed to them. Janet was a slow, considerate reader, and liked to take a month to savour a novel. But when she picked up *Imaro*, she found herself spellbound for three intense days of reading, voyaging through Nyumbani before returning disoriented to Ottawa. She could not believe the man she worked with at the university had such vast universes inside him. "He created miracles with how he married words together. I honestly never read another person who does it in the way he did," she said. "Even in his letters, I would reread a sentence because it would be so unique."

Consider the following from *Imaro.* It comes early in the saga. Imaro has been forced to flee his Ilyassai home and is living like a beast of the Tamburure. He speaks to no one. Our wild warrior has become the supreme predator of the savannah and has just killed a man who sought to kill him. Imaro seems barely human. He then sees Keteke, a war captive who was meant to be his wife before he was kicked out of the clan. Her people, the Zamburu, had hunted in Ilyassai territory. In revenge, Imaro's Kitoko clan raided Zamburu territory, "burning, killing, and taking cattle and women." Imaro leaves with five new cattle for his herd, and a woman who will become his wife. He reflects on how unfair it is that his mother was exiled for mating with a non-Ilyassai man, while Ilyassai men are free to partner with any woman. "But he did not vent his anger on Keteke. To her, he had finally opened a heart that had remained inviolate since the slaying of Kulu. And Keteke had responded in kind." The young couple agree to delay marriage until he has fulfilled his *olmaiyo* and become a warrior. The *olmaiyo* completes the *mafundishu-ya-muran*, the warrior training. Each young man must kill a lion to free the Ilyassai spirit inside, and to prove he has Ilyassai courage. Using an audacious new technique at the high point of his *olmaiyo*, Imaro dispatches the lion like no other. "Imaro dropped the weapon and hooked strong, dark fingers into the lion's mane. Effortlessly, he raised the huge, heavy head of the lion above his own. Blood from the stump of its neck showered like hot, salty rain onto his shoulders and upraised face."

But disaster strikes after what should be a triumph. His tribe's shaman uses *mchawi*, sorcery, to trick the other warriors into thinking they saw Imaro flee the lion. He is declared an *ilmonek,* an unman, a coward, and sentenced to disgrace and death. He escapes, and after killing his Ilyassai rival he finds himself alone with Keteke.

She urges him to build a new life with her people. With his strength, smarts and skills, plus his knowledge of the feared Ilyassai, he can rule her people, she promises, and together they can drive the Ilyassai from the plains. Imaro says no. He must be alone to pursue his personal destiny. In despair, she wades into a lake to drown. Here is how Charles wrote it in the first edition: "Refusing to look at Imaro, she had begun to chant a Zamburu death-song. Exasperated, Imaro had shouted her into silence. In his own past, thoughts of ending his own seemingly unendurable existence had sometimes crept into his mind. They were snake-thoughts; with the iron edge of his determination, he had slain them. Yet, snake-like, those thoughts continued to writhe long after they had been slain . . . he had not wanted to be reminded of them . . ."

Charles relies on the violent imagery of sword and sorcery but forges the words into a commentary on Imaro's inner fight with the "snake-thoughts" of suicide. Charles's sentences carry the weight and balance of the epic poetry he emulated. And he always found the exact right word: *Exasperated, Imaro had shouted her into silence.* The mighty warrior is not in this moment angry, or threatening, but merely exasperated. With one word, the larger-than-life hero is humbled into a man trying to work things out with his fiancée, and failing. A human who would choose a fist fight with a demon any day, rather than engage the "snake-thoughts" of his own mind. All his muscles and rage are no help at the edge of this water.

While Charles waged his own inner battle with creative writing, he struggled in the outer war. The universities kept jostling him from term to term, offering no stability or seniority, nor a sense that they valued his contributions. His teaching work at one university ended abruptly in 1976. His life frayed. He told a friend that it all culminated in disaster in May 1979. "All my problems (prolonged unemployment, no money, imminent eviction, a very deadly, lengthy writing slump, etc.) had become just too much for me to bear. I became mired in negativism," he wrote on June 12 of the same year.[55]

"So, three weeks ago, I cracked up. First, I got drunk. I had to, to remove inhibitions against what I had planned to do. In the course of my drinking, I ended up at the university where I used to work. I had a steady job as an instructor teaching Introductory Psychology there up until three years ago. I ended up getting the short end of the stick in a dispute with the department chairman, and my contract wasn't renewed. In the three years since then, I had only six months of salaried work. The rest was the pits. The pits had gotten too deep for me.

"By now you must have guessed that I intended to take my own life that night. But first I wanted to go out in a blaze of glory. So I went up to the former department chairman's office and set fire to it. Nobody was around; nobody saw me do it. Then I went down to the lavatory on the floor where I used to work. I guess I was thinking symbolically that night. I went into a toilet stall, sat down, took out the razor blades I had bought earlier, and sliced my arms open. There were four wounds, one on each wrist and one on each crook of the elbow. The blood flowed out just like it does in our stories. I weakened, fell down, and figured I was about to die, and didn't feel too badly about that. Then I lost consciousness.

"I regained consciousness, not in the special hell for suicidal fantasy writers, but <u>outside the lavatory</u>, lying half-in and half-out of the elevator across the hall. Question: <u>How did I get there?</u> My only answer is that Imaro decided that he wanted me to continue to write his adventures; he wouldn't allow me to die. Anyhow, firemen found me in the elevator, and rushed me to the hospital, where

---

55 Letter to David C. Smith.

I received blood transfusions and other emergency care. After an overnight stay, I was put in jail by the cops on a charge of arson. I spent the morning behind bars."

Friends bailed him out. He got a lawyer. He prepared for trial and the possibility of a criminal conviction in Canada. "For a few days afterward I was in a sort of emotional limbo. You don't know what 'low' is until you've made a serious suicide attempt and failed. But the doctors said that if I hadn't been found when I was, I would have died of shock and blood loss. I think I began to recover when I realized that my survival was not a failure. Right now I am trying to sort things out and find a more constructive way to solve my problems. My friends have really rallied behind me, and that has helped a lot. I just feel sorry that I've disappointed them. I'm sorry I disappointed you," he wrote to his friend.

He apologized for "laying it on him," but said he wouldn't be honest if he didn't tell him.

"You are right in the defence of writing as an obsession. Without that obsession, our lives would have little meaning. No matter what I do to make a living, what I am by definition is a writer. I feel that with my introduction of true rather than ersatz African mythos and setting, I am making a contribution to fantasy literature. And when, in those dark days of May, it seemed as though I had lost the ability to make that contribution, I just didn't feel like living any longer."

But he was creating again. "So Charles Saunders the writer is still with us." He wrote about Imaro killing demons to slay his own demons. He credited Imaro with hauling him off the toilet and dragging him to the elevator, where he had a chance to live. He poured that new life into returning the favour and would spend decades writing Imaro's journey to its extraordinary conclusion. He knew he and his writing were permanently entangled: His real-world health depended on him creating a healthy Nyumbani. "I am trying to rebuild; to put the pieces back together with stronger glue. I know now that there are many people who wish me well, and that knowledge will be part of the glue."

He pled guilty to arson, and due to his "serious crime" the court delivered a suspended sentence with a year of probation. And not a single offer of help for his severe mental health crisis. After five years, he could have his conviction removed from his record. He could remain in Canada. "Right now my mental state is fairly stable. It was good to discover that my writing ability has not deserted me. I still get depressed when I remember that right now I'm surviving on friends' charity. Pride goeth before the fall, but without pride, what's the use. I am keeping my head on straight, though."

He later told the story to Janet LeRoy in their shared office space at the college. She remembers it as a Friday afternoon, when everyone else had left. Charles had something he needed to tell her. He was afraid it would affect their friendship, that it would cause her to see him differently, but he needed to tell her anyway. She sensed a lot of shame in him about what he was preparing to tell her. What he said stunned her—in part because she'd already heard the story from a friend of her family. Jim Van Egmond and his parents often visited her family for Christmas dinner. One Christmas, when Jim was a rookie firefighter, he told them about one of his first experiences earlier that year. He was part of a crew called to an Ottawa university fire. The experienced firefighters tackled the blaze but noticed the elevator was stuck on a lower floor. The chief sent Jim and another rookie down to investigate. When they got to the elevator, the door was opening and closing on a man lying prone and unconscious. Blood was everywhere. The man was Charles. Jim saved his life but did not know his name, or anything else about him as he told the story. Astonished to learn that Charles was that anonymous man at the fire, Janet told him about Jim, and later passed his gratitude on to Jim.

Janet once visited Charles at home and discovered his walls were covered with images of African people cut out of *National Geographic* magazines. Charles pointed at the photographs and explained that he used the images as models for the people in the Imaro saga. "The wall covering now made more sense to me! It was his writing haven," she later said.

On November 10, 1979, he shared big news in a letter to a friend, written just six months after he was in such despair that he tried to end his life. "Pray for me; I've just started the Imaro novel." He also started a course on bookkeeping, thinking it could be a steadier trade to pay the bills. He began teaching developmental psychology at a community college. In his letters, he appears rejuvenated. "I think the turning point was when I decided to stop regarding what I did as a failed suicide attempt," he explained. "I am still alive, so I am still successful. I am alive for a reason, which is to educate and entertain people via my African fantasy. So I'm going to do that. It doesn't matter whether I make a living at it or not; I'm just going to do it. Now, we'll see just how strong my resolve is when the next crisis hits . . ."

Charles had lost touch with everyone he'd known in America outside of family, but in 1984, he got a letter from an old peer at Lincoln University: Morris Fried. Charles had by then published *Imaro*, and Morris spotted it at a bookstore and saw the name Charles R. Saunders, and wondered—was it the same Charles he had once known?

"To satisfy your curiosity, yes, I am indeed the same Charles Saunders who graduated with you from Lincoln University," he wrote back.[56] "I know you must have been surprised when you saw

56 Letter to Morris Fried, March 31, 1984.

my name on *Imaro*, but then again you probably remember I had a pretty good imagination back at Lincoln."

He typed the letter on high-quality paper that came with distinct African art in the corners, and he added his characteristic stickers and illustrations to the envelope. In his first letter to Morris, he included a signed copy of *Imaro II: The Quest for Cush* and the magazine *Books in Canada*, which included an interview with him. Charles told Morris he felt the cover for the second novel was "more realistic" than the tanned Tarzan of the first. He assured Morris he was hard at work writing the third Imaro novel. "You know, I kick myself in the ass for not having taken fuller advantage of the African resources available at Lincoln. I should have majored in African Studies rather than psychology. But I was too busy trying to make up for lost social life, drinking, and otherwise screwing up. It wasn't until I got to Canada that I began to realize that African culture, history, and folklore would make a terrific setting for heroic fantasy. And it took a terrific cognitive leap for me to suppose I could write it. But I did, and got published, and now it's a career, although I don't make a living at it," he wrote.

"And, in case you haven't guessed, I came to Canada to avoid the draft. Yes, I finally smartened up about a year after we graduated. I can legally return to the U.S.A.; my case was dismissed during the Ford Administration. However, I have become a Canadian citizen, as I like it better up here. It's quieter, and you know I always was quiet except when I was drunk, which I don't get anymore."

Charles never seriously entertained the idea of returning to live in the United States. According to the back-cover blurb about *l'auteur* in the French Imaro, he'd become a Canadian citizen in 1975. Other than Morris, he didn't keep in touch with old friends, but he made new ones, people who'd only ever know him as an American exile writing in Canada. Charles read fantasy magazines, read the letters pages, and often wrote to the magazines. He made several long-term correspondents in that fashion. One of them was a white American fantasy writer named Ron Fortier. They connected quickly over a love of speculative fiction. They were American men of a similar age, but Ron had fought in Vietnam from 1965 to 1968. He suspected Charles was in Canada because he had objected to the war, and worried that Charles wouldn't want a vet for a friend. He worked up the nerve to tell Charles about his service; Charles addressed it in his return letter. This time, Charles was the one worried that his draft-dodger status would cause Ron to ditch him. Ron recalls Charles telling him he didn't believe in the war, thought it was morally wrong, and so moved to Canada. "I hope that doesn't end our burgeoning friendship," he added. Ron told Charles he respected his moral courage, and Charles in turn respected Ron's decisions. They would remain good pen friends for the rest of Charles's life. By 1977, Ron and Charles had joined a small-press writers club and bonded over their mutual love and respect for Gene Day, the zine publisher who first introduced Imaro to the world. Ron and his wife lived in New Hampshire. "Any chance you guys could ever come up to Canada? Maybe we could go visit Gene," Charles wrote in the early 1980s. In about the summer of 1982, Ron Fortier and his wife flew to Ottawa. She asked him how they would recognize Charles. Ron grinned. "I've seen pictures. From what I understand, he's this big, Black man."[57]

That was enough of a description for Ottawa in the 1980s. Soon a giant man with an Afro and beard materialized before them. "Hi, I'm Charles," he said—and swept her into the air. She was charmed by his warmth. "Welcome to Canada," he said, returning her to

57 Ron Fortier interview with the author, 2021.

earth. She told him the last person to pick her up like that had been Santa Claus. "I'm the Black Santa from the South Pole. Ho ho ho," Charles answered with a laugh.

Charles gave Ron a handshake that turned into a hug, though he couldn't get him off his feet. For three days, they talked writing and life, and took in the sights of Ottawa. Then they made a road trip to visit Gene Day. After *Dark Fantasy*, he'd gone on to illustrate Marvel Comics' *Star Wars* series, and now they found him deeply involved in the MC title *The Deadly Hands of Kung Fu*. Day delighted in showing them his works-in-progress featuring Shang Chi and Iron Fist. Comic fans loved the cinematic, richly detailed images Day created, and he seemed on the cusp of an important career as a fantasy illustrator.

The trip was over too quickly, and Ron and his wife returned to America. A month later, Ron's phone rang. He was disturbed to hear Charles's voice—he'd never once phoned him, and certainly not late at night. "What's up? Why the phone call?" Ron asked. "I've got some really bad news, Ron," Charles said. Earlier that sunny day, while crossing the street, Gene had suffered a heart attack, and died. He was just thirty. Charles had loved him and was devastated to lose him.

Charles's bond with Ottawa was fraying. He was divorced and frustrated. He enjoyed teaching but hated the instability. In the summer of 1985, his friend, the writer Spider Robinson, invited him to visit Nova Scotia. Robinson was born in New York but had moved to Nova Scotia in 1973, sometimes living at a hippie compound in the woods. He wrote a string of successful science fiction stories that would win him most of speculative fiction's highest prizes. Spider raved about eastern Canada's quality of life and urged Charles to visit him. And that spring, Halifax would host its eighth Hal-Con Sci-Fi Fantasy and Comic Convention. The organizers invited Charles and Spider to come together as the main attractions.

Nearly nine hundred fans packed the Nova Scotian Hotel to meet Charles, Spider, and the writer Eva Whitley.

Notes from an unpublished fan history of the event mention problems with the Dorsai Irregulars, "a group of costuming/gaming fans interested by the Dorsai (interstellar mercenary) characters created by Gordon R. Dickson." The eager irregulars had volunteered to provide security for the convention. "Unfortunately, they gained a reputation for strong-arming convention-goers rather than simply checking badges at the door." Aside from that, the event was a hit. "The programming was superb. Highlights were the costume contest, the art show and auction, the chocolate symposium," the fan history recounts. Many attendees enjoyed a lecture on the theory that we live in a flat universe. Charles noticed the fans in their cosplay outfits, including an eye-catching group called the Cape Breton Barbarians. But it was another group of people who quickly captured his heart: African Nova Scotians.

9

HOME IN AFRICADIA

Africans have been in the land now called Nova Scotia for more than four hundred years. The first African to visit was likely a man named Lusofonia, who came from the trade city Elmina in the Gold Coast, today's Ghana. He spoke several languages and earned his living as a *grumete*, often hired by Europeans for his language and cultural expertise on journeys exploring what was to them a new world across the ocean. Lusofonia adopted a European name for these trips: Mathieu Da Costa. In 1604, French explorers retained him for a trip to New France, which the British called Nova Scotia and the Mi'kmaq called Mi'kma'ki. Da Costa spoke Portuguese, and many Mi'kmaq had also learned the language to trade with Portuguese fishermen. It's possible he had travelled to North America before and may have spoken Mi'kmaw. He helped the French contact the Mi'kmaw leader Membertou and establish Port Royal, the first non-Indigenous settlement in what would become Canada.

Black people formed small free and enslaved communities in Nova Scotia's big colonial settlements of Halifax and Louisbourg in the eighteenth century. The American Revolution drove thousands of people out of that country for a freer life in Nova Scotia as the Black Loyalists. Several thousands of people settled in Annapolis Royal, Preston, Little Tracadie, and other areas. The Black Loyalists came with the white Loyalists—and many of the second group brought slaves with them. For more than twenty-five years, the free Black Loyalists lived alongside enslaved Black people. Halifax had held slave auctions since its founding in 1749, and in 1808, a group of slaveowners in the Annapolis Valley sought clarity on the matter. Their Member of the Legislative Assembly petitioned the Nova Scotia government "most humbly" to confirm that "property in Negroes was maintained and acknowledged if not encouraged." The Nova Scotian slaveowners explained that no law prohibited human slavery in the colony, yet "Negro servants" were walking away daily. They said it should be "incumbent" upon all free Black people in Nova Scotia to carry their certificate of emancipation at all times, or proof that they were born to free parents. That way, any other Black person could be assumed to be an escaped slave. The twenty-seven signatories claimed ownership of thirty-eight men, twenty-seven women, and nineteen children. The bill passed second reading but was not formally passed into law. The Slavery Abolition Act of 1834 began the process of ending slavery in Canada. As the historian Dr. Afua Cooper has observed, reparations were indeed eventually paid when slavery was dissolved—reparations to the slaveowners.[58]

The Jamaican Maroons arrived in 1796 and helped build Citadel Hill, the fortress that has protected Halifax since the city's birth, and dug out the streets of the growing city. The War of 1812 displaced more people, and a group later known as the Black Refugees fled to Nova Scotia in the 1810s and settled in Preston, Hammonds Plains, and other communities. In the early twentieth century, Black Caribbeans immigrated to Nova Scotia to work in the steel mills and coal mines, with many settling in Whitney Pier on Cape Breton Island.

---

58 Afua Cooper, *A History Exposed: The Enslavement of Black People in Canada*, exhibition at the Canadian Museum of Immigration at Pier 21, 2024–25.

In June 1985, Charles Robert Saunders added himself to the long list of African-rooted people to settle in Nova Scotia. He often explained his decision by saying that in Ontario, he saw lots of black squirrels—but not many Black people. Nova Scotia didn't have black squirrels, but he did meet Black people, and soon found a community that reminded him of the one he'd left in Pennsylvania.

He rented a modest room on Hollis Street in Halifax's South End above a shop in a two-storey red brick building that would later house the Trident bookstore. He had space for a hot plate, a fridge, and a bed. His room was overrun with books, papers, and a typewriter. He decorated his walls with dozens of photos of Africans from *National Geographic*. "Everything is going well here so far, with one exception, which I'll get to later. My pictures are on the walls, and the books are out of their boxes. Of course, the clothes aren't out of the suitcases, but the pictures and books do indicate that I'm getting used to the place. Kind of like a cat taking its first crap in a new litter box," he wrote.[59]

Charles intended to launch a career as a freelance writer, with the constant dream of one day being a full-time novelist. The "one exception" to his good life in Halifax that he'd alluded to was a health issue, and a bad one for a writer. Beethoven famously went deaf—and now Charles was losing his sight. He'd started wearing glasses when he was eight, and in his thirties he learned that he had cataracts in both eyes. "In bright sunlight, the world looks like a defocused camera image," he wrote. Without intervention, he'd go blind. The treatment would leave him unable to write for several months. That worried Charles, as he was a full-time freelance writer. He considered returning to teaching. "I guess I'll just have to see it through . . . no pun intended," he wrote to a friend.

---

59 Letter to Charles de Lint, June 22, 1985.

Charles visited Citadel Hill and stopped by the gift shop to purchase postcards for friends in Ottawa. Nothing mentioned the Black Maroons from Jamaica who had physically built the fort, but his eye stopped on one card showing three ceremonial soldiers guarding the entrance to the fort; two are white and one is Black. "See the guy in the middle of the picture? It's me! I lied when I said I was coming here to be a writer! I really wanted to be a Royal Artillery Cadet! Seriously, I'm here, I'm safe, I'm settling in, and I'm writing," he scrawled on the back before posting it.

He had heard about the *Jet Journal*, a Black-owned newspaper based in Halifax's North End. In August, he walked in without an appointment to apply for a job that didn't exist with the owner, Percy Paris. Paris was involved in business, hockey, education, and politics. He would later become elected to the provincial legislature and serve as a member of cabinet. As Charles waited in the lobby, another man entered—seeking the same nonexistent job. The younger writer's name was George Elliott Clarke, and he was Paris's cousin. He would later become poet laureate of Toronto and the Canadian parliament, but he was just starting out in 1985. "We were both there at the same time, looking for a job," George said later.[60]

Percy told them he barely had money to pay the bills, let alone hire writers. He did offer them keys to the office and access to the typewriter, which George would use often, as he couldn't afford to buy his own. George and Charles stayed in touch. George had published his first book locally in 1983, a poetry collection called *Saltwater Spirituals*. He was floored when he learned Charles was published out of New York. For George, the relationship quickly became a treasured friendship between himself, a younger Black writer, and Charles, an established Black writer fourteen years his senior.

---

60 Interview with the author, 2021.

George visited Charles on Hollis Street. He loved the writer's aesthetic, though his eyes kept drifting to the "distracting, hypnotizing" images of bare-breasted African women on the walls. Charles seemed to fill the entire space, but his ego was small enough that he never "pulled rank" on the younger writer. In return, George filled Charles in on African Nova Scotian history—Africadian history, as he puts it—and introduced him to Africadian writing. "On the Black North Atlantic, it's the most distinctive Black culture that exists. It's ours and it's important we have a name to demarcate it," George said. For George, it was the only literature that mattered, because it was the only writing that addressed the problems Black people faced. George told Charles about African Nova Scotian writers such as George Borden, Maxine Tynes, Carrie Best, Pearleen Oliver, and others. Charles didn't write or read much poetry, and George was unfamiliar with fantasy writing. But they supported each other as best they could.

If Charles had any illusions about Nova Scotia being a racism-free zone, George soon corrected that. Being Black in Nova Scotia meant being a suspect at all times. Take out your own garbage and then walk back into your house? Get arrested for break and enter. Drive your car into town to visit friends? Get pulled over and questioned for auto theft. Enter a shop and look for what you need? You'll find the store detective watching. Wait for a bus outside your apartment? Someone will call you a sex worker, and maybe call the police. George had family across Nova Scotia, and introduced Charles to the dozens of small Black communities they called home.

"Governments always forget that the people are smarter than they are. Even though the government deliberately set up a situation where Black Nova Scotians, like Mi'kmaq people, were going to be the have-nots, and going to be the reserve army of cheap labour, the lumpen proletariat of Nova Scotia; even though, what the people knew is that they finally had a chance to have a piece of property," George remembers telling him.

"What the government of Nova Scotia never understood was that people who had nothing, who had been enslaved, who had escaped from slavery, finally had the opportunity to have their children and to hold them; to have their spouses and hold them. And if you could do that on a little scraggly piece of land, upon which you could put your shack—which for you was a mansion—where you could have your children sleeping under the same roof? Your roof? On your little piece of land where you had a little vegetable patch, a few chickens, berry bushes, an apple tree? Even more important than that, you've also got neighbours. And they're Black like you. You've got a community all of a sudden.

"That folks who never could own anything—not even their children, or their spouses—could finally have all of that: spouse, family, household, community, neighbourhood. Add a church and a school and you're a viable culture."

Charles was charmed. "I was falling into a rut in Ottawa, and I decided it was about time to try something new," Charles wrote in a letter.[61] "Nova Scotia is unique in Canada in that it has an indigenous Black community of long standing. I feel right at home. It's better for me than the U.S.A., which is becoming crazier all the time, as witnessed by the MOVE incident in Philly."

In May 1985, armed members of the Philadelphia Police Department assaulted the headquarters of the Black liberation group MOVE. They cut off water and power to the residential area before bombing the houses and burning them to the ground. Police killed eleven people, including five children. News footage of the burned-out buildings shocked people around the world. For Charles, seeing

61 Letter to Morris Fried, May 18, 1985.

such anti-Black violence in his former home state shored up his decision to pursue his writing life in Halifax. "The move is taking up a lot of my energy, and it will take me a little while to get readjusted and go on with Imaro."

George, meanwhile, took a job as a social worker with the Black United Front. He spent the summer travelling Nova Scotia and working with Black communities. That got him very involved in the case of Graham Jarvis, a Black man from Weymouth Falls, Nova Scotia, who'd been shot dead by a white man in June 1985. The white man shot him from six feet away and said it was self-defence. The white judge freed him on a $100 bail and called Jarvis a "mean drunk," words many Black Nova Scotians never forgot. The white man was cleared by an all-white jury in what Black Nova Scotians understood as a gross miscarriage of justice. For George, one of the frustrating aspects was the media coverage of the case, and how the mostly white press corps often failed to get Black perspectives. In response, the Black United Front asked George to help them start a newsletter called the *Rap*. The monthly publication produced eight pages of Black news and arts and was sent to seven thousand homes. George asked Charles for help. "A grown man with plenty of other things to do! But he would come out and help me. And I needed the help," George said.

When he wasn't volunteering on the newspaper, Charles wrote a rare non-speculative fiction short story in 1985, which he called "Outsteppin' Fetchit." It takes place at the "Motion Picture and Television Home and Hospital." Lincoln Perry, a.k.a. Stepin Fetchit, had died that year at the Motion Picture Country House and Hospital, where he'd lived since suffering a stroke in 1977. His death prompted several obituaries and a return to the racial questions raised by his career. It took Charles's mind back to the time he'd spent at Lincoln University with Perry's son, Donald Lambright.

"The old man's body was so small and frail it barely made a dent in the hospital bed. But the orderly was still hard-pressed to hold him down," it opens.[62] "Those eyes were looking at him as though he were the Klan incarnate—and the only white thing on him was his uniform."

Nurse Henrietta shoves the new orderly aside and calms the old man. She tells the orderly that "Peanut Posey" was the old man's stage name, and he once was a movie star. "They used to say he 'outstepped Fetchit,'" she says. He had a notorious son, she whispers.

We cut to 1969 and ride with a wild young man called Flame as he guns his T-Bird down the New Jersey Turnpike. Tears storm out of his eyes. Flame has been fired up by a meeting of "Righteous Liberation" at the Harlem YMCA. "The revolution was getting its ass kicked, and something had to be done," Charles writes.

At the meeting, Flame was outed as the son of the notorious comic actor Peanut Posey. His father was a pioneering Black comedy movie star who's now a joke. People laughed at Flame for playing the Black militant while living off the royalties of racism. "The car was loaded with revolutionary literature—much of it written by him. And there was a semiautomatic rifle hidden under the front seat."

We see the New Jersey landscape flickering "like a badly spliced piece of film." When Flame was a boy, his father's clips had made him fall on the floor laughing. His mother would tell him, "That's your daddy, and he sends us money every month." Flame had met his father only five times, the last time when he was fourteen and towered over his tiny old man. "I know what you are," he'd said. He'd taken the name Flame to burn his past to the ground.

---

62 Unpublished manuscript. "Outsteppin' Fetchit" was eventually published in *Masques II*, 1987.

"Peanut was cavorting across the curve of the windshield. There he was, ear-to-ear grin on his face, chicken in one hand, watermelon in the other. There he went, out-steppin' Fetchit. Jersey was gone from Flame's windshield. There was only one way to bring it back. Still doing 85mph, Flame reached under the seat and pulled out the semiautomatic. He eased back on the trigger. Bullets rocketed into the windshield; slivers of glass swarmed around his head. Peanut was still there—grinning right at him. Peanut threw the watermelon to his son. Flame shot it. It exploded, spewing gobbets of red flesh and black seeds. Peanut laughed." Cars crashed and people ran. State troopers screeched up next to Flame and gave him ten seconds to surrender. They shot him dead on eight.

Back at the hospital, the new orderly stares at his untouched coffee as Nurse Henrietta finishes the story. "So you see, sometime when Peanut see a strange man on the ward, he thinks it's Flame coming to do him in—even though Flame been dead for sixteen years."

After the nurse leaves for the day, the orderly returns to the old film star's room and finds Peanut sedated. The orderly plucks a pillow out from under Peanut's head and holds it firm over his face, suffocating him to death. "Peanut Posey had gone through a lot of women," the story ends, "and he had more than one son."

Writing about this story later, Charles would say: "It was inspired by my hearing of the death of Stepin' Fetchit, a stereotype Black actor of the 20s and 30s. One of my fellow students at Lincoln University was Stepin' Fetchit's son. But nobody knew that until the son went on a shooting spree on the Pennsylvania Turnpike. Fetchit's son was a real militant."[63]

---

63 Letter to Charles de Lint, December 20, 1985.

That fall, Charles invited George on a walk along Barrington Street in downtown Halifax. They stopped outside a bookstore and Charles proudly pointed to the window display. Next to Spider Robinson's new book was *Imaro III: The Trail of Bohu*, published October 1985. *So this is what Black writers can do*, George recalls thinking.

Charles believed the new novel showed his growing powers as a writer. He liked the covers for the second and third novels, both done by James Gurney. "Imaro is so big he makes that rhino (or should I say *chipimbere*) look like a horse! My only disappointment was when they didn't use the Makonde sculpture forest," he wrote of the second cover. In his early days in Halifax, he still had hopes to continue publishing with DAW. His agent was talking to them about a deal for *Imaro IV* and *V*. "I don't think I'm going to be able to get much more done on *Imaro V* until after the [cataract] operation," he wrote. "Hopefully, I can get it done before the end of the year."

Don Wollheim, the DAW publisher, also ended up in hospital that year, putting plans for *Imaro IV* on hold. Charles kept in touch with Wollheim's daughter, who ran the company in his absence. "She also said she was just getting ready to read IMARO IV. Still don't know when I'm getting a contract, but she did assure me there would be one forthcoming."[64]

He lived near Halifax Harbour and its fog often grew so thick he couldn't see across the street. He stayed inside much of the time, waiting to hear from DAW.

"As far as my emotional climate goes, things have calmed down some. It has done me good to get away from the shit at Algonquin and other places. This city has a lot of places that are interesting just to look at, and most of them are within walking distance for

64 Letter to Charles de Lint, July 11, 1985.

someone who is used to walking," he wrote.[65] He'd discovered Point Pleasant Park, a forest filled with trails opening onto the ocean at the inner edge of Halifax Harbour. He loved the smell of salt in the air. Charles had also quickly learned that Hollis Street in the 1980s was Halifax's main stroll for sex workers. When one approached him, he demurred, saying, "I'm sorry, but my performance would not be worthy of your skill."[66]

He found his performance as a writer was changed by age, too. "I once tried to write when I had an earache. Couldn't do it. But then those were the days when any excuse not to write would do," he wrote.[67] "You'll like what Spider has to say about writing. 'I write because it hurts more not to do it.'"

He returned to Imaro, reworking a story about Bushmen and giant scorpions. He read a lot about Bushman, or San, culture and was eager to weave it into the story. As a younger writer, he'd found himself tacking such research onto an already written piece, but now he worked it into the foundation of the story. His eyes got worse. He kept pounding away at his typewriter.

Near the end of 1985, he got the devastating news that DAW Books was killing the Imaro series. "If this had happened a year ago, I would probably have been ready to jump off a bridge," he wrote.[68] He was in a bind. DAW still owned the copyright to the first three novels, and what publisher would buy the end of a cancelled series?

"Well, this sure has been a year of changes. But I wanted to make some changes in my life, so that's probably what's keeping me from getting sucked under. I can't say I feel good about getting turfed

---

65 Letter to Charles de Lint, August 8, 1985.

66 Letter to Charles de Lint, August 21, 1985.

67 Letter to Charles de Lint, September 7, 1985.

68 Letter to Charles de Lint, September 23, 1985.

out by DAW, but then if they're not going to promote and distribute my books . . . At least they did get me started," he wrote.

He had good news, too, which had come just as he was preparing for eye surgery. "Four days before I was to go into hospital I got a call from my agent in New York. It seemed she had gotten a call from New Horizon Studio in Hollywood and they wanted to adapt one of my short stories into a movie!"

It wasn't an Imaro story but one about a female hero he'd been developing named Dossouye. He published a short story about her that Roger Corman of New Horizons wanted to fly Charles out to Hollywood "ASAP" to start writing as a movie called *Amazons.* Charles usually listened to Anita Baker, Robert Cray and the Fat Boys, but that summer nobody could escape Tina Turner's new hit, "We Don't Need Another Hero." Charles was inspired to rewrite the lyrics: "We don't need another Tarzan, always swinging' through the trees. What we need is an Imaro, knock that sucker to his knees!"

He worked away at the screenplay for *Amazons*. "It's kind of tough going, because it's not really 'my' story, but I can only help myself by giving it my best shot, and I wouldn't be giving it my best shot if I rushed through it. Still, Hollywood knows how to put the pressure on. Yesterday I got a call from the studio asking how I was progressing!" he wrote.[69]

The deal had a catch. The studio planned to shoot in Argentina and told Charles they'd struggle to find Black actors there. So would he mind rewriting the story so that everyone was white? Ditch Dossouye's other-Africa for an alternate Europe? And could he turn Dossouye's black war-bull into a white horse? Charles decided to do this one white sword and sorcery film, with the belief that it

69 Letter to Charles de Lint, October 23, 1985.

would prove his ability and lead to a deal for an Imaro movie—and hopefully not a white Imaro.

"Wanna hear something funny? Now there may be a Black girl in the film after all, as the second lead. This was the director's idea. He challenged me to find a way to 'integrate' a Black character into an all-white cast. I invoked the magic of adoption," he wrote.[70]

He got new paper for his letters, with a Nigerian ceremonial drum pictured on the bottom. It's shaped like a squat animal, with two heads looking in opposite directions. He studied it, and began to write in his head a story where it suddenly sang and danced all by itself. He wrote nonfiction for *Jet Journal*, usually two or three articles per issue. He didn't get paid, but he did make contacts with the Black community. He kept writing *Amazons* and was in talks, ironically, to turn it into a novel. "The script has evolved into something so different from the original story that you'd hardly know where it came from," he wrote. "Imagine that. Me—writing a whole novel about *white people*! Kinda makes you wonder what the world is coming to, eh?"

But just before Christmas, he got more bad news. "Now there won't be a Black girl in *Amazons* after all. The director said he couldn't find one who could act well enough to carry the load of the second lead. It's kind of a vicious circle—there's not that many parts around for Blacks, so Black actors don't get much experience to develop their craft. He told me he didn't want to see the lone Black in the cast make a mess of the role, and I had to agree. I wonder what's going to happen when I do Imaro as a flick? Well, I'm not near that bridge yet," he wrote.[71]

---

70 Letter to Charles de Lint, December 9, 1985.

71 Letter to Charles de Lint, December 20, 1985.

The tumult of his career was balanced by a deepening love for his new homeland. He was content in his days. "Personally, I feel a hell of a lot better at 39 than I did at 29. Back then, I hadn't accomplished much. Now I have. Well, I knew things would change when I moved out of Ottawa, but I didn't know they'd change like this."

10

CHARLES FALLS IN LOVE

A strange change happened to the author Charles R. Saunders in the late 1980s: He stopped publishing fiction. His entry in the Internet Speculative Fiction Database shows twenty-seven published stories in the 1970s. In the first half of the 1980s, his CV builds into the three Imaro novels. In 1986, it records only two new short stories. Two more follow in 1987 and two in 1988, including one called "The Last Round." In 1989, a lone title: "Drum Magic." And then not a single piece of fiction published between 1990 and 1999. It seemed his career in fiction had sputtered to a stop, leaving him the author of three out-of-print fantasy novels and a handful of uncollected stories. He spent less time reading and writing fiction, and more time studying his new outer world in Africadia. Fantasy fans in the United States began to worry he had died. In fact, he was about to burst into real life in Canada in a way he had never before.

Her name was Dale Farmer, and she was preparing for a night of dancing with her girlfriends at Halifax's iconic Derby Tavern on Gottingen Street in January 1986. Her niece Nicole was sixteen and has dreamy memories of watching Dale and the girls slip into their best dresses to dance the night away. Black people from all over Halifax turned up at the Derby for its famous steaks, live bands, afternoon hootenannies, and night-time dances. "I remember as a teenager sitting on the stairs watching them get ready, thinking,

'I can't wait to go to the Derby with those dancing Queens!'" Nicole says with a warm laugh.[72] "They'd be dancing around the living room. Dale would always be wearing those long chiffon dresses, high heel stilettos, dressed to the nines. They were always on point, making sure their hair was done. She loved to go out."

Everyone at the Derby knew and loved Dale, and as she danced, people would call out, vying for her attention. How exactly her eye fell on the quiet writer celebrating at the bar that night remains a mystery, but it's clear Charles never stood a chance. For a man starved of family, starved of Black people, starved especially of confident Black women, she was a revelation. "I never went there very often, but I did that time because I had just finished the third draft of *Amazons* and I thought going out might relax me. Little did I know . . ." Charles told a friend.

Charles and Dale talked in the noisy bar. He told her he'd just finished writing a movie script and was throwing a sad one-person party to celebrate. He told her he was an American by birth and had recently moved to Nova Scotia. She told him about her family roots in Nova Scotia dating back to the 1760s. They compared notes on their homelands. Charles liked to joke that the main difference between American and Canadian racism was that in America, white people would say, "You can't eat here," while in Canada they said, "Sorry, you can't eat here."

Charles and Dale exchanged telephone numbers and soon called to set up their first date. She introduced him to her family. She was about thirty-two, eight years younger than Charles, and she'd never lived anywhere but the busy family home on Fern Street in Halifax's North End. He made a huge first impression on Nicole, who lived with Dale. "When I first met him I was like, God, look

72 Interview with the author, January 2024.

how big he is, and look at that Afro! Wow! He had the big Afro, the big beard—he was just a big man," she says. "He had to duck in our hallways. And the Afro made him two inches taller!"

In April, Dale told Charles she had to relocate to Prince Edward Island to work for the summer. "She knew she'd be lonely out there—ain't too many Black folks on PEI. So she asked me to come with her. Now that I'm freelance, I can be pretty mobile, so I accepted. We lived together in PEI during that time, and got along just fine. We decided that if we could get along in PEI, we could get along, period. We'd been talking marriage before, but at some nebulous time in the future. The time together in PEI kind of solidified things. We knew we were in love, so there was no reason to wait. The wedding will be in Halifax in September of this year," he wrote.[73]

When his lease expired in June 1986, Charles and Dale moved into a two-bedroom rental on Sullivan Street in Halifax, and one of the bedrooms was turned into his office—his first writing office. He and Dale suspected they were the first Black people to move into the middle-class white neighbourhood. "No crosses burned on our front lawn as yet."

"You know, I had decided to boycott the word 'happy,' because every time I applied it to myself, it turned into a pile of shit. Not any more. I am really happy here in Halifax. I feel as though I have come home. And with Dale, I have found a family. For all the close friendships I made in Ottawa, that was the thing that was missing. Now, it's there," he wrote.[74] "The Black folks here are very much like the ones at home, the exception being that there is much less Black-on-Black violence here. But then there is less violence in general in Canada. Some say that makes us dull. I'll drink to dullness (the

---

73 Letter to Charles de Lint, May 12, 1986.

74 Letter to Charles de Lint, June 1986.

beer's stronger here)." He turned forty that summer and celebrated with Dale and his new network of friends and family.

On September 20, 1986, Charles and Dale married at her family's spiritual home, the Cornwallis Street Baptist Church, one of the biggest and oldest Black churches in Canada (today it's called New Horizons Baptist Church). Nicole remembers the buzz of excitement as her beloved Aunt Dale prepared for the huge wedding. The Farmers made the celebration wine at a cousin's mother's house. "I was sixteen—me and my cousin stole all kinds of wine and hid it," she says with a laugh. "Nobody knew, because there was so much and it was free." Charles brought no family to the wedding. It seems that Dale's family was so big that nobody noticed the imbalance. Charles did invite friends, including the very first one he'd made in Halifax: George Elliott Clarke. George was still a broke writer in Ontario, and Charles was enjoying a time of financial success, so Charles paid for George's tuxedo. George also happened to be Dale's cousin. "An evening of memorable intoxication," George later said.[75] "Dale was gorgeous in a white gown with a bouquet of red roses. Charles—all six feet plus of him—was a tuxedo'd, gentle giant." George saved the brass razor handle Charles gave him as his usher gift, and still had it in 2021. George enjoyed visiting the newlyweds at their townhouse, where he and Charles continued to discuss writing.

Charles later told his Ottawa friends about the ceremony. "No major fuckups, such as the bride dropping her bouquet or my pants falling down. Everyone who was there enjoyed themselves immensely, and it was a good way to start a marriage," he wrote.[76]

---

75 George Elliott Clarke article on the Delmore Buddy Daye Learning Institute website, 2021.

76 Letter to Charles de Lint, October 5, 1986.

Nicole remembers Charles trying to remain a quiet outsider amid her bold and beautiful family. "He was an introvert, but you couldn't be an introvert at those gatherings. You couldn't sit over by yourself, because someone was going to come over and talk about anything. You couldn't hide in those shadows. Even if you tried, someone would just come over and say, 'Hey! You're Dale's husband. Nice to meet you.'" She said the family accepted Charles as a new son without hesitation. They came to love his dry wit and warm presence. He spoke slowly, with long, drawn-out words. He loved eating a big plate of home-cooked food. She remembers that at first he rarely smiled, which seemed odd for someone Dale would choose for her partner. But he relaxed with their acceptance of him and soon started beaming.

He handed out his books to her mother, siblings, nieces, and nephews. Nicole is a lifelong fantasy reader and devoured the Imaro novels. The family knew all about dastardly DAW and the backstabber Tarzan. Imaro soared in their imaginations. "I love it. Back then, there were no Black superheroes. We didn't see ourselves as any of those fantasy characters. That was not a thing. It warmed my heart. Wow! Look: a Black hero."

Nicole says Charles embraced his role as Dale's husband. "I remember thinking, Aunt Dale's with a superstar now. He's going to be famous. But I knew him as just Charles." Charles learned that the house Dale grew up in and still lived in had been earned by her grandfather through his service in the all-Black No. 2 Construction Battalion. The Canadian Army was racially segregated in the First World War, and only under great pressure did it allow Black men to enlist, and then only in non-combat roles. After the war, some men got paid in new homes. Despite those heroic origins, some of the white neighbours campaigned to keep the lone Black family off the street. Charles dug deep into the Farmer family history but didn't divulge his own origin story. "Nothing. I knew about his mother back in the United States, and nothing else. I never heard anything else," Nicole says.

In August 1987, Charles and Dale were proud to buy their own home, a nice place on Mayo Street in Halifax. Charles used the money he'd made from movies to make the down payment. "For a long time, I have been nomadic, moving an average of once a year. I think that pattern may have changed at last. My wife and I have moved into a newly constructed semi-detached home," he wrote. "We moved in last week, the boxes are all unpacked, and it is beginning to look like home. I never thought I'd see the day . . ."[77]

Charles wasn't publishing fiction then, or even directly working on Imaro. It's clear, however, that deep inside his soul, Imaro was watching this wonderful woman win over his creator. So was Tanisha. When Charles ended his long fiction drought decades later and started revising his Imaro novels, his first order of business was to recreate the love of Imaro's life. This is her new arrival: "Sharp intakes of breath greeted the sight of what the all-enveloping garment had concealed. Tanisha was tall for a woman. Her obsidian-black skin gleamed in the sunlight. Two long, narrow rectangles of pale-yellow silk hung from a chain of gold looped low around her waist: one in front of her, the other behind. The translucent rectangles were her only garment, other than the strands of gold that circled her neck, arms and ankles. Gold hoops hung from her ears, and studs of the same metal pierced her navel and the tips of her large, round breasts. Her waist was so narrow that Imaro could have circled it with both his hands. Her hips, however, were far from

77 Letter to Charles de Lint, August 29, 1987.

narrow, arcing from both sides of her scanty garment. A cloud of woolly, black hair framed Tanisha's face. Full lips parted beneath her nose, showing a flash of white teeth. After seeing her, (they) knew that the tales of the beauty of Shikaza women were true."

When Nicole read the revised Imaro novels, a smile bloomed on her face as she encountered Tanisha. "It's Dale. I would hear little tidbits of conversations and Aunt Dale would say, 'You know that's about me, right? That's me. He wrote about me.'"

Nicole understood how Dale provided the inspiration for the new Tanisha. "She was a strong woman. Growing up in the North End of Halifax at that time, building herself up, getting a job at the Department of National Defence. She was a single woman. Dale and her siblings were raised by a single mother. Their father was a corporal and he died in a tragic accident at 34. My grandmother was a widow at a very young age with five children. They only knew strong women. Maybe Charles, being around the women of our families, being in our lives, he was surrounded by strong Black women who raised their village. Strong women warriors keeping their village together and raising these strong women. And then he came into our family." It fell to the women to fight off the racists of Halifax, to stop them hurling insults at their children, and to determine their right to live where they chose.

As a husband and homeowner, Charles turned his attention to work that paid well, and ideally up front. Mostly, that meant films. *Amazons* shot in Argentina in February, with a targeted release date for the summer. He and Dale took an all-expenses-paid trip to the set near Buenos Aires. He enjoyed the work and the money, if not the writing. "Because of the intervention of the camera, screenwriting is a kind of shorthand compared to prose," he observed.

Charles turned his talents to a new film, a local project that was a contemporary horror movie from a Black perspective. "This one's about hypothetical Maroons living isolated in a Louisiana swamp.

This one, I think, should be shot somewhere other than Argentina," he wrote. "It isn't Hollywood, but I'll get a fair bit of cash out of it."

In a letter, he congratulated his Lincoln friend Morris Fried on the birth of a child, and noted he was "still batting zero on that score, but that's a matter of choice, not chance. I think my creative writing takes the place of children in my life." They discussed their upcoming class reunion, which Charles did not attend. He did write a letter to his classmates and asked them to read it aloud: "How does all this 1968 nostalgia affect you? I find myself having more than a few flashbacks to that year. And I think a lot about all the things I did and didn't do."

Charles ended 1987 celebrating the holidays with Dale and their extended family. They always had big family Christmases, with partners, kids, friends, food, drinks, and card games like Rummoli. The happy couple had invited everyone to their new home for Christmas dinner. "There's her mother, three sisters, a brother, and their respective children, so you can imagine how packed it ended up being," he wrote.[78] "Still, it was great. We all enjoyed ourselves. I exchanged my Scrooge hat for a Santa Claus costume. Literally. We bought one of those $2.99 jobbies from Shoppers Drug Mart and I gave gifts to everybody. It was fun—something I've been having a lot of lately."

Nicole remembers that Christmas fondly. Her Aunt Dale glowed with happiness, thriving in an equal partnership with a man she deeply loved and admired. "I remember when they married. He wasn't there, and then he was there in our lives," she says. "He went and got the little Santa Claus hat, he gave gifts to all the kids." That Christmas marked the end of Charles "kind of looking like a grouchy guy," she laughs.

---

78 Letter to Charles de Lint, January 1987.

Imaro returned in the form of a surprise cheque; the novels had been translated into French (without Charles knowing) and had sold a few copies. He sent the complementary French copies to close friends, "autographed in French." His agent told him she'd been unable to sell *Mwindo*, his African high fantasy novel. He did sell a short story about a mythical bout between Muhammad Ali and Jack Johnson to *Twilight Zone Magazine*. Charles was pleased, but it was an unwelcome step backwards in a publishing career that had started in zines more than a decade ago.

He bought his first computer: a Tandy 1000 SX, which he proudly noted was IBM-compatible. "But I don't know how to use it well enough to do my correspondence on it. In fact, I'm getting ready to throw the %#@*&%# thing through the window, because it doesn't do what the manual says it's supposed to do," he wrote.[79] A month later, he was back to his electronic typewriter.

He and Dale took a road trip to Annapolis Royal, and as they bounced down the highway, his retina detached. He still hadn't gotten the needed eye surgery. "I started seeing something like a black curtain crossing over my field of vision in the left eye."[80] Dale turned around and drove him directly to the Halifax emergency room. Eight hours later, he was unconscious for emergency surgery to reattach the retina. He stayed in hospital for a week, during which time he regained dim vision in his left eye, leaving his right to do most of the work. When Dale got him home, he could hardly make out his typewriter, but he kept writing. It seemed to fix the problem, as Charles doesn't mention it again.

The *Amazons* movie was finally released, and Charles spotted a copy in the local video store. "I make no claims for it as a great

---

79 Letter to Charles de Lint, March 1987.

80 Letter to Charles de Lint, March 1987.

movie, but I'm sure not ashamed of it, either," he wrote. He had made decent money screenwriting, but his heart wasn't in it. He'd been writing for the *Jet Journal*, but it folded. He continued to publish the *Rap* to fill the void. A new type of writing was taking shape in his mind, one that emerged when he wrote to a white friend who had asked his advice about including the n-word in a novel.

"Hit me with the word when I'm not ready for it, and my stomach knots up. Still, it's there. It'll probably be here a hundred years from now. I can't knock your using it. I use it myself," he replied. He expanded on his thoughts in an essay entitled "Word Power." He compares the slur to a psychological experiment. When Pavlov rang his bell, the dogs salivated. When Charles heard the word, he tensed for a fight. He didn't like that, and tried to find a way to react that rejected the word but retained his self-control. He recalled that, back at Lincoln, his friends used *splib* to avoid the n-word. The slur rarely appears in any of his writing, though we do learn that the hated Mizungus had a term of derision for the people of Nyumbani that means "despised people" and echoes the English word.

Meanwhile, his old friend George Elliott Clarke had been writing a Black-focused column on public affairs for the Halifax *Daily News*. But he felt writing it from Ontario wasn't good for him, or for African Nova Scotians. "When I bowed out, I suggested that the paper ask Saunders to take over the column. It did so, and Halifax and Nova Scotia have not been the same since. Hallelujah and all praise to Saunders for his meditative art—and for all the beautiful changes," he later wrote.[81]

Charles had moved to Halifax to become a full-time freelance writer. He'd done it, but not on his own terms. Instead of living off novel royalties from his fiction creations, he worked on

---

81 Forward to Charles Saunders, *Black and Bluenose*, 1999.

commissioned true stories. He had responsibilities to meet and bills to pay. One friend remembers calling on Charles around the time he was waiting for the job offer from the *Daily News*. He would not leave the house and hung out near the phone most of the day. When it rang, he said yes to a new life as a public nonfiction writer.

Where did that leave Imaro? When Charles lay dying in an Ottawa university bathroom stall, he felt Imaro lift him off the toilet and thrust him toward the elevator. Imaro had for years been a source of strength and inspiration for Charles. But now it seemed that Charles would fail Imaro. He would not finish his story. In Nyumbani, nobody sees Imaro's worth. On Earth, nobody could see it either. Imaro, the son-of-no-father, was now the person-of-no-author.

It was a remarkable transformation. Charles had come to Halifax as the star guest for Hal-Con, but once he made Nova Scotia his home, he wove a spell of forgetfulness. When he emerged as one of Nova Scotia's most famous nonfiction writers just a few years later, his new fans didn't know he'd ever written fiction. He abandoned writing about Imaro. He started an unrelated fantasy novel and plugged away in private. Despite this, his private letters to friends reveal that he thought about Imaro constantly. He writes of Imaro as if he were a prodigal son, or perhaps as if Charles was a prodigal father, having squandered the chance to bring Imaro fully into our world. Trapped in this cage of letters, Imaro seems stymied, frustrated—*exasperated*, no doubt—and forced against his will to stay on his side of the veil. Confined in Nyumbani, unable to enter our world through Charles, he paced in his master's mind during a long imprisonment. Certainly, the DAW disaster had smashed Charles's confidence, and there were legal and logistical problems in rebirthing the Imaro trilogy in print. Most book contracts stipulate that when a book goes out of print, the author regains the copyright.

Imaro was well out of print, but Charles never indicated he was trying to get the warrior back into books.

He seemed creatively scattered, more the perpetual disorder of *Bohu* than the creative breath of *Rouah*. In letter after letter in the late 1980s and '90s, he wrote to his friends about a series of ideas for new worlds, often birthed and abandoned on the same page. He kicked around an idea for a story called "Heroes in Hell," which would see Malcom X and Bob Marley team up in hell to fight the early twentieth-century white South African president Hendrik Verwoerd and Jefferson Davis, the Civil War–era white president of the U.S. South. "Haile Selassie, ex-Emperor of Ethiopia, would also be in it, running from a horde of famine victims," he wrote.[82] His ideas for fiction set in our world rarely got out of the thinking stage, and this was no exception.

He pitched a screenplay called *The Hazard*, which would explore the supernatural stories he'd learned from African Nova Scotians, but the project was rejected. He told his writer friend Charles de Lint about another idea that would involve modern South Africa, but enriched by ancient mythological lore. "No, Imaro would not be brought to modern times. The thought is tempting, but I'm not ready to try it," he wrote.

He still had hopes *Imaro IV* would somehow get finished and published. He'd abandoned it half-done after DAW killed the series. "And then of course there's the fifth novel in the series, which I was working on before I stumbled onto the screenwriting trade," he wrote to a friend in 1986. "Meanwhile, other aspects of my life have become more unpredictable than before. Last week, I was in New York to talk to the director who did *Amazons*. He wants to make a

82 Letter to Charles de Lint, June 18, 1986.

fantasy picture independently of Roger Corman this time. And guess who he wants to write the script?"

The new film would become *Stormquest*, about a world where women rule and men are kept for breeding. It's a dark sword and sorcery comedy flipping sexism on its head, and Charles wrote a charming, funny script. He spent three days locked in a room in Greenwich Village, hammering out the story. "Made me glad I live in Canada. The place looked like some giant bazaar gone to seed."

He'd become friendly with another new Scotian, David Woods, an artist and writer who was thirteen years younger than Charles, and who had been born in Trinidad and moved to Dartmouth in 1972. The two occasionally ran into each other at the Derby Tavern, and on one such occasion Charles told David about a project he was developing. It was about Sam Langford, the iconic Nova Scotia boxer who in the early twentieth century was called the greatest heavyweight never to win a title—largely because he fought in an era where white champions ducked Black challengers. Charles had been commissioned to write a radio play about Langford for CBC. It combined his lifelong love of boxing with his newfound love for Africadia. Charles asked David to audition, and he ended up playing Sam Langford Sr., the father. Charles sat in on the taping and gave notes to the actors. CBC turned it into an hour-long radio play.

"During that time CBC was actively courting Black writers for radio drama, TV movies, and mini-series possibilities," Woods later said.[83] "I was active as a playwright but worked almost exclusively in the Black community and was not known by the mainstream literati.

83 Interview with the author, 2021.

"Charles was always humble and seems to have respected my opinion on literary matters. He often sent me his stage scripts, screenplays, and asked my opinion. My impression of him is that he welcomed the comradeship of a fellow writer whose work he felt was serious and accomplished and who perhaps was well-entrenched in the local Black community."

Imaro burst back into his life one day when Charles answered his phone in Halifax. He was stunned to hear the voice of Ivan Dixon, the famous Black actor and director who had played a prisoner of war in the hit TV show *Hogan's Heroes* and starred in a 1960s movie called *Nothing But a Man*, which Charles had watched at Lincoln. Dixon was in Toronto shooting a miniseries called *Amerika*, about an alternative future in which the Soviet Union has taken over the U.S. On a break from shooting, Dixon visited Bakka Books, which holds iconic status as Canada's oldest science fiction and fantasy bookstore. Rifling through the second-hand section, he picked up *Imaro.* He bought it and read it at the hotel before quickly returning to buy *Quest for Cush* and *Trail of Bohu.* He devoured all three novels, somehow figured out Charles was in Nova Scotia, and got a number for him. He told Charles he wanted to make an Imaro movie. "There is no guarantee that he will be able to pull it off. But at least now the chances of an Imaro movie are better than ever. And I know this guy won't try to get me to turn everybody white," Charles wrote.[84]

In 1988, Charles was invited to Halifax's Black Cultural Centre, and there he read the short story he'd published depicting the imagined bout between Ali and Johnson. It was in the style of his

84 Letter to Morris Fried, March 1987.

pre-Imaro short stories, where he clashed boxing titans against each other in fictional fights. At the centre, he learned more about Nova Scotia's long Black history, and met an array of people from all parts of that society. He found their stories irresistible, and felt a growing urge to tell them. "Thus I get dragged, not exactly kicking and screaming, into the world of reality," he wrote.[85] "For years, I had dreamed of developing a lifestyle which did not require my participation. What've I got? The complete opposite!"

85 Letter to Morris Fried, October 1987.

11

SWEAT AND SOUL

Five summers after he moved to Africadia, Charles Saunders made his way from his Halifax home, across the bridge, and down the long road to Cherry Brook, Nova Scotia. This Black community sat just outside of Dartmouth and near the Preston Township communities that are some of the oldest Black settlements in Canada. He approached a red-bricked building with a sloped roof, perhaps glancing across the street at the former Nova Scotia Home for Colored Children, an orphanage started by the Black community when other orphanages turned the Black children away.

On that fine summer evening of August 2, 1990, he stepped inside the Black Cultural Centre, the cathedral of Africadia, and prepared to address Nova Scotia's Black royalty: Wayne Adams, a politician who had won five council elections in Halifax County and in 1993 would become the province's first Black Member of the Legislative Assembly; Alma Johnston, a teacher and community leader; Dr. Bridglal Pachai, author and director of the Nova Scotia Human Rights Commission; Ricky Anderson, a former welterweight boxing champion; Dave Downey, a former middleweight champion. And beyond, the hallowed halls celebrated the ancestors: Viola Desmond, a businesswoman who fought segregation in Nova Scotia; George Dixon, the first Black world champion of boxing; Sam Langford, the greatest uncrowned boxing champion; the warriors of the No. 2 Construction Battalion.

The living had gathered for the book launch of Charles's first nonfiction title, *Sweat and Soul: The Saga of Black Boxers from the Halifax Forum to Caesars Palace.* Each guest was given a four-page program that divided the evening into a "six-round main event." The cover of the program, and of the book, shows Langford in profile, fists raised.

Charles took the stage, no doubt to loud applause, and addressed his people. It was not so much a homecoming as a homemaking. He had spent most of his writing life in Nyumbani, and this was his first book about our real world. He dedicated it to his wife, Dale, "and to her family, which has become mine." Charles had spoken to every gym rat he could find, listened to the old boxers and trainers, read the yellowed newspapers, and scoured every book on Maritime boxing to create *Sweat and Soul*, a comprehensive history of boxing in the Maritimes, and of Black boxing in general. The Black communities of Nova Scotia, New Brunswick, and Prince Edward Island knew of the great boxers they'd produced and wanted a book to celebrate them. Dr. Pachai and the Black Cultural Centre had approached Charles and asked him to take on the task.

"The author writes with sensitivity and strength, giving life and depth to issues which transcend victories and losses in the ring, to bring to the surface issues of race and colour, of management and money, of determination and duty, of what it takes to overcome tremendous odds, to make good and bring credit to the sport, to the family and community, to the province and beyond," Pachai wrote in the publisher's note at the start of the book.

"Although he never put on the gloves, he has been a boxing fan since the day his grandfather plunked him in front of a round-screened TV set to watch Jersey Joe Walcott win the heavyweight title by flattening Ezzard Charles in 1951," the book's about-the-author section says.

In the book, Charles shares deep insider stories, like the disastrous debut of a Halifax fighter known only as Merciful Heavens. Merciful was set to fight for the first time in Moncton, New Brunswick, in the 1950s. He was supposed to fly but got scared of the plane, so his team jumped into cars and drove for many hours to the arena. Merciful filled up at every rest stop: fish, chips, cookies and chocolate milk, despite his friends' counselling against such irregular fight preparation. "In a nose-to-nose confrontation during the referee's instructions, 'Merciful' gave his bewildered opponent a graphic account of the total destruction that was to come soon," Charles wrote. "One body punch later, 'Merciful' was on his hands and knees, spraying ringsiders with a gourmet's delight of fish, chips, half-digested cookies, chocolate milk, and excess stomach acid."

The fight was called off, and Merciful's career came to a merciful end. The book documents Black boxing history, from the days when white champions dodged Black challengers, to the rise of Floyd Patterson, Sonny Liston, and Muhammad Ali, all the while showcasing the Maritime boxers, including names, fight details, and records. Little of the material had been gathered before, and Charles clearly poured his soul into the work. And that title—*Sweat and Soul*. It would stay bubbling in the gumbo for another two decades before he saw in it the potential to describe a whole new genre of fantasy writing.

His author biography lists him as a Pennsylvania native, a Lincoln University graduate, and a Canadian "who has had three novels published by DAW Books of New York." It doesn't name the books, nor describe him as a fantasy author. He called *Sweat and Soul* "the most satisfying book project I've ever been involved in. Well, the Africville project was just as satisfying, but in a different way."

His oldest byline in Canada comes from the December 1987 edition of the *Rap*: He's credited for two of the three front-page articles. The lead story must have been a fantasy come true for Charles: "At approximately 3:00 p.m. on Tuesday, November 24, the corner of Gottingen and Cogswell streets became the hottest spot in Halifax," he wrote in the *Rap*. "Why? Because former world heavyweight champions Muhammad Ali and Larry Holmes were there!"

Charles got to meet the legends. "Pretty awesome, shaking the hand of one of the most famous men on the planet. Before that, the most famous hand I'd ever shaken belonged to Stephen King," he later wrote.[86]

A promoter had brought the boxing icons to Nova Scotia to draw attention to a fight card. They met at the headquarters for the Black United Front, which helped publish the *Rap*. You can imagine the excitement as the limousines pulled up to the curb and Ali and Holmes stepped out. Ali started playfully sparring with a young Black man, word spread, and soon the offices and streets outside were filled with shouts to the greatest of all time. Ali was retired, and Holmes was preparing for a fight with a rising heavyweight named Mike Tyson. Charles covered the fights, which featured the Canadian contender Donovan "Razor" Ruddock and Halifax's own Trevor Berbick.

The "Africville project" had first established Charles's name as a nonfiction writer, and it shows the moment his fiction and nonfiction styles crossed over. Africville was a harbour-side Black village just north of Halifax that traced its history back to the first days of the city in 1749. It had been a centre of Africadian life for centuries until the white-run Halifax council voted to bulldoze it in the

86 Letter to Charles de Lint, December 1, 1987.

1960s. White people had dumped the town dump on Africville in the 1950s, and then used that as the excuse to destroy Africville itself. For white people, Africville was a synonym for the dump. The white lie had been the official truth until the late 1980s, when a Black-led grassroots movement forced the city to re-examine the destruction of Africville. In 1983, Africvillians formed the Africville Genealogical Society to restore the community's name. By 1985, people were picnicking in Africville each summer as a family reunion. Eddie Carvery, whom I would meet decades later and write about in *The Hermit of Africville*, was fifteen years into his protest. And in 1989, filmmaker Shelagh Mackenzie created a thirty-minute documentary called *Remember Africville*. White Halifax had been used to seeing Africville from the outside—and so had many Black Nova Scotians, swamped by white culture. But the documentary showed the community from the inside, in the words of its people. It featured extraordinary testimony given at an informal inquest into what had really happened to Africville. White city officials provided their perspectives, and so did the Black former residents. It all culminated in a history-changing book called *The Spirit of Africville*.

Charles's work for the *Jet Journal* and the *Rap* had caught the attention of the wider Black community, and they recruited Charles to write what was first called the catalogue for a museum exhibit about Africville. Charles had never been to Africville, as it was destroyed when he was at Lincoln University, and the last house was bulldozed in 1970, his first year in Ontario. On page 9, we read "A visit to Africville, Charles Saunders (with the help of others)." Charles clearly spent hours with old-timers, learning their stories until they became his to tell. In his novel-writing career, Charles had been the first to see the richness of Africa as a setting for speculative fiction; "A Visit to Africville" had a seismic impact in Nova Scotia, and for similar reasons. Up until Charles, nearly every written account came through white eyes, and saw Africville as a slum built by the dump, rather than the truth—that it was a harbourside village that had a dump thrown on it, along with every other unwanted service. The white version of Africville was forever plagued by criminals and vice; newspaper articles and popular accounts portrayed it as an exotic, dangerous place to visit. White Haligonians would drive "to the dump" and thrill their friends with stories of rats running under their cars, and of close encounters with Black people. The long, simmering animosity boiled over in the 1960s, when the white city overlooking the Black village destroyed it in the name of "urban renewal" and lies of newer, better housing that never materialized.

"A Visit to Africville" recreates a day in the summer of 1959. We meet our guide, a boy aged about ten, where the pavement ends and the dirt road begins. Charles perhaps had an eye on the children of Africville, who would now grow up in Halifax, and to white people in Halifax, as he starts his story at the meeting point of the two communities.

"The Road's startin' to rise again now. See that ocean view? You couldn't buy a better view than that. When the wind's not blowing, the Basin looks like a sheet of glass. Maybe that's why there's so many houses here. Go ahead, wave to the people; you're among friends," he writes. "You're noticin' the different colours people paint their houses. Like flowers, right? Folks do what they want to with their houses. If you want to have a different-lookin' door or window, that's OK. Keeps things interestin'.

"Let's go over to the church, and stop for a minute. Look at the way that white paint gleams in the sun. Look at the steeple standing against the sky. Now, be perfectly quiet. Tune out the sounds of the kids and the cars and the dogs.

"Listen close . . . can you hear it? Can you hear that sound, coming from the church? It's like a heartbeat . . . the heartbeat of

Africville. This church is the living, breathing soul of our community. As long as this church is here, *we'll* be here."

He mentions that musician Duke Ellington is a regular visitor, as he married Mildred Dixon, whose father was an Africville Dixon. And how the world champion boxer Joe Louis came to town to referee a wrestling match and asked the hotel manager where all the Black people were. The manager told him Black people weren't really permitted to stay at the hotel, but they'd made an exception for him. He left the hotel and went to Africville. "You know, that's one of the reasons why we don't pay much mind when people talk down to us. If we're good enough for folks like Joe Louis and Duke Ellington, we figure we're darn well good enough for anybody else."

Our guide invites us home for supper and shows us a spare room where we can spend the night. "And when you get back home, if anybody asks you about Africville, just tell 'em we been through good times and hard times, but we're still here. 'Relocation' they call it. But we've heard that kind of talk before. Long as it's just talk, we got nothin' to worry about, right?"

It was a haunting last line that sealed this new understanding of Africville. It captured the community so well that people often thought Charles himself was from Africville, and writing about his own childhood. It marked a profound moment in the journey to redeem the village, to admit the racism that destroyed it, and to hold it forever in the soft summer sun of 1959.

"You don't know what a trial it was to do the Africville thing," he wrote.[87] "What I wrote in the introduction doesn't begin to explain the trouble I had inside my head. It took me two months to battle the worst damn case of writer's block I've had since the 1970s.

---

87 Letter to Charles de Lint, August 18, 1989.

I know one thing. I've really gotten away from fantasy. I think I really was using it as an escape years ago. Now, I've got to find another way to relate to it. If I believed in fate, then I'd say the Africville piece was the reason I came to Nova Scotia."[88]

Charles worried that as a "Come From Away," a somewhat insulting east coast expression for residents not born in Atlantic Canada, he would fail to capture the voice of his new community, his new family, in Africadia. But he thought about the Black people who had fled the United States for Canada in 1776 and 1812. "Those people involved in those two migrations of hope, along with those who were held in slavery in Nova Scotia, formed the basis of a unique Black community," he wrote.[89] "I've often wondered what my choice would have been had I lived in slavery in the U.S. 200 years ago. Would I have taken my chances with the revolutionaries, with their declaration of independence that was written by slave-owners? Or would I have trusted the British, the ones who brought slavery to their colonies in the first place?"

Charles thought he'd have bet on Britain, and been born a Nova Scotian, not a Pennsylvanian. And he ultimately answered the question for himself by settling into Nova Scotia and making it his home.

For months in 1989, friends and family had been telling Charles about the racism heating up among students at Cole Harbour High between the mostly white communities of Eastern Passage and Cow Bay and the mainly Black communities of North Preston, East Preston, and Cherry Brook. In January, a snowball fight between two groups of grade ten boys escalated to a brawl that left students

88 Letter to Charles de Lint, September 27, 1989.

89 Introduction, *Black and Bluenose*, 1999.

bleeding. Police charged fourteen people—students, but also older friends and relatives who had raced to the school to join the fracas. Many students would for years resist calling it a race riot, as they saw it as just two groups of students fighting. But one side was Black and the other side was white, and for the rest of their school years students on both sides felt the sharpened racial divide, and it caused them to doubt old friends from the other side.

Charles watched two students—one Black, one white—trading punches in a clip played repeatedly on the news. Nova Scotia had just seen a Mi'kmaw man named Donald Marshall Junior freed from prison, where he'd been serving a life sentence for the murder of a young Black man named Sandy Seale in 1971. A 1989 Royal Commission fully exonerated Marshall and found that the white Cape Breton police department had framed him, and let the true killer—a white man—get away with murder. Marshall's name would become famous in Nova Scotia as a byword for racist persecution from the justice system, but Seale, the young man who was stabbed to death, was largely forgotten. The "Just Us" system is how a lot of Black Nova Scotians saw it—a justice system built and run by white people, for white people. Just Us.

When the media storm over the school brawls calmed down, the city planned to build a second high school to relieve overcrowding, which was an easy target to blame for the fights. But while much of the media reported on that as a simple, obvious solution, Charles saw the deeper threat to Black students. Separate but equal has never happened naturally in Nova Scotia or anywhere else; white people inevitably give themselves the better deal, be it land, public services, or employment. He feared the same thing would happen in education, if done unwisely.

"Hot on the heels of the controversy surrounding the schoolyard fights at Cole Harbour High School comes the debate concerning the location of a new secondary school," he wrote in one of his first Halifax *Daily News* columns, published June 11, 1989. "Racial integration in the school system is one of the focal points of that debate." Charles landed hard shots on "integration," noting how in the 1950s and '60s it meant Black access to jobs, justice, and lunch counters. He jabbed at the "separate but equal" claim popular with white people by showing Black schools always got less funding, which led to poorly paid teachers with shoddy resources. Inevitably, integration meant moving Black students to white schools, which is what had happened when Nova Scotia desegregated schools in the 1950s. "Today, the concept of 'integration' is synonymous with raised voices, clenched fists and angry petitions. But it doesn't have to be that way," he wrote.

He offered a fresh vision: Don't just integrate the students, but also integrate the staff and the curriculum. Hire Black educators. Put Black authors and Black history on the curriculum for everybody. Have Black teachers teach white kids—and Black kids—about history, or math, or English. Black teachers will then act as good role models for Black and white students, and by their very presence counteract racist images. "This can be of special benefit to white students who have absorbed such stereotypes from parents and peers," he wrote. "A curriculum that fails to take into account the current and historical contributions of Black and other minorities to all aspects of human development and progress is a segregated curriculum."

As a columnist, Charles was a boxer, not a brawler. He picked his shots and built his game on his background in psychology, his genius level of writing talent, and his expansive mind, always ready and able to encompass a new perspective. Halifax's white columnists were caught flat-footed. They hadn't expected to be outsmarted by this new Black columnist. The photo that accompanied his column became iconic. It's a head-and-shoulders shot, with Charles looking slightly to the left, straight at the camera, with short, woolly hair, a full beard, and big glasses.

An unlikely controversy erupted in Nova Scotia in 1989, focused on Citadel Hill, the British fortress that protected Halifax for generations before becoming a museum, complete with re-enactors in historical costumes. Parks Canada, the federal agency that ran it, had declared that it would never hire a Black person to be a re-enactor. "If you're going to go the historical accuracy route you have to have whites playing the roles—it's the only thing that makes sense," one white person was quoted saying in a *Daily News* article. "Blacks can't seem to see that. They should stop crying and moaning."

Parks Canada said the ban had always existed. Charles raised an eyebrow and wrote to his old writing friend in Ontario, Charles de Lint. "I need your help. I'm remembering a postcard I sent you right after I first moved to Halifax in June of 1985. Maybe you remember it, too. It showed several cadets or militiamen on Citadel Hill. One of them was Black. I remember sending it to you and joking that the guy on the postcard was me. I never kept any of the cards I bought. Anyway, I know you keep just about all your correspondence. If you still have that postcard, I would appreciate your sending it to me as soon as possible." He wanted to learn more about that man, and hoped to "catch the officials in a lie . . ."

Charles de Lint still had the postcard and sent it to Charles. Charles passed it onto a reporter, who broke the story under the headline "Blacks wore period garb on Citadel before 1980." Charles stayed undercover, as the reporter mentioned only "a postcard obtained by the *Daily News*," and showed the evidence. It proved that the decision to not hire Black people did not date to the 1860s, as Citadel Hill staff had claimed, but to 1980. It wasn't historic racism on display, it was contemporary racism. "Really? That's very interesting," said the head of the Halifax Citadel Foundation.

The superintendent of Citadel Hill promptly moved the goalposts, claiming those 1970s guards were "for entertainment," but now they wanted to be historically accurate. "If we were to rewrite history to suit the Black, then the Black, I hope, won't mind when we present Black history and have 90 per cent of the animators white," he pouted. Black leaders noted the Maroons had built Citadel Hill, yet were not recorded anywhere on the site. Rocky Jones, a longtime Black activist, said if Citadel Hill was truly concerned about historical accuracy, then surely they should start firing a real cannonball from the traditional Noon Gun. And nobody worried about hiring actual Scottish people to re-enact the 78th Highland Regiment of Foot; any white person would do.

Charles wrote a column on it, drawing attention to William Hall, the first Canadian naval recipient of the Victoria Cross—and the first Black person to win the medal. Hall was from Nova Scotia, yet nobody was animating him at the famous fortress. "The Citadel was intended as a defensive installation against an American invasion that never happened. It would appear that the officials who run the animation program are being overly 'defensive' in their response to criticism," he wrote dryly.

Charles had caught Citadel Hill in a white lie, and they eventually ditched the whites-only policy. The *Daily News* gave him a two-month trial. "I guess I've disturbed enough shit that they're willing to let me continue." In September 1989, he became a permanent employee of the Halifax *Daily News*, for the "foreseeable future. Don't know why I said that; how much of the future can one foresee?" he wrote. He added a regular column reviewing books and magazines and was now writing several essays each week. At the start of 1989, few Nova Scotians would have known the name Charles Saunders; by the end of the year, it seemed he'd always been with us. Charles drew an avalanche of letters to the newspaper, half of them loving this new champion, half hating this pugnacious foe. "It seems I've fallen into a new career. Haven't been doing any fiction at all lately," he wrote. "I'm not exactly making a living at inflicting my opinions on an unsuspecting public, and I damn sure don't want to become a journalist. I'd rather make up stories than run around chasing them down. I'll just have to follow where my muse leads me, and hope for the best."

He found it unsettling—yet freeing—to stop writing fiction. "Through processes that certainly are not due to any intent on my part, I've been moving ever farther away from fantasy over the past few years. I really never thought I'd ever move this far away from fantasy. I don't think I've 'outgrown' it, or any other kind of bullshit like that. Most likely, I'll be coming back to it someday. Right now, I'm just giving my creative horse its head. We'll see where it leads me," he wrote at the time.[90]

Charles had two visitors in 1991. One came from western Quebec: his old college colleague Janet LeRoy, who visited in the spring. Her family was in crisis. She had gotten pregnant, and she and her husband, Burt, had eagerly anticipated the birth of their first child. Yarrow would be named after Peter Yarrow of Peter, Paul and Mary. Later, Janet discovered that yarrow is also the flowering herb that Achilles used to heal his wounded soldiers in the battle of Troy. But Yarrow had died shortly after birth. Grief consumed them. Janet wrote to Charles to tell him. They had bonded when he told her about his attempt to end his life, and he opened up again when she told him about her tragedy. "Charles wrote and told me that

90 Letter to Charles de Lint, April 1989.

he and his first wife had had a baby boy die—a stillbirth, I think," Janet later said.[91] "After Charles came to realize how I was impacted by Yarrow's death, he wrote and told me that he had reconnected with his first wife to say how sorry he was that he hadn't realized how the death of their baby had impacted her. He said it was healing that after so many years, he could communicate this to her. The contact didn't continue, but he was glad he was able to have more clarity—more understanding to say what he now needed to say to Margaret."

Charles rarely spoke about losing his own child in the 1970s. He told Janet and mentioned it to one other friend in a letter years later. We perhaps get a psychological glimpse of the terrible moment in the short story "Horror in the Black Hills," first published in 1977. Imaro has risen to lead the *haramia* outlaw gang that abducted him. After a great victory, he sits as sullen king, watching the revelries but not enjoying the spoils himself. The sounds of celebrating are erased by an awful noise—"Isikukumadevu's last song."

"The sound struck without warning, like a leopard dropping from a tree. It was a sound like the shrieking of a thousand tortured souls united as one. It was a doom-laden orison cried out by the worshippers of a dying god; it was the wail of a woman who had given birth to a stillborn child." The great monster—depicted on the original *Imaro* cover—calls one man, and lays a silver path from Mwesu the moon at his feet. Imaro must face her alone. At the end of the path, he finds confusion. "He turned and saw a huge, lithe figure appear as if by magic from the twisted foliage. In graceful, catlike bounds, the figure leaped toward Imaro. Then it sprang into the full glare of Mwesu's eye. Imaro prepared himself for imminent

91 Interview with the author, 2023.

attack . . . then he uttered a half-strangled gasp of disbelief. For the newest foe Isikukumadevu had sent him was—*himself!*"

Imaro begins his toughest fight.

"Not since childhood had Imaro been rendered so helpless by any foe. Slowly, inexorably, he was drowning . . . dying in a futile battle against his own strength, the strength that was the thing that set him apart from all others—except himself. *Why?* Imaro's mind cried as air emptied from his lungs. Why could he do nothing against an other self that was younger, less experienced, and ever-so-slightly less strong than he? The answer came to him with all the intensity of the pain stitching through his starved lungs: *hate!* It was a core of hatred and resentment that fed his strength, fired it to levels beyond the limits of other men.

"Now he had to redirect his hatred, to aim it against this earlier self, this fool who believed that he could be one with his mother's people, and win the approval of those who hated him. Direct his hatred against himself . . . yes . . . he had done it before." But the other Imaro does not rise again, and Imaro's final battle in this story is with Isikukumadevu. Imaro slays the monster, hacks off her head, and hurls it at the *haramia.* That image became the cover of the *Dark Fantasy* edition in which the story was published.

In the real world, Charles invited Janet to come and stay with him and Dale for a couple of nights. She planned to take a week-long solo bike trip around Nova Scotia to come to grips with her own battle with the sorrow that was threatening to drown her. She travelled to Nova Scotia with her bike in a box. "Charles noticed I wasn't putting my bike together. He said I could keep staying with them, so I did," she later said. "Dale was a lovely woman—kind and gentle. Charles invited Dale's mother over one evening and left the two of us in the living room together. He told me that she had had an adult son die and also a newborn. I remember asking her if one death had been harder than the other. She answered, 'They were equally painful'—her newborn's death and her son in his forties."

Janet recalled that a friend of hers had told her she was "lucky" her child died as a baby. "Had he lived longer, it would have hurt more," the friend said. It broke the friendship and hurt Janet. "Dale's mother helped me deeply," she said. "Charles was infinitely wise—opening a possibility of a healing moment for me by having Dale's mother visit. Both Dale and Charles cared enough to have me as a guest, not for a night or two, but a whole seven to ten days! I smile as I realize that Charles and I helped each other in terms of the death of our infant children." The forging of their friendship was true, and they would remain close for the rest of his life.

Later in 1991, Charles's old friend from Lincoln, Morris Fried, brought his wife and young children across the water on the Yarmouth ferry and drove up to Halifax to visit Charles and Dale. Dale made dinner while Morris took in his changed friend. They had been exchanging letters for six years but hadn't seen each other since graduating in 1968. Morris was amazed at his friend's new life.

But back in the U.S., few people heard about the career change, and soon rumours spread to explain his sudden literary silence: Charles R. Saunders, author of the *Imaro* trilogy, was dead.

12

THINGS FALL APART

Charles wasn't dead—he'd just turned fully to telling true stories. His next nonfiction title seemed another he had been born to write: *Share and Care: The Story of the Nova Scotia Home for Colored Children.* Charles had been raised without a father, and without a mother at times, too. He'd spent the first prime of his writing life creating Imaro, the son-of-no-father whose mighty exterior concealed a hurt child. As an exile who had been driven out of his homeland, he felt drawn to the story of Nova Scotia's orphaned Black children who were denied care in white orphanages until the Black community stepped up and created the Home. The board who oversaw the institute in 1991 approached Charles and asked him to write a book to tell that story ahead of its seventy-fifth anniversary in 1996.

"It would be a history of an orphanage . . . which was founded in 1921. Although the clientele is mostly Black it's taken in whites and Natives as well. Maybe I'm destined to be a historian, one way or the other," Charles wrote.[92]

After some internal wrestling, Charles decided to write the book. "Fiction, ah, fiction . . . the siren call. I'm still trying to get into

92 Letter to Charles de Lint, October 6, 1991.

it, a little at a time," he wrote.[93] But nonfiction came with a publishing deal, money, and a chance to give back to his new homeland. Dale was then on strike from her government job and spent her days marching on the picket line—at least until she caught bronchitis and was bedridden. Charles took care of her, wrote his *Daily News* columns, picked away at a few fiction projects—but mostly he poured himself into *Share and Care.* He spent long days reading original documents and interviewing the key people who had sustained the institute. The people who hired him to write the book also gave him two hundred pages of raw research, boxes filled with photos, and stacks of newspaper clippings. They had tried to get it published, but it had been rejected. They were hiring him in the hope that his professional writing and editing skills could fix the book and make it publishable. They gave him the names of a few people who'd lived in the orphanage and had agreed to be interviewed. He also spoke to many people who knew about its founding and its decades of operations.

Charles called the history of the Home "a microcosm of Black Nova Scotia history." His book details how Nova Scotia's white community refused to care for Black orphans, and how Black community leaders put forth a tremendous effort to dream up a Black-run institution that would care for those children while also training them in skills that could lead to work. In the face of great indifference, they raised the money and built the orphanage. For generations, it was the only option for many children. Charles details the difficulty of sustaining the orphanage, the impact of a staff strike in the 1970s, and how provincial funding kept shrinking, leaving staff underpaid and children hungry. The book does not mention the accounts of abuse that had long percolated in the Black community

---

93 Letter to Charles de Lint, October 6, 1991.

and would soon surge into public awareness, but it leaves no doubt that some people felt that life in the Home could be bad. "There are some kids who come in here saying they heard such horror stories about the Home, and then they come here and think it's the greatest place they've ever been," he quotes one staff person as saying in the 1990s. In the last chapter, he speaks to a few current residents. One says she loves it. Another said it was "pretty good," but he'd rather be somewhere else. Another says staff can "bug you sometimes." And one fifteen-year-old told Charles, "I thought it was all right when I first got here. It was new. But after you've been here a while, your mind changes." Charles asked what changed his mind. "You don't get much freedom. The staff is okay most of the time, but sometimes . . ." Charles leaves the reader with an enhanced knowledge of historic and contemporary racism in Nova Scotia and how Black people found ways to thrive despite that, and he shows a flawed, underfunded Home struggling to cope with troubled children.

"I'm a 'come-from-away,' which is how Maritimers refer to those who were not born in this part of Canada," he writes in the introduction. "However, even though I'd only been living in Halifax for six years, I was well aware of the existence [of the Home]." He admits some reluctance to write the book, but that faded when the research began. "Once I started looking through the materials in that box, I didn't want to stop," he wrote. "We all agreed that my job would be to turn the materials they had given me into a publishable manuscript."

Charles had first heard rumours about abuse at the Home when he moved to Halifax. When he married Dale, he heard more. But these were always just vague complaints, and no one wanted to speak about them in any detail. In 1988, one former resident had contacted him and told Charles he'd been mistreated at the Home. Would Charles help him write his story? "I told him I would help him, but he needed to write the memoir himself," Charles said years later.[94] "He seemed to be OK with that. But he never followed up. It's not that I lost contact with him altogether. But to the best of my recollection, we didn't talk again about his memoir."

No one shared detailed accusations Charles could investigate. "So I've got three incidences, with one person not giving me specifics and the other two not wanting to say anything at all. This was just not enough for me to doubt the validity of the task I was undertaking," he later wrote. He interviewed twenty or thirty people who had worked for or run the Home, and none directly raised the issue of abuse. They did tell him about the difficulty of caring for troubled, abandoned young people who arrived at the Home with a history of abuse. He finished *Share and Care* in February 1993.

Charles's fantasy world returned to him one day in a surprising way. He was editing a story from a cub reporter named Paul Bacon. They'd never met in person, but Charles called him on the phone to clarify a fact. Paul answered his questions. Paul had been reading speculative fiction as long as he could read and often scoured the second-hand bookstores around Halifax for new books. One day in the 1980s, he'd found a novel called *Imaro* and, intrigued by the fresh setting in Africa, scooped it up. He instantly became a lifelong fan of Charles R. Saunders. He searched the stores until he found *Imaro II* and *III*, and even read the first Dossouye story. And now he was talking to a copy editor named Charles Saunders. After they'd met in person a few times, Paul worked up the courage to pop the question: "You're not the Charles Saunders who wrote the Imaro novels?"

94 Letter to David C. Smith, September 28, 2014.

Paul expected him to say no. It had been hard to find the novels in Halifax—why would it be easy to find the author? But Charles laughed and admitted he was the very same. The two struck up a friendship that would last for two decades. Paul admired how Charles could write novels, and nonfiction books, and also turn around a tight column in an eight-hour shift. "To do that day in and day out is quite an accomplishment. Not everyone can do that," he later said.[95]

Outside of work, Charles read some of his new fiction to members of the Black Artists Network of Nova Scotia. "But they weren't critical at all. They were just blown away by the concept, so they didn't pay attention to the details," he wrote.

Share and Care returned to him for the second draft, and he put fiction aside again. "It's worth it, though. It's the best nonfiction I've ever done. That excludes the Africville story, because I can't really classify that. Inspirational writing, maybe," he wrote. He was approached with another nonfiction book deal—a biography of James R. Johnston, Nova Scotia's first Black lawyer, and one of the driving forces that created the Home. Charles was tempted but decided he needed to finish *Share and Care* first before he could really consider it. His life got busier in the fall of 1993, when the *Daily News* hired him full-time as a copy editor, alongside his columns and the new and growing Black History Month supplement, which he had pioneered. He sent off the final prints for *Share and Care* that December. The book was launched to a packed house of more than one hundred people on a bitterly cold winter night during Black History Month: February 21, 1995. It was an amazing evening for Charles and he signed books for ninety minutes, until

95 Interview with the author, 2021.

everyone had what they wanted. "It gave me a little taste of what guys like Stephen King go through. I will never forget the scene at the 1984 fantasy World Con, where King's signing line stretched out into the street!"

But something about the book haunted him. Those rumours ... he wasn't sure he'd gotten the entire story. "Even today, I can still think of other people I'd like to talk to, more documents I'd like to locate, other old newspapers I'd like to read; new directions I'd like to explore," he wrote in the preface. "But the journey has to end sometime, and that time has arrived. Along the way, the Home had become my Home. Hopefully, by the time you finish this book, it will be your Home too."

One line in the book would seem ominous just a few years later, when people abused in the Home started speaking out in public. "Today the [original] building still sits in silent reproach, like an elderly person who lives alone and never has visitors. The windows are boarded shut, the steps leading to the front door are gone, and signs that warn No Trespassing and Do Not Enter are nailed to the walls."

Charles turned fifty on July 12, 1996. "I'll be just as shellshocked as you are," he wrote to Morris. "A lot of more militant Blacks our age used to say that if racial justice didn't come soon, then the next generation would make the '60s militants look like Uncle Toms. Well, here the next generation is, and they don't make us look like Uncle Toms. More like Martin Luther Kings. We may have been tough-talking, but at least we had a cause. The youth of today just seem nihilistic. I wonder if that's the impression we gave to the World War II–Depression set."

To his horror, the life Charles had built in Nova Scotia started falling apart. One person who'd been in the orphanage told a journalist that his years at the Home had been marred by abuse. He gave detailed accounts. Kids were encouraged to fist fight each other to entertain staff, according to some, and to settle disputes. Staff exploited the vulnerable children and abused them physically, sexually, and emotionally. For decades. Many more former residents spoke out, and the province launched an official inquiry, which would confirm the abuse and lead to an apology from the premier of the province. Several former residents launched legal action against the Home and the province, which would keep the orphanage in the news for years.

Charles told several close friends he was "mortified" by the book he had written. He felt he had betrayed the children who suffered and didn't have a voice. He thought he could have provided that voice, but he hadn't. The title alone made him cringe. It was a nightmare. He also felt conflicted about the people who had hired him to write the book celebrating the Black achievement. Why hadn't they told him the truth? Many of them certainly knew about at least one allegation of sexual abuse, and they had also received a report that residents had attempted escape and suicide. He was also contacted by lawyers representing the Home in legal actions and asked to clarify what he had written, and to divulge any accusations of abuse. He had nothing to disclose that wasn't now on the public record. He was told he could be asked to testify at a public inquiry or other legal proceeding. He agreed to do that. He never had to testify, but the lawsuits and accusations dragged on.

Charles never spoke about the scandal in public, but in 2014 he wrote to his old friend David Smith about his struggle to make sense of what he'd done. "In the wake of all this, do I wish I had never written *Share and Care*? In all honesty, there are times ... Overall, though, I'm not sorry I wrote it. I don't think it's a cover-up or a whitewash. I don't think I sugar-coated anything. The book is not all sweetness and light. It is, though, mostly positive. It's the kind of book the Home wanted, and it's the kind of book I wanted to write," he said. "I never found any skeletons in any closets when I was writing the book. But, to be frank, I never opened any closet doors. I didn't even look for any closets. That's something I'll have to answer for at the inquiry, if I'm called as a witness. But I don't know what answers I can give. Even so, I'll most likely volunteer whatever help I can give the inquiry. But I don't much look forward to testifying. What if some hotshot lawyer thinks I'm hiding something? It would have been worse, though, if I'd had to testify during the class-action trial.

"I feel terrible for the people who, as children, had to endure abuse from those who were supposed to care for and protect them. At least now they've achieved vindication and validation. I would never compare my own feelings in the wake of this sordid mess to those of the victims. But it has affected me as well.

"My integrity as a writer is the bedrock of my validity as a person. Now, I feel as though my integrity has been undermined. In writing *Share and Care*, I feel as though my good intentions may have been the proverbial paving stones on the road to hell. If I'd known then what I know now, I most likely would never have written the book in the first place. But I never made any effort to dig deeper. I was too caught up in my role as the writer of an homage to the Home. Rightly or wrongly, I've lost confidence in my integrity as a writer . . . I'm battling depression because of the scandal at the Home." He had heard some of the victims say they hated his book, and he didn't blame them.

Smith's reply came by post a few weeks later. Charles opened the envelope and read: "My friend, I feel that you must relieve yourself of your anguish over this matter as well as you can and as soon as you are able to. You've expressed perfectly how boxed in you are by this situation, but your concern that there is something you could have done differently does not seem reasonable to me," his friend of forty years wrote. "You are a sensitive, caring, and level-headed person; this comes through in all of the reportage and non-fiction of yours that I've read. The regret that we have after the fact when we realize that something may have been going on around us that we were blind to or not privy to, this is hard to bear. But the 'what-ifs' and the 'might-have-beens' are empty vessels; we fill them with the worst that we can surmise when we learn too late about something, but we could play this game forever, to no end. They are empty; there is nothing there."

Smith defended Charles to his worst enemy—Charles. He reminded Charles he was a journalist and could not have reported rumours as facts. What if he'd been wrong about that and falsely accused people of abuse? He didn't have superpowers to read people's minds, nor to see the past or future. People had to tell him things, and they didn't. But now people were mad and looking for a target. Charles had never worked in the Home, nor abused a child. Others had, but they were hard to hold accountable. Nobody was ever charged with any criminal offence. "You're visible, so you become the scapegoat."

Charles was greatly encouraged by his friend's support. Later in 2014, when Charles got an email from an author and social worker named Wanda Taylor, who was writing a new history of the Home—one that told the full, awful truth—he was ready to talk. "Had Wanda approached me a couple of years ago, or even one year ago, I most likely would not have responded to her request. I was just too torn up inside to want to talk about the matter," he wrote to Smith in November. "However, thanks to my opening up to you and another close friend about my angst, and the support you gave me, I felt as though I'd be able to answer Wanda's questions. She sent them to me by e-mail, with which I was comfortable. I do feel a sense of a weight lifting off my shoulders, though. It's as though I have passed the torch to Wanda, so to speak."

Wanda knew that growing up Black in Nova Scotia meant that if you misbehaved, your parents might threaten to "send you to the Home." She knew people who had suffered in the Home. Wanda knew that some people in the Black community were angry at Charles for writing the book. She'd never met him but knew enough about him to think he had not deliberately misled people—that he'd been misled himself. By the time she emailed him, he was a recluse. He'd become, as he'd written evocatively of the Home itself, "an elderly person who lives alone and never has visitors."

But he answered her email and they talked. She didn't blame him for the book he'd written. The code of secrecy around the Home was so deep and dark. What happened behind closed doors was kept hidden. And as someone from the outside, Charles may not have known or been aware of just how deep community secrecy was back in those times. Too many people wanted to believe the fantasy he'd been hired to write. "You're writing the book I should have written," he told her.[96] Wanda herself faced an intense backlash when she published her book, *The Nova Scotia Home for Colored Children: The Hurt, the Hope and the Healing*. "When you're Black and you're writing about something horrible that happened in the Black community, you're seen as selling your people out," she told me. People sent her death threats. People told her publisher to pulp the book—or else. She told Charles about it. "Not everybody loves the truth," he answered. "You're doing the truth. Do it, no matter what. Don't have the regrets that I had."

She urged him to forgive himself. "His book was what it should have been when the founders first opened that Home. That's what they wanted it to be. The image that he put in the book was the image the Home wanted everybody to see. And it wasn't the reality

96 Wanda Taylor interview with the author, 2021.

of what was happening behind closed doors. He genuinely thought he was doing a good thing by shedding a light on it. He went into it with optimism."

He told her to ignore the voices of the critics and listen to the cries of the children. Tell their truth. "After that, it was almost like it doesn't matter what the abusers said, because Charles said what I did was a good thing."

Charles would publish one last nonfiction book, in 1999, called *Black and Bluenose: The Contemporary History of a Community*. It was a collection of his columns and marked the end of his career as a nonfiction author. His personal life was collapsing, too. "I haven't been out of sight; just out of mind. That's just a cryptic way of saying things aren't going all that well. To put it non-cryptically, Dale and I are splitting up. There's no abuse or infidelity involved; just a long, slow parting of the ways. As soon as we sell the house, hopefully before the year is over, we'll be gone from each other's lives," he wrote in 1997, eleven years after they wed.[97] "This was my third marriage—two official, one common-law. Two were to Black women; the other to a white one. Three strikes and you're out."

Charles did not write in detail about the end of his marriages, but perhaps we can gain insight from *The Trail of Bohu*. The third book opens with Imaro as a husband and homeowner working a regular job. His colleague notices the changes in Imaro over the five years he has spent in Cush. "The warrior's bearing had reminded Akhini of that of a lion—a wild one, not the domesticated ones that were a common sight in Meroe and other parts of Cush," we read. "Imaro . . . was then like a creature of the wild confined to a cage."

97 Letter to Charles de Lint, March 31, 1997.

When Akhini asks Imaro why he no longer fights, he replies: "I have fought before. I have a family now. When the time comes, I will fight again."

As an Ilyassai, Imaro was raised as a nomadic person, and Charles used that word to describe himself as well. Did married Charles feel, like Imaro, that "even in the midst of such pervasive protection and security," he was "trapped, like a bird in a snare, ready to be taken"? Five rains in one place "bordered on eternity" for Imaro. "The hard edge he had kept well-honed in anticipation of attack had softened, and he did not like that."

Charles writes that the "initial incandescence" between Tanisha and Imaro had cooled over the passing rains. "As Imaro's dissatisfaction grew, so did the distance between them. Over the past rain, their disagreements had grown sharper, and their nights were, more often than not, spent in angry silence," we read.

Charles first wrote *The Trail of Bohu* in the early 1980s, after his first legal divorce. He was in his thirties. In the years after he divorced Dale, he rewrote the entire Imaro saga. He was in his fifties. The changes those years wrought in the writing are fascinating. Tanisha and Imaro can't agree on a name for their child. In the 1985 DAW edition, Tanisha "finally acceded to Imaro's wishes." But in the modern editions, "Tanisha had ultimately agreed," showing a more mature couple discussing the issue, not just fighting until one gives in. When their son turns five, Imaro wants to begin his warrior training. Tanisha, happy in civilization, says no, and in the DAW edition "becomes almost irrational in her disagreement. 'One killer in this family is enough!' she had shouted at him before he departed for the forge that morning. 'I won't allow you to turn our son into another one.'"

It's a shocking moment. Tanisha sees Imaro as a killer? And she sees his deeply important Ilyassai *mafundishu-ya-muran*, the warrior training, as simply turning their son into a killer? In the 1980s,

Tanisha and Imaro seem strangers to each other, lacking any insight into what motivates the other. They have little empathy for each other and are always quick to see the worst in their partner. When Charles rewrote that scene twenty years later, Tanisha no longer calls Imaro a killer. She now accepts his desire to train their son in the ways of his people, but suggests waiting until he is older. And it's clear this Tanisha knows Imaro well. In place of the "killer" comment, she says, "Do you really want him to suffer as you did?" Modern Tanisha understands that Imaro's warrior training nearly killed him as a boy; it did not turn him into a killer; it made him a survivor. In the modern version, Tanisha and Imaro come across as a loving husband and wife who are baffled and distraught over the collapse of their marriage. In the DAW edition of their last days together, Tanisha's eyes "had a hard glint in them now, and she did not smile often." In the modern edition, "there was less joy in her eyes now. And she smiled less often."

And then there's perhaps the greatest revision. In the DAW version, we get: "Imaro stared at Tanisha. Defensively, she glared back. 'When will you accept the fact that you're not running free on the Tamburure anymore?' Tanisha shouted in exasperation. 'And if you care so much about the Ilyassai, why didn't you stay with them?' Tanisha regretted those words almost before they left her tongue."

Compare that to the modern version, which switches perspective and deepens the encounter: "Tanisha looked at Imaro. Sorrow and anger mingled in her eyes. 'You are gone from me, Imaro,' she said. 'I don't know how, or why, but you are not with me anymore. You are here . . . but you are gone.' She paused, waiting for Imaro to speak. He didn't. He couldn't. 'When the priestess of my people showed me the vision of you, I never thought it would come to this,' she said. Tanisha regretted those words almost before they flew from her tongue. But it was too late."

Perhaps in these words we get a sense of the sorrow that overwhelmed the marriage of Charles and Dale. Perhaps she, too, felt Charles was gone from her. And perhaps Charles couldn't speak. Dale moved into her own apartment. Charles found a place for himself.

After the divorce, and the *Care and Share* disaster, Charles culled people from his life, starting with a longtime pen pal in Denver. "That friendship ran aground on the shoals of racial disharmony," he wrote. His friend was about the age of his mother, he noted, and "just can't shake this attitude that white is right, and Black people should stop bellyaching and conform to white ways if we want to have a chance of being accepted. And that's just to have a chance—there are no guarantees."

He wouldn't "swallow that crap." He persevered with the exchange, hoping she would see more of his view, but what he saw of her view increasingly discouraged him. He had to count to ten before responding to her. He would offer logical, evidence-based counter-arguments, no doubt like he did in the newspaper. "Of course, facts don't matter when your belief is strong or blind enough to ignore them. I admit, I'm guilty of that myself sometimes. But it was very important to [her] to try and convince me that whites can do no wrong and Blacks can do no right."

The disintegration of his new life and home dropped him into a deep depression. He called it a late-blooming mid-life crisis hitting him at fifty-one, and often sang to himself the lyrics of "The Message," by Grandmaster Flash.

He ran out of typewriter ribbon and had to stop writing for more than a week until he could replace it. That caused him to halt a letter midway through, and when he returned to it, he realized he was irrationally getting angry with another old friend about something, when the truth was he didn't want to write about his failed marriage. "Anyway, you can see I'm not in the best frame of mind right now. I mean, I feel good because I'm about to get out of a situation that has turned bad. But I feel bad about the part I played in making it turn bad. Only thing to do is make the best of my freedom once I've got it back. That doesn't mean running around acting like I'm half my age. Just that I want to get this new novel done, and do some other things," he wrote. "Right now, though, I'm just trying to keep from going under."

He tried to sell the house, but the market was cold and the delay was devastating his finances. Charles shampooed the carpets, tore down the wallpaper, and repainted the walls to attract a buyer, but none came. He returned to the States in September to visit his mother and other family, and no doubt to tell them in person about the end of his marriage.

He and Dale lowered the price, but the house still didn't sell. "The thing is, not only is this prolonged breakup hanging over my head, I also got diagnosed with diabetes last fall. That's the bad news. The good news is, I've been able to keep it under control through diet and exercise. I've lost about 40 pounds over the past six months or so, and will probably lose more. Of course, I have no desire to get down to what I weighed when we were at Lincoln. That was just too thin," he wrote.[98] "As for the rest of my life, I had a real scare when our paper got sold to an international chain and there were buyout packages offered in lieu of layoffs. I have two aces in the hole. One, I'm good at what I do. Two, I am the only minority person in the newsroom."

The house finally sold in 1998. His next letters came from a new address: 11 Primrose Street in Dartmouth, Nova Scotia. "After an agonizing year of waiting, and lowering the price again and again, the house was finally sold in early October. With that gone, Dale and I were free to go our separate ways. A no-fault divorce will

---

98 Letter to Morris Fried, March 1, 1998.

follow in about a year. So now it's on to the next phase of my life. I sure do hope it turns out better than the last one did. At least I'm in my own space now, and that's pretty well what I need. I have come to realize that I am essentially a solo act, for better or worse," he wrote.[99]

After the divorce, Charles and Dale broke all ties, by mutual consent. He heard rumours of her health failing with multiple sclerosis, and learned in 2010 that she had moved into a nursing home, despite being only in her fifties. He contemplated visiting her. He worried it would upset her, or him, but decided to risk it. He found she needed to use a wheelchair to move around and could hardly use her arms and legs. The encounter broke Charles's heart. "She was glad enough that I had come. When I left, however, she said I didn't really need to come again, and she didn't want anything from me. That was fair enough. We had pretty well agreed to stay out of each other's lives back at the time of the divorce," he wrote.[100] "I can't really explain why I went. I can't even express a maybe. But I did get the strong impression that as far as she was concerned, once was enough."

In 2017, he was reading the daily obituaries when he got a shock: his one-time wife had died at sixty-three. Her death notice records her name as Dale Rhonda Saunders, suggesting some part of her heart remained with Charles Saunders. "The obituary was laudatory, as it should have been," he wrote to Janet. "You met Dale, so you know what an outgoing personality she had. Even when I saw her at Northwood, it was clear that she had made a lot of friends there. She was coping as well as she could under the circumstances."

---

99 Letter to Charles de Lint, February 14, 1999.

100 Letter to Janet LeRoy, January 20, 2018.

He struggled for years to make sense of how it ended, and to understand why he'd gone to see her in 2010. Janet suggested they needed to say goodbye. Charles agreed. "As I remember, we laughed and reminisced at first, but eventually the conversation died down. You know how it is when there just doesn't seem to be anything else to say. So I guess that was our second 'goodbye'—the first one occurring when we separated."

He didn't go to her visitation or funeral, as he felt it would be overstepping the terms of their parting. He also worried about bumping into her family—which had become his family—and seeing them disappointed in him. But he felt he was no longer part of her life, and preferred to mourn her death in private. "Her personality was pretty much the opposite of mine. Maybe that's what attracted us to each other in the beginning: the old cliche, 'opposites attract.' But sometimes, the initial affinity between opposites wears off. I think that is what happened with Dale and me. At the end of the marriage, there just wasn't anything left between us anymore—at least not enough to enable us to continue to live together." He took comfort knowing she died loved as she began "her transition to whatever lies beyond the life that we know. I think I am pretty well meant to be alone, with all that implies," he concluded.

Nicole Farmer, the niece who had once watched her Aunt Dale get ready to lead the "dancing queens" to the Derby, learned about the divorce with sorrow. Over the following years, she'd see Charles riding on the bus. She always gave him a warm hug and they'd sit together and chat. She still loved the jolly, gentle giant who had been her uncle. She watched the *Care and Share* disaster unfold, and understood how it would have been a bitter reminder for Charles that yes, he was a Black man, but "you were a Black man from the outside. You didn't live the Nova Scotia experience. You don't know that experience. Perhaps some individuals didn't think he was being his authentic self, or was only reading. You don't have that experience. So how could you know?"[101]

Nicole wondered why he didn't go to her Aunt Dale's funeral and says he would have been welcome. She sees the truth in Charles's diagnosis of the marriage: Opposites attract, until they don't. Dale was a vibrant, outgoing woman who grew up in a big, bustling house. Charles loved silence and solitude. At first, they brought great joy to each other. Nicole thinks the marriage constituted the happiest years of Dale's life, too.

Nicole visited Dale often as the multiple sclerosis took over her body. Her aunt never lost her spark for life. On one of her last visits, Dale smiled up from the wheelchair in the nursing home, eyes wet, and asked to go dancing one last time. In those final days, she had no muscle movement at all and spent her time in a giant wheelchair with a bulky headrest. "But I still managed to spin that big Cadillac of a chair one last time."

Alone again, Charles did what he often did: He pulled up the front steps and retreated inside. He might as well have nailed a "No Trespassing" sign to his door. He left the house for work and food, but no longer for fun and friends. He went back to safety: his fantasy worlds. He spent his mornings writing a new novel, *Abengoni* and his evenings editing the newspaper. "*Abengoni* is my new life's work, outside my job and columns. I'll keep trying to get it out there, and if I eventually have to turn to the small press, I'll do it," he wrote.[102] "This kind of support is enough to cause me to rethink

---

101 Interview with the author, 2024.

102 Letter to Charles de Lint, July 28, 1997.

my earlier decision to let Imaro stay buried. The fourth and fifth books are kind of unfinished business."

Charles prepared for Y2K in bleak circumstances. He was single and broke and hadn't published a word of fiction in fifteen years. But Jua, the sun, began to shine again. One ray came all the way from Europe. "Another change is that I've become involved in a new relationship after pretty well convincing myself I wouldn't do so again. But this one is different," he wrote. "The woman in question doesn't live in Nova Scotia, or even Canada. She lives in Switzerland. I met her through correspondence—that's old-fashioned correspondence, not the internet. She's a teacher, artist, and human-rights activist. She came to visit me for four weeks during July and August, and will be back again for two weeks in October. Where from there? Who knows?"

And then he got a message from an American woman named Sheree Renée Thomas, who was creating an anthology of speculative fiction from Black authors. It was the sort of anthology Charles had tried to create in the 1970s, and abandoned when DAW beseeched him to write an Imaro novel instead. Thomas had read that novel and never forgot it. She, too, had heard the rumours that the author was dead, leaving the Imaro saga unfinished. But she'd searched for him anyway, and found the missing author alive and well in Canada. Her anthology was to be called *Dark Matter*—would Charles consider contributing a short story to it?

13

LOSE THE WHALE, HERM

I walked up to the tall green glass building on the Halifax waterfront and double-checked I had the right address: 1601 Lower Water Street. This was the place. I entered through the front doors and headed to the elevator. I'd never been inside before but jabbed the button for the fourth floor and arranged my thoughts as I rose. The doors opened, and I saw a sign confirming I was at the right place. I turned left and stopped at the front desk. "Hi, my name is Jon Tattrie," I began, and explained what I was doing there. The woman nodded and picked up her phone. "He'll be right with you," she said. I waited, nervous, taking long breaths to calm myself. A middle-aged white man with white hair smiled and greeted me with a handshake and led me to the back of the office. A small group of people sat at a semi-circle bench of desks forming a horseshoe around two other desks. I nodded to the people on the outer rim, and to the man facing me from the first chair in the middle. Then I noticed one more person at the second desk, slowly turning his hunched frame from the window to look at me. *Wow,* I thought, *that's Charles Saunders*! He nodded from his desk before returning to the harbour view and the day's editorial.

I settled into my desk and started my first shift as a copy editor on the Halifax *Daily News*. They had plenty of well-known columnists, but Charles was the face that stood out, even though he hadn't written his column in half a decade. He'd aged since his last photo byline. His hair was longer, as was his beard. He wore glasses. When he stood, I discovered I looked up to him—literally. I'm halfway between six-foot-three and six-foot-four, but Charles must have hit the full six-foot-four.

It was June 2006, and I was home, fresh off a plane from Europe and a little disoriented. I had moved to Scotland after university, in 1999. For most of my twenties, I lived in Scotland and wandered around the world every time I saved a few thousand pounds. I had a sense I was seeking something but was never really sure what. A year earlier, I'd been crawling over a fallen temple to Zeus in Athens when I realized I'd been looking for home. Growing up in Nova Scotia, I always felt at home and out of place: at home because people who looked like me were well represented in national iconography, and I had many positive role models; out of place because I knew the Mi'kmaq had lived in the same land, called Mi'kma'ki, for fourteen thousand years or more, and that most of the history I'd been taught was designed to make me forget that. My home could never be some monomythical ancestral homeland of white people, I realized amid the debris of ancient Greece. My home had Mi'kmaq, and African Nova Scotians, and French Acadians. Newcomers, too. Running my hands over the fallen pillars, I realized that I would never find home in Europe. I'd heard enough people say "I'm Scottish" in a loud Canadian accent to know how odd that sounded to born-in-Scotland people. So I started thinking it was time to return to the place that did still feel like home: Nova Scotia.

I'd flown back to Canada to interview for a few newspaper jobs and was travelling while awaiting the results. A week before meeting Charles, I'd been hot-air ballooning in Turkey. I was at an internet cafe in Cappadocia when I got the email from the Halifax *Daily News* offering me a job that started in five days. I told my new boss I'd be there; I didn't tell him where I was, or what it would take to get me there. I flew from Istanbul to Edinburgh, closed up my apartment, and stuffed what I was keeping into a small backpack. I hopped on a flight to Halifax and landed Sunday. On Monday, I reported for my first shift.

A sign hung over us, declaring in the newspaper's red and white colours: "News Rim." Paul Bacon, the night editor, sat at the bottom of the U, and Charles sat behind him, his back to us. The shimmering glass tower was designed to look like a ship's prow launching into the harbour, and Charles had the captain's view. My desk was just before the U-bend. I soon got into the routine. I'd arrive for my shift around three or four p.m. and work until eleven p.m. or midnight. Our schedules shifted over the weeks, so we all took our share of weekends. I can still hear how Charles greeted me at the start of the shift: "Hey, Jaan." That accent, turning the *o* into a long *a*, was my first hint that he hadn't been born in Canada. Up until I heard him say my name, I thought he was from Africville. His essay in *The Spirit of Africville* had blown me away as a teenager. He'd made me feel like Africville was my home and my history, which was the first time Black history had hit me that way. I never looked at it the same again.

The office was busy at the start of our shifts, but the best part was after five p.m., when all the daytimers departed, leaving the newsroom to us on the rim, plus the late reporter, and the techie who sent the digital files to the printing press. The rim could be a rowdy place at night. We'd talk about the news, make the worst puns we could think of ("Why can't you watch TV in Afghanistan? The Tellyban"), and generally amuse ourselves as we edited the newspaper. The *Daily News* had the first newspaper website in the world, but at the time, we literally had to stop the presses for breaking news. I got to do that once—it was quite the thrill.[103]

Charles was held in high esteem throughout the newspaper, both as a journalist and as a person. One of his closest colleagues on the paper was Judy Kavanaugh, who worked alongside him as a copy editor for nearly two decades. "I don't think I can remember any of his horrible puns, though," she later told me. "They were along the lines of 'What do you call a kid who lives on a beach? Sandy!' Only his were much more groanworthy. I think he just enjoyed laughing at my reactions."

Judy wrote the "On This Day in History" note in the newspaper, and Charles provided her with a steady stream of Black history dates. The only thing that could disturb his tranquil demeanor was his old enemy: computers. "Charles lost his temper and slammed his fist down on his desk whenever his ancient Mac crashed and he lost a page. Few things were funnier than watching a roomful of young white journalists turn even whiter when a Black man shouts 'FUCK!' at the top of his voice," she recalled with a laugh.

He was always at his desk when I arrived. Usually he was writing the next day's editorial. When he was done that, he'd help the night editor out by going over our final proofs for the newspaper. We copy editors would work on a page and, when we were certain all the facts were correct and there were no errors, we'd print it off and put it in a basket for the night editor—or Charles—to sign off on. Charles was a meticulous editor and would probably shake his head if he saw that I'd first tried to spell that word "miticulous." It was a

103 I couldn't quite remember the occasion as I wrote this. A political scandal? A shootout? I asked the techie, my friend Michelle Thornhill, and she broke the news to me: It was probably the time I'd sent the same page twice and we had to correct that error. That sounds about right.

rare night when Charles handed my page back with no red ink. We warred over one piece of punctuation. I called it our comma-kaze battle: Charles always liked more commas than I did and would insert them with a small red-ink hook. (Several times while working on this book and writing up something Charles wrote, I found myself removing commas out of old habit. I put them back in.)

One night, my editing was interrupted by a kerfuffle in the corner. A few editors and the entertainment writer had gone to the store and were putting on a spread for Sundaes on Sundays. We had buckets of the best ice cream, sundae cups, sprinkles, chopped nuts, chocolate chips, and a range of sauces. I dug in. I don't think Charles worked Sundays in those days, and he was by then a health-conscious eater, so likely he wouldn't have indulged.

Another time we decided to hold a Best-Dressed Copy Editor competition and we all turned up for work in tuxedos and ball-gowns. The daytimers cocked a curious eye, but didn't say anything. I won second place in the men's division.

Work would grind to a halt as we got to the serious business of ordering food. "Anyone scaling the wall?" someone would ask, and we'd put in our orders for the Great Wall, a Chinese restaurant just down the street from our office. Charles mostly skipped those feasts, opting for his own healthy food. Often it was fish and a bag of radishes, and a few of his colleagues wrinkled their noses disapprovingly when he cracked that container open.

One memorable night, we decided to hold an epic feast on the rim. I got there at three, made my coffee, and got to work on my pages. We copy editors exchanged sly glances. We waited until five, when the daytimers left, and then six, when the editor-in-chief, whose office overlooked the news rim, departed. We had the place to ourselves; we stopped working immediately. Editors piled an enormous amount of food and drink onto a table in the room that housed the morning news meetings. We loaded up one end with wine bottles and worried their weight would collapse it. The feast began. There we were, arrayed around the empty newsroom, some of us more than a little tipsy, and all of us stuffed to the gills, when the door opened and the newspaper's editor-in-chief walked in and saw his crack copy editing team looking like a modern take on Gin Alley. We froze. So did he. He walked quickly to his office, picked up his briefcase, and walked right out of there. He never said a word to us. We resumed our bacchanalian evening. And we made damn sure there wasn't a single mistake in the newspaper the next day. I don't think that boss ever re-entered the newsroom unannounced after hours.

Often, we'd ask Charles for his editing advice, hear only silence, and turn to see his empty chair. I never understood how a beloved heavyweight could slip past a rim of sharp-eyed editors without drawing notice. Yet he did it, night after night.

After I settled into my job on the newspaper, I pitched a feature called "Confessions of an Aspiring Novelist" to the Sunday newspaper editor. She said yes. I interviewed several potential publishers for my own fiction, hoping they'd read the feature and take a chance on my novel. I planned all of this sitting about ten feet away from Charles. I could always see his back out of the corner of my right eye. The *Sunday Daily News* finally published my article, and splashed my photo across the front page of the insert on the writing festival that was on that week. My bosses also included an excerpt from my novel-in-progress. I hoped the publishers I'd interviewed would read the story, see my excerpt, and be inspired to publish it. It worked.

It was around then that Charles greeted me one day at the start of my shift—and he was standing. "Hey Jaan," he said. He offered a wonderful smile. He handed me a bright book that showed a ripped warrior roaring over a pile of fallen foes, and beneath them all was a slain lion. "*Imaro*, by Charles Saunders, featuring an introduction by Charles de Lint."

I was utterly delighted. I had followed Charles's writing career since I was a teenager, but I didn't know he wrote fiction until he handed me his novel. I treasured the gift, and the work friendship. Charles was such a warm, friendly giant, and I can't remember him ever coming to work with a bad attitude, or even showing a bad mood. There was something so compelling about him. I think it was his eyes: so honest, so probing, as though he could see deep inside you, and challenged you to look deep inside of him. It was transfixing.

I started reading *Imaro* that night. I hadn't read much fantasy, but the writing was amazing, Imaro was captivating, and I romped through it in a week or so. I bought *The Quest for Cush* and devoured it, too. I assumed the rest of the series would follow in due time and looked forward to Imaro's ongoing journey. I told Charles how much I loved it. I also loved how he treated me as his writing peer, though I didn't tell him that.

Charles was living a lot of life outside the newspaper from 2006 to 2008, the years we worked together. He'd stopped writing his column in 2000 as the eternal tides of fiction and nonfiction pulled at his soul. "I gave up the column after 11 years because I wanted to devote all of my time away from my job to my fiction. That is what I really want to do, and I found that I couldn't give the column the attention it needed for it to be effective, and also put in the effort that my fiction needed to have in order to make it publishable in a market that is much more competitive than it was when my Imaro novels were first published 20 years ago," he wrote.[104]

---

104 Letter to Morris Fried, fall 2000.

In 1999 and the start of 2000, he'd felt on the cusp of a deal with Warner Books to publish his new Abengoni series. "A deal was imminent," he wrote. "But then, like a real-estate transaction in which the buyer backs out before the deal can be closed, Warner got cold feet, for reasons I still don't understand." First, they'd asked him to break the one book up into three, and then they wanted three turned into two. "Their suggestions as to how to do so would have eliminated all the new, innovative aspects of that story, and would have rendered it not worth writing. I wasn't willing to do that. . . . It would be like a publisher telling Herman Melville, 'Great story, Herm, but you're gonna have to lose that whale.' So, there it is. Lots of effort, and not a cent to show for it so far. I had entertained dreams of being able to leave my job, but it looks as though I'll have to stick it out a while longer. Maybe for the next 10 years, or more."

He had begun using email by then, first for work, and later for personal communications. "But I'd rather go the snail route. There is something inherently demanding about email. Since it arrives instantly, I feel as though I need to respond instantly, and that creates pressures I would rather do without," he wrote. Often, when people did email him, he'd write a short reply and then answer at length in a letter. Email was mostly for checking in on people. He got lots of emails inviting him to the 2002 Lincoln University reunion, but he didn't want to go. "A super-reunion of the Lincoln classes of 1966-67-68? What are they thinking? Does anyone seriously want to get all those nuts together in the same place again? Talk about a critical mass of rabble . . . the Office of Homeland Security would be rounding all of us up in the refectory," he wrote to Morris that February. "I don't know why; maybe it's just that I've gone more 'inward' since I decided to spend as much of my off-work time as I can on my fiction. I don't have that much interest in getting together with the old gang anymore." He did send a message that year: "Charlie Snake remembers."

He was less involved in Nova Scotia, too. "I don't think I'm more conservative now. However, I have pulled back from my former level of community activism, beginning with the discontinuation of my newspaper column. That's not because I've become more conservative; it's because I've become more tired. I'm tired of fighting the same battles over and over again, plus new ones on top of them. Did you ever in your wildest dreams envision that Blacks would lose a national debate over accusations of 'racial preferences,' as happened in the affirmative-action controversy? That was just unbelievable. Yet it happened," he wrote. "I'm doing what is most fulfilling to me, which is my fiction writing. I hope never to retire from that, whether I get another word published or not."

He was a great editorialist and he enjoyed the work. "Not a bad job, and certainly less stressful and demanding than the copy editing job I've done for the past ten years. Actually, it *is* demanding; it's just that the demands of this position are more acceptable to me and less likely to cause me to burn out. It plays to my strength, which is writing."

Charles's ties to the U.S. were fading, too. In the early 2000s, his mother got sick, and he made frequent trips back to Pennsylvania as her health failed. She'd fallen once and been found in agony by workers a couple of days later. She moved into an assisted-living residence and had hip surgery. "I went down to provide moral support and whatever other help I could give. I mean, I couldn't do the surgery myself, right? She came through it fine."

The trips to the U.S. always solidified his decision to remain in exile. "I have lived in the Halifax/Dartmouth area longer than I have any other place in my life, so I guess this is 'home.' Although I am becoming less tolerant of winter, I will probably stay here, at least as long as I can keep my job. When I reach retirement age, I might head for a warmer climate."

By February 2003, he'd given up on publishing. Nobody was biting on the proposed four-part Abengoni series, and he wasn't sure he had the drive to write it with no deal. "None of the big-time publishers is willing to take the chance that I will, indeed, finish the entire quatrology. Boy, that word isn't going to get past my spell-checker," he wrote.[105] "So, my hopes of being able to quit my job and get paid to write my epic have not been realized. Fortunately, I no longer want to quit my job. So I'll continue to labour away on my epic until it's done. Who knows how long that will take? As it is, I enjoy the creative process, so it's not as though I'm working at two jobs, one for pay and the other not."

Typically in a Nova Scotia fall, hurricanes blow up from the Caribbean but weaken into tropical storms before they reach us. However, in October 2003, Hurricane Juan hit the province full force, killing two people. Charles wrote about it at length, giving us a tour of his world at the time. "On one street near where I live, every tree and power pole on a long city block was either snapped or toppled onto power lines and people's houses," he wrote.[106] "The power went out close to midnight, not long after the hurricane made its landfall, so I just sat in the dark for a while, listening to the pounding of the powerful wind. It sounded like the beating of gigantic drums. I couldn't see much outside the window. It was like looking out a car windshield in a rainstorm with the wipers off. The strangest thing I saw was what looked like lightning without the accompanying sound of thunder. I did hear one boom, though.

"Eventually, I went to sleep. When I woke up the next morning, the wind had died down, although it was still blowing briskly by normal standards. The electricity, of course, was still gone. As I

105 Letter to Morris Fried, February 5, 2003.

106 Letter to Morris Fried, October 4, 2003.

looked out the window, I saw that a big tree had fallen next to my apartment building. That was the 'boom' I heard during the night.

"When I went outside, it was hardly a typical, back-to-work Monday morning. The power outage hit virtually all of the city and its suburbs, as well as rural areas and small coastal fishing villages that you see on postcards."

Charles made his way past the white-capped Atlantic and through the deserted, tree-strewn city and took his seat at work. "By late morning, the last traces of the hurricane had passed. The sky was clear and blue; the sun was shining; there was only the slightest of breezes. It was a warm, summer-like day—a jest, or perhaps a consolation prize, from the same natural forces that had generated the hurricane in the first place. The day was pleasant—the destruction was not," he wrote. "Huge trees were either broken in half, or toppled onto their sides, with giant clumps of earth and grass clinging to their roots. Power poles were snapped like matchsticks. Not many houses or buildings sustained damage, but there were some instances in which the destruction was spectacular, and downright dangerous. In one case, the roof and one side of an apartment building were ripped away as thought they were made of paper. Other roofs were peeled off, as one witness said, 'like the pull-tabs on pop cans.'"

Sailboats and small watercraft had been ejected from the storming seas and tossed onto front lawns. Two enormous container ships ended up on top of a wharf. "Fishing sheds, wharves and lobster traps were smashed into a mess of kindling. One observer described a formerly picturesque fishing cove as having been turned into 'gumbo,'" he said, no doubt quoting from the pages he was editing. By Tuesday, politicians had already turned the storm damage into something to bicker about. "We were psychologically unprepared for an event like this. We just couldn't believe that something like a direct hit from a full-force hurricane, regardless of its category, could happen here. I guess the lesson we learned was: Yes, things like that can happen here, and eventually, they will."

In 2005, Charles got an urgent call from his mother's seniors' residence, saying she'd had a seizure and been sent to hospital. Charles rushed to her side in Harrisburg, Pennsylvania. He flew from Halifax to Toronto and then transferred to a nineteen-seat Beechcraft with "little, whirling propellers." Air Canada sent his luggage to Indianapolis, so he had to survive with his carry-on bag. His mother was out of hospital and in the nursing home when he reached her. "When I finally saw my mother, I was glad and sad at the same time . . . glad that she was still alive; sad that her condition had gone downhill," he wrote.[107] Charlene turned eighty-one that year. Charles spent more than a week in Harrisburg trying to get his mother's situation settled so she could be safe and comfortable. "It was just a matter of doing the best I could for my mother, because I'm all she's got," he wrote. "Besides, I wasn't planning on going to Hawaii or the Caribbean for a vacation, anyway."

Charles returned to Canada but expected he'd be back in Harrisburg soon, as her health was uncertain. "I've found that every time I visit the United States, I feel less and less like an American, despite my American roots. Guess it's to be expected; I have now spent more than half my life in Canada."

In March, Charlene's health declined again and Charles returned to her bedside. "I could hear the machine breathing for her, like some disembodied ghost. I would like to think she knew I was there . . ."[108] He had to wear a gown and gloves to sit with her. The

107 Letter to Morris Fried February 26, 2005.

108 Letter to Morris Fried May 1, 2005.

doctors said her recovery chances were slim. "So, I had to decide how the life of the woman who gave me life would end. And I had to make that decision during the last days of the life of Terri Schiavo, and the intense debate that was going on then was inescapable."

The bitter U.S. debate was over whether Schiavo, who was being kept alive by machines, should continue to be kept alive and unresponsive, or left to live or die naturally. After a long and painful court battle, her machines were turned off, and she had died that month.

Charles spoke with his aunt, his mother's older sister. Charlene's twin brother had died before her. He also spoke to two cousins. "What it all boiled down to was that I had to understand, somehow, what my mother would have told me, if she had been able to talk with me. And I had to make a decision I could live with." He wrestled with the decision for two days and nights. Finally, he told the doctor to let her live on her own, so that she could die on her own. They turned off the machines and she soon passed away. "I will not describe my grieving and mourning; that is a personal matter." She was cremated and, at her request, no funeral service was held. Her remains were interred next to the graves of her mother and father in western Pennsylvania.

"But now that I'm back home in Nova Scotia—this place really does feel like home in a way the United States can never be again—I find myself wondering if I really did the right thing. Who am I to decide whether another person lives or dies? The answer is: I am no one," he wrote. "I still feel lingering doubts, and a degree of guilt. My mother's death has become part of my life. The sadness comes and goes in waves. I'll live with it."

It hit hard on Sundays. "I still find myself going to the phone at the usual time, and then having to catch myself, and remember. Sundays aren't the same anymore. But then, no day will be the same anymore."

Charles loved greeting cards and he sent them to his friends religiously (and irreligiously, in the case of Morris, his Jewish friend to whom he always tried to send a Christmas card that was not a Christmas card). He enjoyed selecting Charlene's Mother's Day card and often sent it two weeks early to ensure she had it on the special day. "I only messed up a few times on that, and I was never allowed to forget it."

Later that year, when Hurricane Katrina hit the U.S., Charles wrote an editorial. Canada had sent four relief ships to help the storm victims, despite the tension over Canada's refusal to fight in the U.S.-Iraq war. "All of that is relegated to the background in a time of need such as this one," he wrote, comparing it to the 1917 Halifax Explosion, when help came first from Boston. "The help that's coming from Canada now is in the same spirit, because friends can have their differences, but when one of them has troubles, the other is there for them."

The editorial was printed and posted online, where it found a surprise audience. "I heard the news editor saying, 'Wolf Blitzer is reading from Charles's editorial!'" Charles told a friend.[109] A colleague turned up the volume on the normally mute newsroom television. Charles watched, amazed and tickled, as CNN's famous anchor read his words. "That was my 15 seconds of fame—but it was anonymous, because newspaper editorials are not signed. Still, the people I work with in the newsroom congratulated me, and I raised my arms like Muhammad Ali," Charles wrote.

The old lion still had plenty of fight in him.

---

109 Letter to Morris Fried October 27, 2005.

14

THE DEATH OF THE *DAILY NEWS*

Charles and I both spent the morning of February 11, 2008, chilling out ahead of the night shift. The Halifax *Daily News* had seemingly stabilized under the latest new owners, Transcontinental Media. The newest new editor-in-chief had pulled all the journalists together for a pep talk in January. He'd been parachuted in from Quebec and tried to rally us with his promise to "turn this ship around." He didn't announce any layoffs, so everyone went back to work.

But then mid-morning that Monday, the newsroom was swarmed with suits. They took up key positions across the fourth floor and called another mass meeting. Anyone with a sharp eye would have noticed that a small number of journalists had been extracted from the room and were being stored next door in Tug's Pub. They were the survivors. In the main newsroom, the editor-in-chief broke the news: The Halifax *Daily News* was dead, killed by Transcontinental, and would be replaced by a free daily called *Metro*. Everyone in the room was out of work. Those in Tug's Pub would run the surviving local weekly newspapers and *Metro*. Everyone else had to take their things and get out of the building. The computers were locked down. The suits were there to make sure everyone knew how to leave nicely. Oh, and they could tell us about severance packages and retraining opportunities.

I was across town, enjoying a birthday brunch with my parents. I turned thirty-one that day. My phone was off; I figured I'd catch up with the day's news when I got to work that afternoon. My aunt called my dad and told him she'd just heard on the radio that the newspaper had gone out of business. The world swirled under my feet. I flipped my phone open and started calling people. It only took a few minutes to establish the truth: My dream job was over. I had no work to go to that night. I had no source of income. The future I'd imagined for myself burst like a bubble. Everyone was gathering across the harbour in a downtown Dartmouth pub called Celtic Corner.

I think everyone had managed to get fully drunk by the time I pushed the door open on the dim pub mid-afternoon, and I soon caught up. It was a raucous, joyful vibe, like a doomed band of warriors partying before the suicide mission. Or I guess after it, in this case. I heard about the execution of the newspaper from many people, and learned about the extracted band sent to Tug's Pub to carry on the free papers. We had no hard feelings, and were glad some of us had stayed employed. Plus, we were all looking for work. One person at the party who wasn't a journalist drew laughs when she said she was a freelance writer—we were all freelance writers, suddenly.

The barman yelled us to attention and told us an old editor of the *Daily News*—one of the good ones—had just called and left his credit card details at the bar. Next round was on him. We roared our approval. A radio news reporter turned up to interview some of the better-known columnists and, in a moment of bleary inspiration, my tipsy friends serenaded me with a version of "Happy Birthday" that made the song sound like a filthy sea shanty. We all cheered when the bartender played the hourly news and it started with a recording of our drunken choir to lead into the news of our demise.

As an extra kick, the bastards at the *Chronically Horrid* broke the news of our end and the next day ran a front-page photo of two of us walking down the steps of Summit Place, holding boxes of desk goods. I saved a copy of the final edition of the Halifax *Daily News*. Fittingly, the last front-page headline reads, "Town holds its breath."

Charles spent that morning puttering around his apartment. He tuned into the local TV news at noon to catch up on events and maybe to find an idea for the editorial he would write that night. "The introductory music faded, and the top news story of the day came on: 'The Halifax *Daily News* will no longer be publishing, as of today.' The Halifax *Daily News* is the newspaper I work for—or used to work for, as it turns out. The TV news story went on to say that the paper will be replaced by a free daily handout called *Metro*," he wrote a few weeks later.[110] "After I saw this news on TV, I went to the office to learn more about what's going on. There, I was met by a nice lady from Human Resources, who handed me a severance package. It's not a lot of money, but it will keep me going for a while. I was also told that I could still officially retire, and start getting a pension—which won't be as much as I would get if I had been able to stay until I turned 65, but is still better than nothing," he added. "Did I see this coming? Yes and no. The *Daily News* has always been the underdog; always on shaky financial ground. For years, people cried 'Wolf' about the way the paper lost money, and that it could go out of business at any time. But that never happened. Locally, the *Daily News* was known as 'The Little Paper That Could.' And even with all the cries of 'Wolf,' the paper kept on going. Now, a wolf called Transcontinental has decided it's 'The Little Paper That Can't.'

"My biggest worry had always been whether I, as an older employee who had built up some seniority, would go on the chopping block before I turned 65, at which time I could retire with a full pension. I never thought the whole operation would go

---

110 Letter to Morris Fried, March 15, 2008.

under. I don't know if I was just naive, or what. I just didn't think Transcontinental would shut the paper down after all the ballyhoo that accompanied their purchase of it back in 2002.

"So now the obvious question is: What do I do next? Right now, I need to look into the details of my premature retirement, and find out exactly what the terms and conditions of my pension will be. Then, I can see whether or not the rival paper in town might want to take me on as an editorial writer, or maybe as an opinion columnist. After all, I never wrote anything nasty about them . . . at least, that I can remember.

"These past months have been a trying time. And now, the newspaper that has been my employer for the past 15 years has folded abruptly, with no warning whatsoever. Even the editor didn't know. I wasn't there at the time, but I was told he walked out of the office in stunned disbelief. He ended up discussing the debacle on a TV-news panel later that day. He did well enough, under the circumstances."

Charles didn't go to many of the revelries that followed. I think I went to all of them. After one, I found myself walking home through the quiet streets of downtown Halifax late at night with a few other ex-editors from the rim. We happened to walk by Summit Place and looked longingly up at the fourth floor. Then somebody asked, "I wonder if our pass-keys still work?" They did. And so a highly intoxicated pack of ex-journalists slipped in the back door, up the stairs, and wrenched the *Daily News* sign off the walls. I still have the *s* in my office.

That first week, it seemed like we got together every day. We were a tight group, permanently welded together by the death of the newspaper. The best-known journalists quickly got new jobs in other media outlets, and a few went over "to the Dark Side," as we called it when someone left journalism to work in PR. And a miserable exodus began, as one by one people got jobs in other provinces or the Middle East or America. We held leaving wakes for them all. And one day late that winter, the small inner circle of the news rim gathered at Judy Kavanaugh's apartment in Dartmouth. To our joy and surprise, Charles came out. It was a quiet occasion. We'd sobered up and this was like a classic night on the rim: lots of good food, some tasty drinks, and the vibe of a group of friends sitting around after they'd finished their homework. Or after their school had been destroyed by capitalism.

We took a last photo. There were just eight of us. Paul Bacon and I flank Charles. I'm on his left. Judy's in front of him. We were all in that rainbow mood of sunshine and tears. Charles looks directly at the camera, eyes open and clear. There's a stack of books behind us. The front row is holding the *Daily News* "Rim" sign that we'd stolen from the empty office.

I didn't see Charles much after that gathering. On May 19 that year, he updated Morris on his life post-paper. "What am I doing now, you ask. Well, my severance lump sum is enough to allow me a couple of months to devote most of my time to finishing the Imaro short-story collection, which will be the sixth volume of the series. Of course, while I'm doing that, I will still be looking for a way to make a living once the severance money runs out. If I live frugally enough, it will last me for more than a year. I haven't been very frugal over the years, but I guess I'll have to learn how to be now.

"Some good news is that my print-on-demand book collecting the stories of my woman warrior, Dossouye, is now available. Here's what the cover looks like," he added, including a colour print. Dossouye is ferocious and unforgettable, a furious Grace Jones wielding a massive sword in her right hand while fighting off a man with her left. A pile of warriors has fallen beneath her fury.

He also started his website, charlessaunderswriter.com, and sold a few articles to the *Herald*. By then, part of his pension had started, lifting him out of the deepest pit of poverty. He watched the incredible rise of Barack Obama but still could barely believe Americans would vote for him over Hillary Clinton, let alone over John McCain. "And he just might do it. It's a long shot, though." He was astonished when Obama won the presidential election. "Obama is a real game-changer, coming out of nowhere. I wonder if he even saw himself coming?" he wrote to Morris on November 21, 2008. He noted he was MySpace friends with Obama.

Charles turned his TV on at ten a.m. on January 20, 2009, and spent the entire day soaking up the moment. "When I saw all those hundreds of thousands of people gathered in the cold, patiently awaiting their opportunity to witness and become part of history, with smiles on their faces and a sparkle in their eyes, I felt really good about the country of my birth—the country from which I later departed, for reasons you well know. The whole world was watching this amazing event . . . and the whole world was proud. I'm glad I lived to see January 20, 2009."[111]

The next time I saw Charles was at the book launch of *The Hermit of Africville*, which was held during the Africville reunion in August 2010. As a white guy writing about a Black guy, I felt pretty insecure at the gathering, and having Charles support me at the launch meant more than you can imagine. It had been Charles's Africville essay that had created my image of the community and prepared me to write Eddie's life story. Charles had written many columns on Eddie and his protest, which is how I first learned about him. "Of all the Black communities in Nova Scotia, the one with which I most identify is one that no longer exists—on the map, anyway. That community is Africville," he wrote in *Black and Bluenose*. "What happened to them could easily have happened to the community in which I was raised."

---

111 Letter to Morris Fried February 7, 2009.

He knew that many white people saw Africville the same way they saw Africa. A Halifax newspaper—you can probably guess which one—had in 1967 written that "soon Africville will be but a name. And, in the not too distant future that, too, mercifully will be forgotten." A Toronto magazine ran a 1966 feature called "The Slow and Welcome Death of Africville." Charles wrote about the "Africville diaspora" scattered around Canada and the U.S., much as Africvillians' ancestors had been scattered from Africa. Charles first visited Africville for the 1989 reunion, when the children of the great village returned and parked their campers and tents where their homes once stood, and for a week, Africville lived.

By 2010, *The Spirit of Africville* and the accompanying museum exhibit had travelled across Canada, inviting people to see the redemption of Africville. Charles saw Africville as its children did, and through his writing, he made all of Canada see Africville as its children did.

"Ever go to a reunion of a family of which you are not a member? It can get pretty uncomfortable," he wrote.[112] "Sometimes you feel like an outsider, even an interloper, as family members laugh at in-jokes you don't get and keep introducing you to people you know you'll never see again. Not all family reunions are like that, though. The annual Africville reunion certainly isn't. Everyone is welcome to attend it, and no one is an outsider. It doesn't matter what colour you are or where you come from; the experience is open to all."

I smiled when I spotted his tall, slow-moving frame entering the big white tent in the fields of Africville. Eddie and I had decided to launch the book on the fortieth anniversary of his protest in the summer of 2010, and to do it among his people in Africville. It was

112 *Daily News* column, July 24, 1994.

something of a redemption for Eddie, too, as people slowly began to see his decades-long occupation of Africville not as "squatting" for money, but as a civil rights protest for justice.

I signed a copy for Charles that day, but it would be more than a decade before I learned that he had urged a good friend to buy it, too. Her copy was still there when she checked the daily mail with a sinking heart, wondering why Charles had stopped writing. When she grew worried enough to check on him, she realized she didn't know anyone in Halifax who knew Charles. But then she saw my book.

15

DARK MATTER

In 2000, Charles responded to Sheree R. Thomas's request to publish his work in her anthology *Dark Matter: A Century of Speculative Fiction from the African Diaspora.* He offered her a story he'd published in 1984: "Gimmile's Songs," a Dossouye tale. She asked him if she could also republish his classic 1970s essay "Why Blacks Don't Read Science Fiction." Charles countered with an offer to write a new essay, which he titled, "Why Blacks Should Read (and Write) Science Fiction." In doing so, he seems to have convinced himself that he should start reading and writing fiction again.

Thomas was delighted to have a new essay from Charles. He also alerted her to the W.E.B. Du Bois short story "The Comet," which she added to the anthology. In her introduction to *Dark Matter*, she explains why she chose that title. In science, it's a "non-luminous form of matter which has not been directly observed but whose existence has been deduced by its gravitational effects." Like dark matter, she writes, "the contributions of Black writers to the [science fiction] genre have not been directly observed or fully explored." Samuel Delany and Octavia Butler had received attention, but many were left out. Thomas wanted her collection to study the way Black writing had shaped the genre, even as white readers and critics failed to detect it. Black writers had been made invisible, unread, unacknowledged. Yet their gravitational effects were obvious.

"As the call for submissions was shared throughout the [science fiction] and Black literary communities, and the postcards—then envelopes, then manuscripts—began flooding in, I was humbled by the response. And just as I had hoped, the critical pieces began to arrive. When I finally spoke with author Charles R. Saunders, who had virtually 'disappeared' (as far as the U.S. sf community was concerned) into the far reaches of Canada, *Dark Matter* began to take on a new shape in my mind," she writes.

In his new essay, Charles reflects on the piece he'd written in the 1970s. "It was a rant and a screed in the sense that it expressed my dissatisfaction with the endemic paucity of Black characters and themes in a genre that purported to transcend convention and stereotype," he wrote. He recalled his early days as a fan, when at conventions, he'd see plenty of green and polka-dot faces, but his was the only Black one. He explained that he'd left the speculative fiction world and retired from such writing. "My own attempt at opening such a door, the Imaro heroic fantasy series, did not find the readership it needed to remain in print," he noted. "The onus is on us. Just as our ancestors sang their songs in a strange land when they were kidnapped and sold from Africa, we must, now and in the future, continue to sing our songs under strange stars."

Dark Matter was reviewed by the *New York Times* and put Charles's name back on the map—and assured readers he was indeed alive. He still hadn't published a new word of speculative fiction in more than fifteen years, though.

His name in the anthology caught the attention of Amy Harlib, an eccentric American contortionist who dedicated her life to art and had first published "Gimmile's Songs" nearly twenty years earlier. She wrote to Charles and interviewed him over email for an article she posted to her website. "Alas, due to the vagaries of the publishing world, Saunders's books went out of print and his output declined to a handful of yarns since," she writes in the introduction to the interview.

"Some fans even feared you were deceased! What was the cause of this hiatus in your science fiction and fantasy writing and what prompted your long awaited and welcome return?" she asked.

"It really blows my mind to think that some people believed I was dead!" he answered. "But then, I guess I really did vanish completely from the SF/fantasy radar screen."

He told her about the DAW disaster and Tarzan's revenge. Evidently his opinion of his screenwriting career had declined, as he now referred to his two movies as "so bad I won't even name them." He told his American audience for the first time about his Canadian journalism, his column, and his nonfiction books. He told them about Nova Scotia, and why it was his chosen home. "But you know, that gumbo in my imagination just wouldn't stop bubbling." He said when Thomas "sleuthed" him down to his newspaper in Halifax, it had changed his life. "This brought me back into the attention of fans I never knew I had. The rest, I hope, will be the future. I can't really hold a grudge against DAW for dropping me back in 1985. They took a chance on publishing an unknown writer with a new idea, and it just didn't pan out commercially. It took me a long time to realize that, but now I have, and I'm moving on."

He explained how he wrote in the morning, relaxed in the afternoon, then headed to the newspaper for the evening. He still wrote in longhand at times, but was falling in love with the computer's superior ability at cutting-and-pasting and writing and rewriting. He listed his favourite writers: "Nalo Hopkinson, Octavia Butler, Steven Barnes, Stephen King, Tanith Lee, Harry Turtledove, and Charles de Lint, who is not only a favourite writer, but has been a friend for more than 20 years."

He spoke about his new essay. "I believe that science fiction is the folklore and mythology of our modern, technological society, and fantasy preserves the folklore and mythology of the past," he told Amy. "We need to contribute to this culture's mythology and folklore because we are part of it, and it is part of us."

And at the end of the interview, he told her about a new development: Imaro was being reborn, this time with plans for a hardcover *Imaro* in February 2006, followed by the second, third—and the fourth and the fifth. "That means eventually, the entire Imaro saga will be in print."

◆———

With rumours of his death proven to be exaggerated Charles began a full-scale return to fantasy writing. An editor at Night Shade, a publisher in San Francisco and Portland, had heard about the Imaro series from the 1980s and searched out the first three—and was devastated when he closed the book on *The Trail of Bohu* and realized there were no more Imaro stories. The editor tracked down Charles at the newspaper and emailed him with the suggestion that Night Shade republish the first three Imaros—in hardcover no less—and then complete the series by publishing four and five.

"I believe that now more than ever Imaro is very relevant to the fantasy genre," the editor wrote. "I think Imaro is a compelling character, because he functions on so many levels. If one chooses to, one can see you the author as Imaro. The battles of cultural identity and identification (aka tribal membership and acceptance) that Imaro faces are similar to ones that you describe facing, as a Black reader and writer in the fantasy genre."

Charles said no, he couldn't republish the three novels. A key story in the first novel, "Slaves of the Giant Kings," had become unprintable. In the 1980s, the story had been pure fantasy set in Nyumbani's Ruanda, pitting the enslaved Kahutu against the imperious Mwambututsi, with Imaro leading the Kahutu on a bloody revolt. Imaro meets and falls in love with a Kahutu woman—Tanisha. "At the end of the story, the Mwambututsi are massacred," Charles wrote. The horrific 1994 Rwanda genocide, in which Hutus murdered eight hundred thousand Tutsis, had made the story obscene. "As I read the horrific stories and saw the gruesome pictures of the unfolding tragedy, my shock, horror and sadness were profound." He ruled out an author's note as too glib, and didn't want to change a few details to try and hide the story's African origins. But just removing it would render the novels incomprehensible, as Imaro otherwise never meets Tanisha.

"My fingers were poised on the keyboard," about to say no to Night Shade, he wrote in the introduction to the new edition. "At that moment, a stray neuron fired in my brain. I had not written a word of new Imaro material in eighteen years, and I had become resigned to the probability that I would never write about him again. I had buried him in my subconscious, and I wasn't certain that I could bring him back to life. However, my Ilyassai friend proved to be tenacious.... Imaro had not lain totally fallow all those years, and it turned out I had more to say about him."

There was only one remaining problem: Charles didn't have a single copy of *Imaro*, or *The Quest for Cush*, or *The Trail of Bohu*, or any of the manuscripts he'd laboured on so many years ago. All three novels were out of print and tough to find. Then he remembered that talk he'd had with Paul Bacon back in the 1990s, when Paul asked him if he was *the* Charles Saunders, author of the Imaro novels he'd found in second-hand Halifax stores. He borrowed those paperbacks from Paul and retyped the manuscripts, word by word.[113] In doing so, a wiser, older Charles edited his younger,

113 Paul lent me those same copies so I could get the DAW quotes used in this book. I balanced my phone on the books to hold the stiff, yellow pages open, and was amazed at how Charles had done the same thing with some unknown paperweight and not damaged the spines. It must have been a long, hard job.

brasher self. "The former self was not chopped liver, but there's always room for improvement," he would write in an author's note. He returned the books, signed.

The original DAW *Imaro* edition starts with the prologue, then "Turkhana Knives," "The Place of Stones," "Slaves of the Giant-Kings," "Horror in the Black Hills," and ends with the "The City of Madness." In the fantasy world, these are called "fix-up" novels, where the author has written several short stories that are then connected for a novel. The modular nature of the mostly self-contained short stories means you can often pull out one story and plug in another. However, for the Night Shade edition, the changes went deeper. *Imaro* now begins with the prologue, "Turkhana Knives" and "The Place of Stones"—and then turns to a brand-new story, "The Afua." In the DAW version, this section of the story sees Imaro enslaved and brutalized by the Giant-Kings. In the modern version, Imaro instead meets two men being attacked by a giant crocodile. Imaro swiftly kills the beast and helps the wounded men get home. He is adopted into their tribe and makes friends. He even smiles at one point. He hasn't met Pomphis yet, so Imaro must learn new languages and adjust himself to a gentler life. Instead of cruel slavery, Imaro's first experience of people beyond his kin is now a kind one. The peace is disturbed when the *haramia* abduct him (and the Afua) from this tribe, and we get the full story of how Imaro rose from captive to ruler of the bandits. In the modern saga, Imaro is never enslaved.

Tanisha is transformed. In the DAW editions, she is an enslaved Kahutu who mostly sticks with Imaro as her ticket to freedom. She's a different woman in the Night Shade editions, written after his marriage to Dale. Tanisha is not a Kahutu, but a Shikaza woman (a tribe perhaps based on the real-world Shirazi of the Swahili Coast). She is not a slave. And she immediately sees and loves the truth about Imaro. "No one sent me, Imaro. I am here because I want to be.

Among my people, women are trained from birth to serve men, to please men," she tells him in their first talk. "We of the Shikaza are a small tribe, a weak tribe. But we are also a free tribe, because we trade our women in exchange for safety. To the outsiders, a Shikaza woman is worth more than her weight in gold. The Shikaza women are taught something else as well. We are taught that no matter how many men buy us, and use us, there will be, for each of us, one man to whom we truly belong, whether or not he buys us. For me, that man is you. And I knew that from the moment I saw you."

Imaro comes to see her as a warrior defending her people through different means of bodily sacrifice. He matures under Tanisha's love, but she is again abducted at the end of "The Afua," so it can lead into "Horror in the Black Hills," where Imaro must fight himself. Charles decided to keep revising the novels in light of these developments. Book one of the DAW edition ends with Pomphis, Tanisha, and Imaro together, happy, and Imaro laughing for the first time, in "The City of Madness." An older Charles moved that story to the start of *The Quest for Cush*, and now ends the first novel with a second new story: "Betrayal in Blood." It means that in the Night Shade edition, the first novel ends before Imaro meets Pomphis. And there is no laughter, but instead a bitter Imaro, rejected by the Ilyassai and the *haramia*, on the warpath for abducted Tanisha. Those changes reverberated through the second novel.

During his long fiction drought, Charles often said he needed to find a new way to relate to fantasy. I think he did so by reversing how he thought about his "escape" into fantasy. Etymologically, "escape" comes from the Latin phrase "ex cappa" and refers to eluding someone so narrowly that they are left holding only your cape; a fitting word for a man consumed by superheroes. As he matured, Charles started treating fantasy not as a way out of our world, but as a deeper way into it. Instead of running from his problems, I think he realized he could use fantasy to turn and defeat them. His main weapon was removing Imaro's metaphoric cape and showing us more of the human. As I read the Imaro saga in zine short stories, the unedited proofs for the DAW books, the published DAW books, and the modern editions, I detected improvements that showed Charles adding depth to the work of his younger self.

Consider the following passages. This comes from the 1980s DAW version of *The Trail of Bohu* that Charles wrote in his twenties and thirties. Imaro is meeting with the Kandisa, the sacred and secular ruler of Cush. She tells him his pride has turned the cheers he once heard at the Cush athletic games into jeers calling for his death. He chose to win every contest and make every other contestant feel small and pathetic. Here's the next paragraph in DAW: "Her words cut deeply into Imaro's soul. They were true words. Imaro recalled the sullen glares Arkhaman could not conceal whenever Akhini boasted of the Ilyassai's triumphs. He recalled the smiles that forced their way across the lips of the men he had defeated. Her words were true."

And the modern edition: "Her words had cut deeply into Imaro's soul, for they were the truth. Imaro recalled the sullen glares Arkhaman could not conceal whenever Akhini boasted of the Ilyassai's latest athletic triumphs. He recalled the smiles that forced their way onto the lips of the men he had defeated. He had never considered those reactions before . . . he hadn't felt any need to do so."

Charles tightens the writing by blending the first two sentences and removing the repetition of "true words" and "words were true." And the line he adds at the end take us deeper inside Imaro's soul. At this moment, the warrior starts to question his use of his strength. He who was so wounded when he was abandoned as a child—who is he to use his adult power to make others feel weak? Imaro hadn't needed to think about other people before because they couldn't hurt him back. But now, we sense, he begins to consider the feelings of others, and not just because they could harm him.

And this one-word adjustment as the Kandisa frees Imaro from custody and the warrior sets out to hunt down his unknown foe, whom she names Bohu, the Bringer of Sorrow.

In DAW, the ruler of Cush says: "My failure to anticipate what the Erriten would do to shift the *chephet* is partly to blame for what happened to your family. The least I can do—and the least I think you would accept from me—is to provide you with a means by which you may recognize the killer." Twenty years later, Charles changed it to: "the least I can do—and the most I think you will accept from me—is to provide you with a means by which you may recognize the killer."

Not the least, but the most he could accept. We can see the height of Imaro's pride and he is deepened in our eyes. Over time, core character traits reveal the man beneath the warrior. Consider his love of cattle. Among the Ilyassai, cattle are revered as nearly equal members of the tribe and never eaten or mistreated. Imaro discards many Ilyassai beliefs as he grows, but not that one. When you hear or see a cow or bull or ox, you know Imaro will soon head over to it, pat it with his hands, and croon to it while it breathes to him. He is more curious about new cattle than humans or monsters, and will always take time to learn about them. One day, he's walking down a city street with friends when he hears a beast moan in pain. His predator neck swivels until he finds the source: a man beating a cow pulling a wheeled cargo cart heavy with jugs of an alcoholic drink. Soon, the massive cart is upended, the containers all smashed, the alcohol bleeding into the stone street, and the merchant is crawling away, begging for his life, as Imaro cradles the head of the dying animal in his lap. Another time, Imaro and a troop of warriors encounter two boys herding cattle. One sees the blood-stained soldiers and immediately runs away, yelling over his shoulder that he's going for help. The other stands his ground. Imaro shows approval for the young defender and an avuncular scorn for the boy who fled. Imaro, who at that moment is in the middle of several cosmic battles, is soon stroking the cattle and asking the young defender about this particular breed's habits and preferences.

In the novels, a person who knows Imaro well describes him as a "warrior and a wanderer." The deeper into his journey you go, the deeper this proves true. As a young man of twenty rains, he'd never left the flat, open Tamburure. The first time he sees a forest, he stops and wants to turn back. But he presses on, overcomes his fear, and comes to love the landscape. Having never seen running water, he is at first deterred by a strong river, but conquers his concerns and crosses it. Later, despite a brutal bout of seasickness, he becomes an excellent ocean sailor. Charles hinted many times that the fifth novel sees Imaro leave Nyumbani—on a ship. He climbs mountains, learns new languages and skills, and becomes a mentor to younger warriors and wanderers. His private love of learning is rarely spoken of in the books. We just see it in Imaro growing wiser.

Charles was delighted with the retold Imaro tale. "So, no author-editor wrangling this time. Maybe in the future. But the insight you showed in your suggestion to tell the whole story of Imaro's experience with the haramia has impressed me greatly," he wrote to his editor. "May this be the start of a great relationship between me, Imaro, and Night Shade!"

Imaro was reborn in 2006, with a bold and evocative cover of Imaro, bloody sword in hand, roaring over a pile of his fallen foes and the dead lion. It ended up being a softcover. Charles added an introduction called "Revisiting Imaro." "A writer can go home again, do it over again, and apply the experience of the present to the circumstances of the past. On the blank page, all things are possible," he writes. He mentions his dream to bring all of Imaro into paper and ink—including "a complete fourth novel and an uncompleted fifth one." He retells the origin story of the warrior born to kick Tarzan's ass, and how the series was cancelled when he was "partway through a fifth one." And that looked like the end of Imaro. "Obviously, that was a turning point in my life as a writer. I branched out into other areas of the field, ranging from screenplays to journalism, with varying degrees of success. Imaro drifted farther and farther away, until he became what I thought would be permanently unfinished business."

Charles was now back in Nyumbani, seeing old friends in new light. "Imaro's character changed, too. Not to worry—he's still the 'Baddest Man on the Planet.' . . . He is a little more mature now than he was when I first wrote about him—hopefully, a reflection of his creator's own character development," he wrote, perhaps forgetting his statement that "not even" 10 per cent of Imaro was rooted in his creator. "The fires of righteous indignation that motivated me during the early 1970s have been banked by the passage of time, but they have not been extinguished. I can, indeed, go home again and finish Imaro's journey."

In 2006, he also travelled to California to explore a relationship with a Black woman that had started as a pen friendship but grown into . . . something else. "At first, I thought Elaine might be able to come here during the week between Christmas and New Year's. But family considerations prevented her from doing so. I will be going to California again later this year. September was the first time we had met face-to-face, although we had been corresponding for about two years beforehand," he wrote.[114] "I really think we will

114 Letter to Morris Fried, December 2, 2006.

be together . . . it's just a matter of a lot of preparation, as I would be returning to live in the United States, which I never before wanted to do." In California, Charles and Elaine went on a date to Universal Studios and enjoyed the live performance of *WaterWorld*. "The *Shrek* show was terrific," he added. He loved how when the donkey sneezed, water sprayed the audience. They also visited the main branch of the Los Angeles Public Library. "She took me there because she had seen a copy of the original 1981 version of the first Imaro novel in the library's reference section. She wanted me to see it, too," he wrote. They found the library had the DAW versions of the first two, but not the third. However, it also had eight copies of the Night Shade Imaros, and they were all checked out. "Well now, that was a good sign," he wrote.

He and his lady friend went up to the reference room and met the librarian, "a middle-aged lady who embodied the basic librarian stereotype." Elaine informed the librarian that Charles was the author of the novel. "You wouldn't believe what happened next. The staid librarian suddenly transformed into a groupie. 'The author?! The author?! Please have a seat! I'll go get your book myself!'" It was a magic moment. The library had protected the book with laminate, essentially turning it into a hardcover—his first. Charles held it in his hands, marvelling. He and his friend "left the library with big grins on our faces. Guess you can see why this was a highlight of highlights. I'm actually thinking of moving to California in a few years. If I can retire, and do fairly well with my books, I may just go ahead and retire at 65. If not—who knows?" But he ruled out the idea in the same letter. "You know, cramped and surrounded as I am by books and magazines, I really don't want to move."

In May 2007, Charles took a momentous step: He finished *Imaro V: Vengeance in Velanga*, completing his magnum opus. He gathered other Imaro short stories for a collection he hoped to publish as a sixth volume to be called *The Warrior's Way*. "Then, after that, I'll start writing other things. As much as Imaro means to me, I don't want to be known only for those novels—though it's great to be known for them. Hell, I even have an entry in *Wikipedia*," he wrote.

But disaster struck in late 2007. Night Shade pulled the plug on Imaro, two books into the five-book deal. They blamed poor sales. And something else. "The publisher of Night Shade said the response he got from a lot of booksellers could be summed up in these words: 'Fantasy is a white realm,'" Charles told a friend. "This was the attitude of white and Black distributors alike—not all of them, of course, but too many. Given my background and experiences, I guess that tacit racism shouldn't come as much of a surprise. What really boggles my mind, though, is that the people who had that attitude didn't seem to see anything wrong with it. Hello! What's wrong with this picture, people? Don't you know literary apartheid when you see it? It's as though they'd also be OK with segregated drinking fountains, public toilets, bus-terminal waiting rooms and schools. In the case of the Black booksellers who think fantasy is just for white folks, would they also say that golf and tennis are white sports, so Blacks shouldn't participate in them? I'm not comparing myself to Tiger Woods or Venus and Serena Williams, but still . . ."

The poor-sales claim doesn't square with what the same publisher told Charles in 2006, after the first *Imaro* had hit bookstores. Then, he told Charles it was being sold in Powell's and Borders, and one individual bookseller had already sold one thousand copies and wanted more. That alone would likely have lifted the *Imaro* sales above the DAW run, and made it one of Charles's bestselling books, along with *Sweat and Soul*, which also hit a second print run. There was another factor in Night Shade's decision, but they didn't share it with Charles. Charles may not have known it, but the same editor who had resurrected Imaro in 2006 had since converted to Christianity and renounced all of his publishing work in the fantasy field as "dung" and lamented that he couldn't destroy every single book with which he'd been involved. Losing Charles's champion editor in such dramatic fashion likely played a role in Night Shade's decision. But to Charles, the publisher only blamed sales. And racism.

"I feel like I'm in a time warp, because that was the same reason [racism in the fantasy community] my original publisher, DAW Books, dropped the series more than 20 years ago. At least DAW published three of the Imaro novels. Night Shade only managed two. I don't think I really need to describe how I feel about this," he wrote.[115] "Two words sum it up: despondent and disgusted."

He said Night Shade had tried their best, but too many booksellers declined to put the books on the shelves, and reviewers declined to review them. "Now, if the people who did read and review the Imaro novels considered me a lousy writer, I could at least come to grips with that. But I don't think it is egotistical of me to believe that I am a good writer. Not only do I know that deep in my heart; I know it because the people who do manage to break through the barriers of nay-saying middlemen and get a chance to read my work have given it great praise. The internet is full of praise for my work, both 20 years ago and now. Yet for all this interest and enthusiasm, not enough people actually *buy* to sustain the print run of even a small press. I can't help but be filled with a sense of futility," he wrote. "I can't say much more, other than it is very difficult for me to see my lifelong dream be killed—not once, but twice. What am I going to do now? Who knows. I sure don't."

He found solace in his readers. He cherished a 2010 blog post by Vincent S. Moore about "the ghost of 'Black Folks Don't Do That.'" Moore wrote with great insight and compassion:

115 Letter to Morris Fried, August 8, 2007.

For when the brilliant writer Charles R. Saunders cannot sell many copies of the new edition of his Imaro series, to the point where his publisher drops the project, then the power of Black Folks Don't Do That hasn't fully waned. Not when booksellers and distributors, both Black and white, can effectively tell him that writing fantasy is a white realm. What is sad about that story isn't that white booksellers wouldn't buy the book. I mean, a series of novels about a Black Conan-esque hero wandering across a fantastic version of Africa would definitely put a cramp in the style of many white readers. What is sad is that Black booksellers wouldn't buy the book.... A Black man with a sword and a purpose in a fantastic land was beyond the understanding and imagination of these people. That is sad in a way I cannot fully put into words. I mean, most days when I rise to look at my face I am proud of the imprint of Mother Africa upon it. At times like these, I wonder if I could trade my medium chocolate skin in for a shiny new white model, just so I could feel less out of place. But that isn't what I really need. Or what my people need. What we really need is a new movement, a Civil Rights movement for the imagination of Black people. A movement to teach them how to stop thinking about pure survival that could reduce them to animalistic behaviours and to start dreaming of how to make the future a better place for them and all. A movement to dream the dreams that are equal to those of whites and Hispanics and Asians, dreams that have our particular flavour to them.

What we in the Black community need is to finally move away from Black Folk Don't Do That, to Black Folk Do That. That Black people can ride in spaceships and change the course of mighty rivers and slay dragons. That we too can dream.

It was a dream Charles shared, and such support relit the fire. He was a writer. He had readers. Screw the publishers who kept screwing it up. He now had a narrowed focus: "To get the rest of the Imaro novels and my other work out to the people who want to read it. It doesn't matter to me anymore whether that number is large or small. In a way, that's liberating," he wrote on February 8, 2008, just three days before the *Daily News* died. "Does that sound like I'm giving up on a dream? In a way. Doesn't every author wish his or her books hit the big time? I'm no different from anyone else in that regard. What I've learned through the Night Shade experience is that for me to write what I want to write, I have to alter my expectations. And that's ok. Like I said, it lifts a load off me—a load that was there before I'd ever heard of Night Shade."

And for the question of finding the time to write? Well, the Halifax *Daily News* was about to solve that problem for him.

16

THE FACE OF IMARO

Charles's final books burst out of him like a supernova. The death of the *Daily News* cleared his schedule of all other commitments and launched the third stage of his writing career. His first phase saw him create Imaro in short stories, publish three Imaro novels, create Dossouye in short story format, and write two movies and several radio plays. The second phase saw him switch to non-fiction books, master the art of the opinion column, and profoundly shift his adopted home province's attitudes toward its own Black history. The third phase—his return to fantasy—was big news on the message boards of an internet group called Black Superhero Forum.

An admin on the group went by the name Uraeus, a pen name taken from the cobra atop the Egyptian pharaoh's crown. Uraeus was a writer of Black superheroes and had created Jaycen Wise, an immortal warrior from antiquity. Uraeus called him the anti–Tomb Raider, because instead of travelling to foreign lands to steal priceless artifacts, Jaycen raids Western museums to return the stolen treasures to their rightful owners. Uraeus, a Black man with three Black sons, had created his hero so his children could see faces like theirs in heroic settings.

In the 2000s, the Black Superhero Forum was an early form of social media and served a similar function to the old letters pages of the zines Charles read and created in the 1970s. Fans and creators shared their works and the works of other writers they loved. One day, a member posted about Imaro, and the idea of a Black Conan possessed Uraeus. He tracked down a rare DAW edition of the first novel and devoured it. He then hunted down the second and third novels, and was wild to read the fourth. But he couldn't find it, nor any trace of it ever having existed. DAW ended at three. Night Shade had stopped at two. But the saga had not finished. Uraeus needed to know what happened to Imaro. He found Charles's email address. Uraeus told him he was a huge fan and loved his work. Where could he get the fourth book?

"It's great to hear from you. I appreciate very much your kind words about my Imaro novels. You are the reader I always wanted to reach, but I never before knew whether or not I had—now I'm sure finding out," Charles replied. "It continues to amaze me that the books found new readers long after they were out of print."

Charles later told Uraeus that he had reached him at an important moment, just as he was in despair of ever finding his audience, and doubting they even existed. And then he got messages from Uraeus, Taaq Kirksey, and Troy Wiggins: young Black American men, the audience he always believed would love Imaro the most. Some read the faded DAW versions while others encountered the bright Night Shade editions. But when Uraeus wrote to Charles, the Night Shade deal had collapsed and Charles and Imaro were outlanders again. So Charles slowly let Uraeus down: The fourth novel existed only in manuscript form. Uraeus revealed that he worked as a designer for one of the biggest and oldest independent Black book publishers in the United States. With Charles's permission, he made the introduction. But before they could go any further, Charles learned Night Shade still owned the rights to Imaro, despite having killed the series.

"You might not be able to do Imaro, but I have this other character," Charles told Uraeus. "This is a female counterpart to Imaro. She's called Dossouye."

Charles sent him the manuscript. It was instantly one of the best books Uraeus had ever read, but the publisher passed. That was another blow for Charles. "Well, maybe I can self-publish it," Uraeus offered. "People deserve to read it and I love it so much. Would you be comfortable with me doing it?"

Charles mulled it over and finally said yes. Uraeus was much more up to date on self-publishing, which was a vastly better option than it had been in the 1980s and '90s. Now you could print on demand, so you didn't need to try and sell hundreds or thousands of copies—you could print as many as were bought. Uraeus had written to Charles as a fan seeking the fourth novel, and had suddenly become his favourite writer's editor, designer, and publisher. They called their operation Sword & Soul Media, and the books bear that imprint. They seem to have held rights for some of the Imaro saga and planned to republish the third, then fourth and fifth, as the first two were still widely available in the Night Shade editions. They'd return to the first two novels once the entire saga was in print.

As the new caretaker to his favourite writer's legacy, Uraeus had to pinch himself: Was he really suggesting improvements to Charles R. Saunders, the greatest writer he'd ever read? But Charles never put on airs. He was a hard-working writer from start to finish. For Uraeus, as a writer, it was an ongoing masterclass. And Charles learned from him, too—especially when it came time to design the new cover. Charles had never loved any of his covers. None were born of his own vision. Uraeus introduced him to his friend Mshindo Kuumba, a New York–based artist exploring Afrofuturism through images. Charles immediately said: "This has to be the guy."

He'd finally met an artist who independently understood his work and could capture it in an original visual form. Mshindo was hungry to collaborate with someone in order to get past his current work, with which he was dissatisfied. It was a perfect partnership. Uraeus and Charles would talk and come up with a few key scenes from the novel and send those to the artist.

Charles told Mshindo that when he looked at Imaro in his mind as he wrote, he envisioned the boxer Ken Norton, but with the hair of the football star Mean Joe Greene. Mshindo took those reference points into his laboratory and came back with iconic covers that blew Charles away. The first Sword & Soul Media edition was for *Imaro: The Trail of Bohu*, in 2008. "This is Imaro," Charles simply said. It was the face he had seen all of his life, but only with his mind's eye. Uraeus was stunned to find himself playing a critical role for mega-characters like Imaro and Dossouye. Charles, for the first time, had a publisher who truly believed in him. And a Black publisher at that. Imaro finally had someone who loved him—someone other than Charles.

The Sword & Soul edition of *The Trail of Bohu* gives us our first glimpse of Imaro as Charles saw him, filtered through the artistic genius of Mshindo Kuumba. Imaro is rippling with muscles, glaring ferociously at a lioness reared on her hind legs and preparing to attack, while a huge lion leaps on Imaro's back. It's likely the moment Imaro faces the armed guard of Cush after finding his family annihilated. Any lingering bad taste from the tanned Tarzan cover was cleared away by the visual feast. Charles dedicated it to the members of BlackSuperHero.com. It comes with no introduction or foreword but jumps right into the story. We find Imaro settled into an uncomfortable life as a father and husband, working in a blacksmith's forge, creating treasured weapons for other warriors. "Amid his growing restlessness, unspeakable tragedy strikes, sending Imaro on a grim mission of vengeance. His adversary has no face, but he does have a name: Bohu, the Bringer of Sorrow."

And in 2009, four decades after he first dreamed of Imaro, and twenty-five years since his last new novel about Imaro, Charles published the fourth and longest novel: *Imaro: The Naama War.* "This was kind of like launching a spacecraft in which the crew goes into suspended animation for a long time, then wakes up and lands the ship at its destination," Charles said of returning to the novel he'd last worked on in 1985.[116] Imaro had first appeared three decades earlier in a short story in *Dark Fantasy*, the community zine sustained as much by writers as by readers, and with the two often switching positions. Uraeus had emailed Charles as a fan two years prior, hoping to read the fourth Imaro novel. And he did—when he published it himself. "That was the Holy Grail for me," Uraeus later said.[117] "The search for that is what initiated our relationship. But I didn't allow myself the opportunity to read it as a fan of his work. I kind of kick myself for that. I just jumped in completely as an editor because we were trying to get it done as quickly as possible."

For Uraeus, it brought much of the series to a heart-pounding close. "Man, Imaro is a tragic figure," he said. "It's not the happy ending that you might have wanted. I mean, it was perfectly brilliant, and it was Charles."

The cover is electric. It shows an immovable object in Imaro grappling with an irresistible force in Bohu. Charles had the general idea of a clash of the titans. Uraeus put together reference images of the Incredible Hulk fighting the Thing, two massive superheroes caught at the moment of collision. Fight fans will

116 *Polar Borealis*, circa 2010s.

117 Interview with the author, 2021.

recognize the thrilling second when the bell rings and the bout begins. Charles was speechless. *The Naama War* was an instant classic with fans. After three novels of heroic fantasy, Charles shifts into a more epic style, as Imaro becomes a critical part of a continental war for the soul of Nyumbani. The story seems to outgrow him, or perhaps he outgrows the story, and we find ourselves flying through the pages hoping for a glimpse of the warrior. Imaro's personal grudge with Bohu is revealed to be at the core of the cosmic battle, and both warriors fight with causes they only dimly understand. This is the destiny for which Imaro was forged. The final clash takes place at the southernmost extent of Nyumbani, in the Naaman capital that is divided into a High City that "crowned a plateau that rose deeper inland" and a Low City "sprawled at the foot of the plateau." The geography matches Cape Town and its Table Mountains, which contain many ancient legends. The Naama of Nyumbani likely draw their name from the Nama people of southern Africa. "Soldiers fall. Cities burn. Blood reddens the sea. Sorcery sears the land."

Uraeus never met Charles in person and knew little about his life outside of the novels. He didn't need to. "His work is just different. A lot of work is so predictable in that way, especially in sword and sorcery and that genre, but this—you never knew what was going to happen, and there was a deep, emotional pull. It was just perfectly Charles."

When he put *The Naama War* down, he couldn't think of a single writer who had done it better. Robert E. Howard and J.R.R. Tolkien had faded. Only Charles remained atop the mountain; Charles and Imaro. "When it's someone who looks like you, someone who is moving through the culture that seems familiar to you, it's just a different experience. It was a game-changer for me. His work is life-changing."

Uraeus's last message from Charles came on October 19, 2019, in an email, and it ended with these words: "I cannot thank you and Mshindo enough for rescuing Imaro from oblivion and bringing Dossouye into print. When Night Shade gave up, then you came along. I will be forever grateful. Keep keeping on.—Charles."

Uraeus spent early 2020 trying to reach Charles through the pandemic fog, only to learn he'd journeyed to the far shore. I learned all of this when Uraeus and I spoke by video. There was one question I needed to ask but dreaded posing. It was the same question Uraeus had once put to Charles, only I was desperate to read *Imaro V*, not *IV*. Charles mentioned it many times over the decades, and at one point said he'd completed it. But when he died, everything he owned was thrown in the trash. That included his writing computer, which was unconnected to the internet, and his stacks of backup CDs. As Uraeus prepared to close the call, I finally blurted it out. "I want to ask about book five, but I'm afraid it's . . . I don't know. What do you know about book five?" I spluttered.

Uraeus smiled.

"Ah, I have it," he answered. "Absolutely. And the hope is to publish it."

17

DOSSOUYE'S ODYSSEY

Charles turned his thoughts toward his legacy in the last decade of his life. While for most people, a legacy indicates what you have left behind, for Charles it was about what lay ahead. An older sense of the word connects it to *legion* and refers to "a body of people sent on a mission," or "to appoint by a last will," and that's what compelled Charles to resume writing for one last Herculean effort. Or perhaps that should be one more Imarean effort.

The revival of interest sparked by *Dark Matter* and the Night Shade editions alerted Charles to the fact that he had legions of fans. He was strengthened by their support. Charles being Charles, he noticed that many of those readers were also writers. They, too, wanted to read and write Black-focused fantasy. He realized his legacy would include their books, yet to be written. He understood in his sixties that he had founded an important sub-genre of fantasy. His final books show an author determined to broaden its foundation beyond one male warrior.

Sword and sorcery is overrun with grotesque sexism that reduces women to toys and trophies for men to play with or win. As poorly as Black people were portrayed in the genre, you could argue that all women got it worse. Marion Zimmer Bradley observed in her introduction to the first *Sword and Sorceress* anthology in 1984 that women were often used as "bad conduct prizes" for strong men.

"Women were the reward or the incitement for his adventures, but never shared them. Women, in sword-and-sorcery fiction, when not a mere 'screaming maiden' to be rescued . . . remained strictly offstage, emerging now and again to reward the hero," she wrote. "But women read fantasy too, and we get tired of identifying with male heroes."

American author and editor Jessica Amanda Salmonson also decided to rectify that by starting an anthology of sword and sorcery stories called *Amazons!*, which would feature women writers and women warriors. In the anthology, she says that classic sword and sorcery adventures actually prefer to keep women off the written page entirely. "By far the largest role women play in heroic fantasy or 'sword and sorcery' is not in the text of the authors, but in the illustrations," she writes. Tarzan with a tan can seem downright progressive in comparison to the exposed women supine on countless covers. "It has been escape fantasy for the least mature aspects of the male ego: escapes into worlds where simpletons are rewarded for unprovoked violence and undisguised misogyny. For readers (men or women) who cannot revel in warped attitudes toward women, it isn't even fun."

The 1979 first edition of the DAW-published series shows an armoured woman standing triumphant over a pile of fallen foes, spear in her right hand, sword in her left. It contains thirteen stories, of which twelve were authored by women, including Andre Norton, the author who had such a critical early influence on Charles. Only one man made the cut: Charles R. Saunders.

Charles was still writing only short stories in 1978, and most were about Imaro. When Salmonson contacted him for a contribution to her anthology, his mind roamed to a line of history he'd read that gave him an idea for a marvellous woman with shining eyes and unbreakable courage. "I came across references to the Amazon soldiers of the West African kingdom of Dahomey. Unlike the

Amazons of Greek mythology, the Dahomean women's corps existed in real life, during the 18th and 19th centuries," Charles wrote.[118] Dahomey achieved independence in 1960 and became Benin. When Salmonson issued her challenge to Charles, he heard a woman warrior named Dossouye answer the call from the ranks of the women's army in the country of the Leopard King, called Abomey, on a never-named other-Africa. "Is it, or is it not, Nyumbani? There is no unequivocal answer to that question," Charles later wrote.[119] "When I first wrote about Dossouye in the late 1970s, her setting was, indeed, Nyumbani. Later, I decided that Dossouye stories needed to take place in a world different from Imaro's. There are infinite possibilities for parallel worlds, so I chose another one for Dossouye. Is this a case of blatant inconsistency? Probably. But then, dreamers do have the prerogative of changing their minds.

"Dossouye's world is different from Imaro's, as are her circumstances. The two characters have one thing in common, though: they're warriors. And if they ever met, each would recognize that quality in the other."

An obvious reason women are poorly portrayed in sword and sorcery is the sword side of things. The Conan-inspired men are always physically overpowering and rely on their great strength to propel their adventures. You can depend on the sorcery side to even things out, but that removes women from the core heroic role at the centre of the genre: the sword-wielding solo fighter who generally uses not sorcery but strength. Often, through the magic of writing, smaller women warriors just overpower the men and it's not explained how. Simply blessing Dossouye with supernatural strength was not Charles's route. Instead, Dossouye relies on her

118 Foreword to *Dossouye*, 2008.

119 Introduction to *Nyumbani Tales*, 2017.

military training, superior fight IQ, and her trusty buffalo, the trained war-bull Gbo. It makes for a compelling heroine whom sword-wielding men constantly dismiss—until she leaves them begging for mercy.

"Orphaned at a young age, Dossouye becomes a soldier in the women's army in the kingdom of Abomey. In a war against the rival kingdom of Abanti, Dossouye saves her people from certain destruction but a cruel twist of fate compels her to go into exile," goes the blurb.

"Mounted on her mighty war-bull, Gbo, Dossouye enters the vast rain forest beyond the borders of her homeland, seeking a place to call her own."

"Agbewe's Sword," the story Charles submitted to *Amazons!*, begins with Dossouye saddled on Gbo, looking up nervously as an unnatural thunder rumbles a sorcery-darkened sky. Gbo snorts nervously, and she pats him calm. They are in the formation of Abomey's women warriors, called the *ahosi*. Each *ahosi* is formally married to the Leopard King and remains chaste during her service, as signified by brass ankle bracelets. Her people have domesticated the mighty plains buffalo and made of them fierce fighters. Today, they are drawn up for battle with a bitter rival bent on invading the Leopard King's territory.

"Dossouye was tall and slender, but strong, like her lance. She came from a long line of *ahosi*, stretching back to the time when Abomean women first fought alongside men," Charles writes. The bigger, stronger male troops would attack first, then the mounted women would ride in to harry the ranks. The archers are split into male and female divisions. This equality is necessary: the Leopard King needs the women warriors to have enough soldiers to protect his kingdom.

She is in her teens or early twenties as the battle begins and has few thoughts other than the hard fighting ahead. Sorcery undoes the Leopard King's army, and they are soon in the most shameful of retreats: defeated without killing a single soldier, or losing one. The Leopard King has a dream; so does Dossouye. They realize only she can break the sorcery that defeated his army, and that she must do it alone. She accomplishes her victory, but at a great cost. Her people understand humans have three souls: one to connect to the body, one to connect to the ancestors, and one to connect to the gods. Her effort to defeat the sorcerer kills two of her three souls, making her a source of shame for her tribe, so she is sent into exile. Charles shows us the Leopard King's private thoughts, and we learn the true reason he banishes her: Everyone knows it was she, not he, who won the war. "There is a price to pay for your continued life. You must depart from Abomey," he tells her.

At the end of the first story, she goes into exile. "I do not think we will see her again," the Leopard King says. "She is legend now."

After "Agbewe's Sword" was published in the anthology, Charles followed it up with three more Dossouye stories: "Gimmile's Song," "Shiminege's Mask," and "Marwe's Forest," all published in the 1980s in Marion Zimmer Bradley's *Sword and Sorceress* anthologies. He had hoped to make them into a fix-up novel for DAW, but DAW was no longer interested.

Sheree Renée Thomas's 2000 anthology brought Dossouye back to life, and to print, and inspired Charles to write a new Dossouye story called "Yahimba's Choice" for *Dark Matter: Reading the Bones* in 2004. "By then, the idea of amalgamating the Dossouye stories into an episodic novel had taken firm root," he writes. He turned "Agbewe's Sword," from a short story into a novella. "And I wrote a new story called 'Benga's Drum.' It is based on the real-life experience of a man named Ota Benga, of the Batwa (also known as 'pygmy') people of the Congo region. Ota Benga was taken from his home and placed on exhibition at the 1904 St. Louis World's Fair. Later, he was exhibited with monkeys and chimpanzees at the

Bronx Zoo. His story is both tragic and outrageous. It inspired both my creativity and my sense of justice to transpose Ota Benga into Dossouye's world."

Charles's first novella, written in the 1970s, was not about Imaro but his mother, Katisa, and her life before Imaro. Where did she go during her first exile, and what led her to return pregnant with a child of wonder? He wrote to find out. It was never published, and he only mentioned it in passing once in a letter. But perhaps some of Katisa's story stayed with Charles over the decades and finally came out as Dossouye. Perhaps it was also, at least at the start, a way for Charles to begin to understand his own mother, and the tough choices she must have faced raising her son with no father.

Dossouye fights more in sorrow than rage, and generally either avoids conflict or strategically positions herself to ambush and overwhelm attackers, with Gbo a constant equalizer. She has none of Imaro's "fierce joy" for bloodletting. Gbo has been trained to fight with Dossouye, but there's a stronger bond between woman and beast; Gbo is loyal to her alone. Exiled by her king and pulled on by desire, Dossouye and Gbo wander across her other-Africa after the battle, but "her road still led to nowhere." Charles published the first Dossouye novel in 2008, with a Grace Jones–like woman warrior battling a horde of foes on the Mshindo Kuumba cover.

Dossouye begins to find her purpose in the third story, "Shiminege's Mask," when she encounters a young girl named Shiminege crying alone in the forest. Shiminege is fourteen and facing a dire destiny. Her people fear a demon named Umenya Kwi, and to appease him, they sacrifice a young woman to him every rainy season. Shiminege has been chosen to die this year. Part of the ritual allows for a champion to defend her, but her champion is her boyfriend, and he has no chance to defeat the demon. Dossouye is interested to learn this. Her mind opens as she realizes not everyone believes as her people do. She knows her people say she is dead because two of her souls have died, but here she is, in front of Shiminege, alive. Maybe her people were wrong. Maybe Shiminege's people are wrong. "During her wanderings, Dossouye had encountered many instances of false faith; of lies that were believed to be true," Charles writes. "She had seen; she had judged: but she had done nothing. The beliefs of others, whether they were valid or not, had nothing to do with her."

Sitting with this terrified and helpless teenager, she starts to change. A resolve forms "like steel from iron," making her stronger. She is familiar with the demon who will kill this girl. The same type of demon once haunted her people, but the mounted *ahosi* defeated them and drove them out of the kingdom. She tracks down the demon-man and challenges him to a fight. The foul spirit recognizes her *ahosi* armour and fears her army. When he realizes he's facing just one warrior and not an invading legion, he laughs and attacks her. Gbo enters the fray and the demon is slain. Dossouye stares in contempt at the demon-man's corpse. She strips him of his costume. She dons it herself. Dossouye now goes and "fights" Shiminege's champion boyfriend. Posing as the feared demon, Dossouye runs away, liberating the tribe from the false belief, and lifting the status of the women in the village. Dossouye demands only one thing in return from Shiminege. "You must never let your people know you saw me. Allow them to think that Umenya Kwi fled in cowardice, in shame. When the time for the next ceremony comes, and Umenya Kwi does not appear, your people will be free."

Dossouye is a city person but learns to live in the forests of her vast continent. When she finds women in trouble—for example, facing ritual mutilation in the next story—she fights to free them from physical danger, and to free their tribes from the false beliefs that always seem to harm women to the benefit of men. In "Marwe's Forest," she and Gbo encounter a shape-shifting spirit that flits between the form of a woman and of something cow-like, enticing both Gbo and Dossouye. The spirit chooses human form, and the two women fall in love. They plan to live together. They share intimacies. But Marwe has a secret that reveals itself in time: She is pregnant. "Dossouye felt neither anger nor jealousy that Marwe had lain in intimacy with others before her. And it did not matter to her that Marwe had lain with men as well as women. Dossouye herself had once shared love with a man," Charles writes.

Dossouye stands naked in the rain that night, hoping it will wash away her discontent. But her warrior training will not yield its grip. She finds pregnancy repulsive and learns she has no desire to raise this child with Marwe, or to have a child of her own. Marwe returns to animal form to give birth, freeing Dossouye from their bond of love. "A moment later, Dossouye was in the saddle and urging Gbo out of the clearing. She did not look back, and she did not stop riding until the trees grew straight again."

The first book concludes with the new story, "Obenga's Drum." Through it, Dossouye learns her souls have been reborn, and she is now "a whole woman again" and could return to her homeland. But, like her creator, she considers it only briefly. "She would find a new home elsewhere," Charles writes.

The second book, *Dossouye: The Dancers of Mulukau* was published in 2011 and dedicated to Amy Harlib, "in thanks for your Amazonian support all these years." The cover image, and the many interior drawings, utterly undo the whitewashing Dossouye had been subjected to in Argentina in the 1980s. On these pages, the ebony warrior roars out of a blue sky, mounted atop her black Gbo. Charles was overwhelmed with emotion when he saw her face. It's one of his greatest novels. The world-building work he'd been doing in private for decades pours out across the pages. The words are windows. You can't shake the feeling that Charles is reporting breaking news from another Earth.

The Dancers of Mulukau is, like *The Trail of Bohu* was for Imaro, the first time Charles had written a novel for Dossouye from scratch.

Nothing in his letters suggests he had been working on it before; it seems to have leapt out of him in the two to three years after he created the fix-up novel. The second book opens in the city of Djarro, set on a great plain beyond the rainforest that now separates Dossouye from her homeland. Djarro appears to be based on Djenné, an ancient city in Mali. It's a trade centre built out of dirt and held together by a sorcery that permits the buildings to withstand the wet seasons. As with *The Trail of Bohu*, we pan over the city and its people and the extraordinary things happening there lately. "But no one in Djarro could ever recall having seen anyone who even remotely resembled Dossouye," Charles writes. She and Gbo arrive on a dusty day, and the locals give them plenty of space. "Before now, no one in Djarro had ever imagined that they would see someone riding one of these irascible beasts, let alone a woman. And no one thought they would see a woman armed and armoured like a soldier or a sellsword."

She finds a band of hired men preparing to leave on a protection journey and offers to join them for coin. They laugh at her. A woman among the warriors? She challenges any of them to battle her in single combat to test her worth. A snickering warrior emerges and strikes at her with his sword. Dossouye dodges, sending him stumbling to the ground and exposing his side. The glimmer of mirth in her eyes causes him to charge her again, but she steps out of the way at the last second, sending his weight uselessly to the ground. When he attacks for a third time, she trips him and presses her sword to his throat. A circle of men surrounds her menacingly. She calls for Gbo and he stands beside her. The men relent. Even attacking as one would not guarantee the men could defeat the *ahosi* and her war-bull. Their commander tells her to leave. Yes, she can fight, he admits, but he cannot accept a woman sellsword. Dejected, she leaves—but a voice calls her to stay.

"The voice . . . was high and reedy, like that of a young woman or a child, or a boy on the brink of manhood," we learn. Dossouye's eyes widen in surprise when she sees the speaker, who looks like no one she's met before. The tall, thin person wears a splendid tunic that falls from shoulders to ankles. Jewels sparkle on the neck, arms, and ankles, bringing gold dust to the dark skin. The person's long hair is braided with gold. "Dossouye could see that the Dancers could, indeed, be considered to be feminine-appearing men, or masculine-appearing women—or both at the same time. As well, the shape of their thin bodies conveyed subtle suggestions of both male angles and female curves."

The Dancers are wealthy and draw their power and money from their unique ability to dance away droughts and other dangers. "Our dancing is more than just entertainment. Our dancing has *kyame*—magic—in it. The gods and goddesses act through our dancing," this lead Dancer, Ukenge, explains. "Here in Djarro, our dancing enhanced the sorcery of the *djiffares*, to make certain that the buildings of the city will remain intact during the wet season.... In Khutama, where we are going next, our *kyame* will help to ensure that the wells upon which its people depend do not run dry." Dossouye is impressed and says that in her country, the Dancers would be esteemed as People of Name.

Their work and wealth make them a target as they travel, so they hire mercenaries to protect them. And Ukenge is drawn to Dossouye and asks that she join the Dancers as their innermost guard. For the rest of the novel, the Dancers are *s/he* and *hir*, never male or female, but both, and more. "We dancers are not what we are by choice. We are born as we are. We are indeed both man and woman.... In the old days children like us were killed at birth without remorse or question ... until one child was born whose mother and father did not want hir to die regardless of tradition," Ukenge says. "Instead of allowing hir to be killed they took hir away to a faraway land called Ujini where others of our kind were known to dwell. As this child grew up the *kyame* of MawiLesi—the deity who is both man and woman—grew in hir and s/he discovered how to work hir *kyame* through dancing. Hir name was Mulukau."

Today, all such children are brought to be raised with the Dancers. The main threat comes from a religious order. "The Walaq are fiercely intolerant. They believe that only they possess what they call the Truth, and that everyone else is unenlightened and deficient. They consider what we do and what we are to be *hukuza*—an abomination of their Truth that must be eliminated at all costs."

The sellswords still reject Dossouye but must accept her as Ukenge's personal bodyguard. This tension mounts as the danger rises on their journey, and the action drives the rest of the novel. So, too, does the whirlwind romance between Dossouye and Ukenge, forcing Dossouye to question her decision to live alone.

In the final pages of the book, as the dead are mourned and the battered Dancers struggle to hear the music again, Dossouye confronts the man she humiliated in the opening duel. She braces for this man's murderous revenge. But he asks for help. "Someone I can trust to guard my back. Someone other fighters respect. Someone like you, Dossouye," he says. She blinks in surprise, and tells him she is honoured. "But I do not want to be second-in-command. I am going to form my own troop." He is astonished, but agrees with her that many men would now follow her command. "Who said anything about men?" a smiling Dossouye counters.

Charles's friend and colleague Uraeus was stunned when he read the novel. "It's some of the most incredible fiction I've ever read. As much as I love Imaro, I'm partial to Dossouye. I don't know why, but I think I enjoy the character of Dossouye a little bit more."

By writing her two full novels, Charles built Dossouye to stand equal to Imaro. The rage and doubt that plague Charles and Imaro do not trouble her. She had good parents who died too young, but their love endures as balm for her heart. She is driven not by a personal quest for vengeance in the typical sword and sorcery way, but out of a higher calling to protect women and girls, and to challenge the old fables that say women and girls are weaker and therefore less valuable. And while Imaro's world is portrayed as entirely heterosexual, Dossouye brings a queer presence to Charles's writing. "Bringing Dossouye to life has been as gratifying for me as the creation of Imaro," Charles wrote.

He had broadened the foundation of his new genre to two warriors. Expanding that base would drive the last stage of his life.

18

DAMBALLA AND ABENGONI

Charles wasn't content to unsheathe old weapons. New metals were being heated in his soul, but it would take a call from a very old friend to forge them. Imaro and Dossouye largely follow the sword and sorcery style created by Robert E. Howard: They're set roughly in a medieval world before the advent of modern technology, rife with monsters and magic, and the stakes are personal and immediate. But Charles's old pen friend Ron Fortier kept urging him in a different direction. The men had connected over *Dark Fantasy* in the 1970s, despite their opposite stances on the Vietnam War, and had corresponded for decades.

Charles shared with Ron that as far back as the 1970s, he'd plotted out Imaro's life, spread over five books. He kept a notebook in which he recorded key moments in Imaro's life and used it as a road map. Then, he sat down and listened for Imaro's voice. He told Ron that when he was writing, he'd get caught up in the magic of the experience and really go live in Nyumbani. He was no dictator writer, telling everyone what to do; rather, like a good journalist, he took dictation down from what they told him in those trances, leaving him often as surprised by what they did as any reader. "They were real people. I don't care how fantastic the stories were, they were real people. He was such an amazing talent," Ron said. Ron always sensed Charles wasn't writing sword and sorcery, that he'd gone beyond it by combining J.R.R. Tolkien's epic fantasy worlds with Howard's intensely personal heroic fantasy adventures and adding the soul of a Black person. "It was that combination. He could blend what two of the greatest writers in the world had ever done and merge it into his own unique style," Ron said.

In 2006, Ron and his friend Rob Davis accomplished a dream by launching Airship 27 Productions with the plan to publish new pulp fiction based on the 1930s classic pulp heroes they both loved. Charles admired the idea, and offered his support. Ron needed a solid proofreader, and Charles volunteered. At the time, he spent his nights editing the newspaper, and much of his days working on the Night Shade editions of Imaro, but he carved out hours to read new fiction and edit it. He devoured the stories starring Secret Agent X, the Black Bat, Domino Lady, the Purple Scar, and Ravenwood, the Stepson of Mystery. Charles got a hoot out of it, but he told Ron he'd found an old problem in the classic characters: "We can't help but trip across the racism of the 1930s."

Ron agreed but contended he couldn't revive classic Black pulp heroes because there were none. Perhaps Charles could change that? No, Charles said. Repeatedly. For five years. But then ... "If it'll shut you up, I think I've got an idea," he finally replied. The idea was *Damballa*, and it fused Charles's primary passions in an original synthesis: "From the heart of Africa to the streets of Harlem, a new hero is born sworn to support and protect Americans of all races and creeds; he is Damballa and he strikes from the shadows."

Damballa is a joyful book, and it became the first new fiction world from Charles R. Saunders in twenty-six years when it was published in 2011. He mixes his love of African history into Damballa's origin story and adds his passion for boxing by centring the book around an upcoming heavyweight tilt. It's the only novel Charles ever set in our world. "Music stirred the sultry night air of Sugar Row. The syncopated sounds of smooth jazz wove magic in the June heat and brought quick smiles to the lips of the men and women of all shades of darkness who walked past the mansion from which the music emanated," it begins.

It's the 1930s, and a Black American man is heavyweight champion of the boxing world. The Nazis hate him and send their own supreme white champion, powered by a mysterious potion, to destroy the champ in the ring. Damballa must thwart the Nazi plot to give the Black hero a fighting chance. In true Charles fashion, even the drugged-up Nazi pugilist is portrayed with all his rich humanity intact. Damballa uses a mix of modern science and ancient African magic to thwart the Nazis.

Ron could hardly believe his luck when he read the manuscript. It was a moment of literary history that he was proud of: the first Black pulp hero of the 1930s, except eighty years later. It was so different from everything else Charles had ever written, and yet fit immediately into his growing canon. The reviews were ecstatic. "Having revolutionized the genre of epic fantasy with the creation of Imaro, a Black warrior easily equal to such classic characters as Tarzan and Conan, Charles Saunders has done it again," the writer Derrick Ferguson proclaimed. "Damballa is no pale imitation of the Shadow or the Avenger. In fact, after reading this excellent book, I think that they would be proud to consider him a brother in the ceaseless war against crime and injustice."

Derrick, a young writer from Brooklyn, created the adventures of a modern-day Indiana Jones named Dillon. Ron had met Derrick at a pulp convention in Arkansas, and they became great friends. "You know, Charles would love your work," Ron said casually. Derrick studied him carefully. "Charles … who?" In the 1980s, Derrick had been scouring Manhattan's second-hand bookstores, stocking up on Robert E. Howard, Edgar Rice Burroughs, Lin Carter and other white writers, when he saw a sword and sorcery paperback with a Black hero on the cover. "It was enough to drive all the air out of my body," he wrote later. He bought *Imaro* and read it twice that weekend. The next weekend, he read it twice again. "You have to understand that I didn't get much encouragement from Black folks as to the stuff I like to write. Even other Black writers didn't have much respect or liking for my pulp-influenced action adventures or science fiction or sword and sorcery. 'That's stuff for white people,' I would be told, or, 'You need to write books that will educate. Our kids don't need that.'" He compared his finding Charles to Indiana Jones finding the Ark of the Covenant. Holding *Imaro*, he was holding proof that Black people could (and should) write and read speculative fiction. So when Ron Fortier sidled up to him at a speculative fiction convention and said "Charles" would love his work, his heart stopped.

"Charles Saunders," Ron replied. "You know Charles Saunders?"

It took Derrick a moment to compose himself. Derrick later wrote that for much of his life, he suffered from "imposter syndrome," and doubted he could write. "Charles Saunders expanded my notion of what a Black writer could write about. He, along with Octavia Butler, Chester Himes, Ishmael Reed, Samuel R. Delaney and Langston Hughes helped me to have the courage to write what I wanted to write," he wrote in 2020.

Charles won the Pulp Factory award for best novel for *Damballa*. The awards team engraved the prize, packed it up, and sent it to Charles. Yet somehow, they actually sent it to a very confused Derrick Ferguson. He called them, alarmed, and asked why an award with his hero's name on it was in his hands. The awards team told him just to return it and they'd get it to Charles. "No way. No way. I'm sending this to Charles on my own dime. Can I put a letter in?" Derrick asked. "By all means," they replied.

He did, and Charles added a new pen pal to his roster. Derrick never quite got over his amazement that his writing hero was writing to him. For so many of Charles's fans, his words possessed a unique power to inspire them, and for a select few, that was just as true of his private letters as it was of his published fiction. "He is now known as the father of sword and soul, but man, did it take him a long time for that acknowledgement. It's not an easy thing to be the founder of a genre. But that's what it means to be a trailblazer, leading the way for others to follow. Quite often, it's the scout that comes back to the wagon train with a lotta arrows in his back," Derrick wrote.

Given the success of *Damballa*, Ron pushed his luck and asked for a sequel. Charles returned to a steady diet of no. But then Ron suggested a new approach. Many Conan stories were written after Howard died, and Tarzan has been reshaped by many writers. "Hey, look, I've got an idea. I realize you're way too busy with Imaro and Dossouye. Is there any way you would authorize someone else to write these stories?" Ron asked Charles in a letter. "Don't get me wrong: they're yours, you'd keep the characters, and you'd be in charge. It'd be like 'Charles Saunders Presents Damballa, by . . .'"

"Well, the only person who's going to do that is Derrick Fergusson," Charles wrote back. Ron asked Derrick if he would consider it. "He was on board immediately. I remember Derrick being totally wound for sound," Ron later recalled.[120] "Especially when he learned it was Charles who had suggested him to me. And so that was all going to happen . . . eventually." Ron wasn't surprised to see his friend of more than forty years take such an interest in a new writer. "When he met people, his focus and intention was on them. He would hardly say anything about himself," Ron remembered after Charles died. "When he spoke to you, he was so 100 per cent interested in who you were, and your life, and your goals, and your setbacks and challenges. Anything he could do to help you

---

120 Interview with the author, 2024.

out. And it was sincere, genuine. He was a great soul. An awesome soul." He paused, thinking about his late friend. "The world needs to rediscover him."

In 2013, Charles wrote a new short story for a magazine called *Black Pulp*. "My contribution, 'Mtimu,' is a Black take-off on the Tarzan mythos—which Imaro was not," he told a friend. The story begins with a modern African American woman attempting to fly solo across Africa but crash-landing into a jungle. There, she is menaced by a leopard, but a man arrives and kills it. "His face was quintessentially Negroid: broad nose, fully everted lips, woolly black hair forming a shot cap on his head," Charles writes. She learns her rescuer is on the run, pursued by a white trophy hunter. The thirty-page story gives us a glimpse into the world Charles might have created, had he truly wanted to write the epic novel of a Black Tarzan. He created another new character, an African witch named Lulama, in a separate story for the same magazine, and had plans to expand her into a novel.

A new friendship finally brought one of Charles's oldest unpublished novels into the world. The Night Shade editions had caught the eye of a writer and publisher of Afrofuturism in Fayetteville, Georgia, named Milton Davis. Milton had grown up loving speculative fiction and hating the racism baked into so much of it. He set out to change that, only to discover that Charles R. Saunders had already started the work. They connected, and soon became deep friends, though they never met (Milton once flew to Toronto and thought he could pop over to see Charles in Nova Scotia, before realizing the true size of Canada). Milton had founded MVmedia to publish Black speculative fiction, and Charles pitched him on a series set in that other other-Africa he'd been living in and writing about since the 1990s. He had come close to publishing the first installment on several occasions, but it remained in his writer's trunk. Milton loved it, and in 2014 published *Abengoni: First Calling*. "Sword and Soul originator and Sword and Sorcery master Charles R. Saunders storms back onto the literary scene with an epic new fantasy sure to become a classic," reads the back blurb.

Charles explains his goals in the introduction. Fantasy fiction generally falls under heroic or epic. Heroic zooms in on one hero—Conan, say, or Tarzan—and documents their adventures. The hero is rarely off the page. Epic, by contrast, pulls back to focus on the world itself, with several main characters and critical plot lines—see Tolkien's *Lord of the Rings*, or George R.R. Martin's *A Song of Ice and Fire*. *Imaro* was heroic; *First Calling* is epic. The two styles are also called low fantasy (heroic) and high fantasy (epic.) Robert Howard had inspired Charles to write Imaro, and as a young writer Charles felt he lacked the skills to build a world and people it with the stories that would hold together a high fantasy. That changed in the 1990s as he developed a life as a columnist in Africadia. "At that time, another alternate vision of Africa sprang from the depths of my imagination. The name for this new other-Africa was Abengoni. And instead of the travails and triumphs of one central character, as in Imaro, the Abengoni saga would involve a broad spectrum of contact between two cultures—one Black, one white. *First Calling* is the initial volume of that saga," he writes in the introduction.

White people are rarely seen in Nyumbani, and when they are, they're the enemies. In some ways, Charles had reversed the situation he'd found in Tarzan. There are no admirable white people in Imaro's world, and most of them die quickly. "For Abengoni, a different creative drumbeat thrummed in my mind. What if there were another Earth in which people from parallel versions of Europe and Africa encountered each other on an equal basis, rather than fictionally reprising the racism and colonialism that have for centuries wracked the so-called 'Dark Continent' of the world we know? What if European and African folkloric traditions could be integrated within the context of an epic fantasy saga, rather than remain at racial loggerheads?" he writes. "The distorting lens of racism does not exist in Abengoni. Wow, what a concept . . ."

Charles was thrilled to finally publish this new world, and in a handsome hardcover edition—the first hardcover book in his long writing career. It would prove to be the last novel he published in his lifetime, and it calls the reader to an entirely new adventure. "When I was writing Imaro, I often felt as though I were channelling the spirit of Malcom X—the spirit of rebellion. When I was writing Abengoni, I felt as though I were channelling the spirit of Dr. Martin Luther King, Jr.—the spirit of reconciliation. Both spirits are vital components of my creativity today. My spirit of rebellion has been on display for 40 years, in the Imaro stories and the tales of Dossouye, my Black Amazon warrior. In *First Calling*, the time for reconciliation is here."

In 2016, Milton and others hosted the State of Black Science Fiction Convention in Atlanta and dedicated it to Charles, an "icon of Black science fiction and the creator of sword and soul." The author Balogun Ojetade paid tribute to Charles, saying he'd first encountered him in 1987 in *Dragon Magazine,* issue 122, in an essay called "Out of Africa." Charles wrote about the amazing demons, beasts and monsters of African folklore in great detail. "I looked at my friends and said, 'Wow, this white dude got it right!' Because I had no idea that anyone like me was writing science fiction/fantasy who was Black," Ojetade told the audience. It was only when the Night Shade editions came out that he learned Charles was Black. In the same magazine, writer Roger E. Moore supplied twelve of those creatures with Dungeons & Dragons game statistics. "That opened up how I was able to play Dungeons & Dragons," Ojetade said. Soon, everyone who played at his high school wanted to play Charles's version of the game. Charles was unable to attend the event in Atlanta, but they recorded the proceedings and posted it online so he could watch from Nova Scotia.

Charles and Milton teamed up again in 2017 to publish *Nyumbani Tales*, a collection of fourteen short stories set in Nyumbani, the world Charles had been calling home for nearly fifty years by that point. "When I wrote the first Imaro stories back in the early 1970s, I knew that even though the Ilyassai was a larger-than-life character, his epic wasn't big enough to crowd out all the other stories that emanated from the people of the setting he dominated," Charles writes in the introduction. "Even as I was shaping Imaro's saga, other stories came into my mind. The more research I did into pre-colonial Africa, the more legends and folktales I saw that could be adapted to the milieu of Nyumbani. Often, I would write an Imaro story, then a non-Imaro story, then two Imaro stories, followed by another non-Imaro yarn. I was really winging it back then, writing whatever it was that wanted to come out of my head."

That's why his worlds feel so lived in; he lived in them, for decades, and wrote many Nyumbani stories not about Imaro. Some happen during Imaro's lifetime but do not feature him. Others take place long before or long after his life and don't mention him. The first story in *Nyumbani Tales*, "Katisa," puts Imaro's mother centre stage and perhaps gives us a glimpse of Charles's unpublished first novella, which told her story. Pomphis stars in a few stories, regaling us with his life before he met the warrior. Some retell African folktales, altered through Charles's fantastical mind. One was inspired by a song. He rewrote some of the older ones "even though my younger self might have resented it." Charles said he planned to publish his remaining Imaro stories in a collection to be called *The Warrior's Way*, though that book has yet to been published.

The reviewers were bowled over. "A Charles Saunders tale is a griot's song, an alchemy of history and magic, both brutal and unflinching. And a reminder that all who write sword and soul work in his long shadow," one wrote. "With his visionary take on African-themed sword and sorcery, Charles Saunders was decades ahead of his time. He's a true original. The rest of us are still trying to catch up with him," wrote another.

Uniquely for Charles, each story in *Nyumbani Tales* is preceded by an author's note divulging the material he drew upon from African history and folklore. "During the 19th century, the infamous explorer Henry Morton Stanley published a book called *Through the Dark Continent*, which chronicled his wanderings in East and Central Africa," he writes. "In contrast, *Nyumbani Tales* could very well be called Through the Bright Continent. As you journey through these stories, you don't need a pith helmet or a bunch of porters carrying supplies on their heads. All you need is an open mind—and a touch of imagination."

Charles spent his final years birthing new worlds. Some, like *Abengoni* and *Nyumbani Tales*, had been gestating for decades. Others, like *Damballa*, were bright new planets shot out of the nebula of his soul. In 1985, when the DAW deal died, Charles was thirty-nine and had published three novels and a pile of short stories. He could have left it there. But in the last decade of his life, he published four new novels and a new short story collection and brought the original *Imaro*s back to life. Twice. A passage late in *The Naama War* takes us deep into Imaro's soul—and perhaps into Charles's inner sanctum. The insight comes from Bohu, Imaro's nemesis, in their final confrontation. "Bohu understood how badly he had misjudged his adversary. He thought Imaro was like him—a seeker of power, domination, supremacy. But Imaro was nothing like that. He sought none of the bounty another person with his advantages would have coveted. Imaro sought only peace within himself. And all the power in Nyumbani—and beyond—was not sufficient to deter him from that purpose."

Charles sought the same peace, and all the power on Earth did not deter him from that purpose. Racism did not defeat him. Dashed dreams did not destroy him. Charles knew the meaning of his life and dedicated his days to serving it alone. There are signs Charles found that peace, which to him was worth more than the gaudy riches of our world. His letters from these final months portray the artist as an old man at one with himself.

"It's Good Friday, and rain is pouring from the sky," the seventy-two-year-old wrote in April 2019.[121] "The forecast says it will be rainy during the entire Easter weekend. So I'm glad to stay indoors. Besides, I don't do anything special to observe Easter anyway—not like I do on Christmas, when I spend the day reading boxing books and drinking de-alcoholized wine. To me, the taste of the de-alcoholized brew isn't different from the real stuff, and not getting high off it is a bonus." He loved boxing, from age five to the very end. He read new books about Muhammad Ali, always glad to learn about the icon. One "tidbit" was enough to make the latest biography worthwhile for him. He enjoyed reading and watching women's boxing, too, especially as Laila Ali, the daughter of the greatest of all time, became a champion in the 2000s.

In 2019, the *New Yorker* wrote an article about the Jamaican-American writer Marlon James, author of the fantasy novel *Black Leopard, Red Wolf*. It included a short history of Black-authored speculative fiction, from Du Bois to Butler. "In the nineteen-seventies, the writer Charles R. Saunders began publishing the stories that became *Imaro*, a fantasy novel set on an Africa-like continent called Nyumbani. Fantasy and sci-fi construct imaginative versions

121 Letter to Janet LeRoy, 2019.

of where we have come from and where we might be going; for Saunders and others, writing such stories with Black characters is a matter of recognizing that Black people have shaped the past and will play a vital part in the future."

Charles was elated. "Hard to believe that in 2021, 50 years will have passed since I first attempted to write an Imaro story. So much has happened since then. Never in my wildest dreams did I think that I would one day be mentioned in the *New Yorker*," he wrote.

In his last days, he returned to his earliest days. With Sword & Soul Media, he worked to republish the first Imaro novel. This time, the cover would show Imaro as Charles saw him, refracted through the brilliant artwork of Mshindo Kuumba. Uraeus returned briefly to pure fandom as he listened to the two geniuses talk about the details of Imaro's face and body for the ebook cover first, with a plan to eventually print it. Charles studied again the text of the first novel. He did so while enduring near poverty after an unspecified "financial reversal" put him so far behind on his bills that his phone, TV and internet were all cut off in 2016. Friends offered to pay the debt for him, but he declined such graces. He said he owed far too much.

"So I had to proofread the manuscript yet again. Ordinarily, it would have taken just a day or two to do that job at home. But, since I don't have internet at home anymore, I had to do that proofreading at the library, which allows only limited time on its computers. So it took a lot longer to do it, but I've finally finished," he wrote to his old Ontario friend Janet LeRoy. "You asked what I do when I'm not writing. Mostly, I read—books, magazines, newspapers. And I read stuff online, when I can get to a computer. I never take anything out of the library. Is there a reason for that? Not really. As it is, my living space is crowded with piles and piles of books. That's why the place is so cluttered. Taking things to the used bookstores around here is not an option. They don't buy used books anymore; they just offer store credit. So I'd end up taking books there, and then getting more books in return. Kind of defeats the purpose."

He told his friend how he'd fallen that summer and been confined to the hospital for a time. He was behind on his letters and had set aside Natal Day, Halifax's birthday on the first Monday in August, to write. He woke up feeling poorly. He felt worse the next day, but headed across the street to pick up a newspaper from a kiosk. "On this day, though, my right leg felt numb, and I generally felt weak. I managed to make it across to get my paper, but on the way back, I felt weaker, and my leg felt even more numb. Luckily, an employee at the drugstore who was in early, as well as a passerby, helped me to get back across the street," he wrote. "But there was no way I was going to get back up the steps that lead to my building. So my guardian angels called 911, and stayed with me until the ambulance came for me. From my position lying on the ground, I was loaded onto a stretcher and then into the ambulance. From there, I was taken to the local hospital. It was the first time I had been in a hospital for nearly 30 years. Back then, it was for eye operations, which were successful. This time, the matter was more serious."

The doctors told him he had an infection and that problems from his diabetes had returned. His right leg was too weak to walk on. He spent ten days in hospital, taking piles of pills and hooked to an IV. He needed a walker to move at first, but later returned to a shaky, independent step. His main source of suffering in the hospital was the dearth of reading material. He mulled donating some of his books so future patients would have worlds to explore while confined to their beds. It also gave him time to reflect on his life. "Do I feel more accepting of myself these days? Well, more so now than I did when the Home for Colored Children scandal first broke, and then the ensuing writer's block, followed by my descent into pennilessness. That was a very depressing time. Thankfully, with your help and the help of others, I've been able to climb out of that pit," he wrote.

But the pit was never far. In 2018, he'd been approached to republish *Sweat and Soul*, his Maritime boxing book. "I was all for this. However, that book was first published in 1990. I wanted to do an update chapter that would have chronicled later milestones in Black Nova Scotian boxing history. For example, one fighter, Kirk Johnson, later became the No. 1 contender among the heavyweights," he wrote.[122] "I thought this would be a simple matter, and I figured I'd send the contract as soon as I finished. But . . . the block struck again! Not for my creative writing, but just for this one thing. I just could not get myself to write that final chapter—or send in the contract. It was as though I were frozen, and I could not understand why."

Upon reflection, he connected his writer's block to a chain reaction of thoughts, fears, and doubts that wore him down to the point where he could not write. "The thing is, I am a very messed-up guy psychologically. Always have been. One would think that after being on this Earth for more than 70 years, I would have learned better, or acquired some wisdom, or at least fixed my psyche. But that hasn't happened—at least, not in a consistent manner. I think it was Edgar Allan Poe who coined the phrase, 'imp of the perverse.' My 'imp' is a tendency toward self-sabotage. I do things that are detrimental, or even destructive, to what I need to do to fulfill my ambition, or sometimes even to make ends meet. Or else I react badly to reverses.

"One example is the five-year-long spell of writer's block I suffered in the wake of the abuse scandal at the Nova Scotia Home for Colored Children, about which I had written a book in blissful ignorance of what was really going on there. Now, with much

122 Letter to David C. Smith, December 19, 2016.

introspection, I've gotten to the root of the problem. Or, at least, I think I have. It may be that I'm not 'over' the Home for Colored Children problem. Somehow, I just can't shake the feeling that my name and reputation have become tainted in the Black community here. And if *Sweat and Soul*, which is closely connected to this community, comes out again, the taint will affect that book, too, even though it has nothing to do with the Home. So that may be what blocks me from doing that final chapter. I know that's irrational. But . . . the imp is not rational."

He asked a mutual friend to apologize to the publisher, as he felt he had burned that bridge down. David Smith had by this point known Charles for forty years. They never met, and spoke just once on the phone. But their letters show a deep, intimate love between two brothers determined to never leave the other's back bare. David told Charles he, too, suffered from devastating collapses in confidence that led to writer's block. He'd found a few ways around the block and shared them. He told Charles that in his worst periods of writer's block, he felt he had "effectively killed some membrane or tissue or part of that old Writer Me." He could still write scenes and dialogue, but the plotting that had once flowed out naturally had been dammed. "Looking back, I now realize that it was because I had stopped reading fiction; familiarity with the plots and basic storytelling of other writers gives us the foundation on which to set up the scaffolding of our own stories. On the other hand, words flowed; scenes happened well as I wrote them. So I tried to get those coals to come to fire again," he wrote.[123]

For David, who had become a later-in-life father, part of that spark came from a Cinderella story he read endlessly to his child. His writer brain became interested in the pure structure of the story,

---

123 Letter to Saunders, December 2016.

which sets up the situation, reverses things, then has good things happen to Cinderella, then another reversal. As basic as a ballad, and just as powerful. Its mechanisms ensure we are always learning about Cinderella and feeling more deeply for her.

Charles often lamented his devastating bouts of writer's block, but in fact he never stopped writing at any point in his life. When I started getting Charles's letters, I saw them from the recipient's point of view: the amazing gift of a letter from Charles, three or four times a year. But consider it from Charles's perspective. He had between ten and forty pen friendships ongoing at any time from the 1970s to his death. Most people exchanged letters with Charles three or four times a year. That means Charles opened his own mailbox to find a new letter every week or two. He sent letters every week or two. Each one is deeply personal, drawing on that specific friendship, asking questions about that person's life, their fears, and their joys. That's why so many people thought they were his only friend in the world. It dwarfs imagination to understand that he was never alone, that he wrote hundreds of letters to people he loved, and received hundreds of loving letters in return. He, too, had never met most of them in person, never seen them move, nor heard their voice. Yet he knew them as deeply as one human can know another. And they knew him. He wrote letters through the worst of his writer's blocks.

Charles wondered what would have happened had the *Daily News* lived, and had he been able to work until 2011 to retire at sixty-five on a better pension. He figured he might have stayed on past retirement, as he enjoyed writing the editorials and working at the newspaper. He thought way back to his college teaching career, and how his life would have played out if he'd stayed in Ontario. But then, would he have written what he'd just produced over the last decade? He came to appreciate that the disasters had at least given him the gift of time to write undisturbed. He wrote and mailed one of his final letters on March 8, 2020.

"Here it is, a sunny Sunday that will stretch into tomorrow," he began. "The rest of next week promises to be typical March—wet and wild."[124]

He had read news accounts of a Black woman named Santina Rao, who had been shopping at a Halifax Walmart with her baby and toddler when she said she was racially profiled, falsely accused of shoplifting, and violently arrested by police in front of her children. It would take months before the Just Us system dropped the charges, while also clearing the white police officers. It struck home for Charles—the image of a mother alone with her children, hassled and attacked by menacing men. And he remembered being harassed in the same Walmart, accused of stealing as he carried an item from one part of the store to another. "What was going through his head at the time?" Charles wondered.

He described the full encounter in another letter.[125] "I went there to get a cheap CD player and a few other items. I obtained one of those smaller, upright Walmart carts and headed to the electronics section (where coincidentally Santina Rao went as well several months later). I found the CD player I wanted, and put it in my cart," he wrote. "Then I pushed my cart to the men's clothing section, which is located at the front of the store. There, I picked up some socks and put them in my cart on top of the CD player. So far, so good."

124 Letter to Janet LeRoy, March 8, 2020.

125 Letter to David C. Smith, March 29, 2020.

He then went to browse the paperback books. And so one of the greatest writers in Canadian history found himself grilled by a guy in a Walmart vest, insinuating that Charles R. Saunders was about to steal a cheap novel. "'Did you bring that into the store?' he asked. 'What?' I responded. He repeated the question. I thought, 'What the hell?' Or maybe a stronger word. Why would I be bringing a cart with Walmart merchandise into the store? I didn't want to return the stuff in my cart for a refund when I hadn't even bought the items yet. I just wanted to buy the socks and the CD player, along with any paperbacks I may have wanted. So I just kept repeating, 'What? What?' And he kept asking the same question. Finally, emphatically but not really loudly, I stated: 'I went down to the electronics section to get this CD player. Then I went and got these socks. Now I'm going to the paperback-book rack—if you don't mind!'"

The Walmart greeter backed off. "The guy could have thought I was dangerous, and called security or the cops. I could have been the one face-down on the floor, with cops all over me. I could have been the one who made the headlines in the next day's paper."

Many people in Halifax rallied to the young mother's side and held protests. "In my old activist days, I would have attended that rally." And in his columnist days, he no doubt would have crafted a powerful essay that would have cornered her opponents and left them flat on the canvas. "The Santina Rao story has been pushed off the media radar screen by other events, such as growing unease over the coronavirus outbreak," he wrote.

His life was peaceful and quiet. He went to the library to edit manuscripts, and to send short emails assuring his many friends he was safe and well, promising a letter would follow. Once in a while, he journeyed across the harbour to Halifax to have lunch at Mary's African Cuisine. He loved the restaurant, and was friendly with the owner, Mary Nkrumah. He had only recently learned her last name, and was delighted, because back in the 1930s, Kwame Nkrumah, the first president of independent Ghana, had studied at Lincoln University.

Charles settled into the lockdown and awaited better days. He had no symptoms of the virus, and no aches or pains. His eyes no longer troubled him. Once or twice a week, he crossed the street to the pharmacy, which also sold groceries, and resupplied himself. "So it's not hard at all to maintain social distancing," he wrote. He was isolated, though, as the libraries had shut on March 16 and kept delaying the reopening date. Charles would not live to see it. In 2019, when Taaq visited, he brought a big cheque from the *Imaro* movie project. Charles had considered using it to reconnect his internet and phone, but "fiddled and farted around" and didn't get it done. So he was unconnected in his home.

"Changing the subject . . . Do I ever worry about losing my mind? Yes, I sure do. As a septuagenarian, it is natural to contemplate such an eventuality. So far, I haven't shown signs of encroaching forgetfulness or lessening of reasoning capacity. But then, I might be just deluding myself through the good old reliable process of rationalization. The next few years will tell the story. Actually, I am more worried about the possibility/probability of debilitating physical disorders."

As he came to the end of the letter, one of the final things he would ever write, he reflected on his life, spurred by his old friend Janet's questions and comments. "Sometimes, emotions can snatch us the way a riptide does to a swimmer in the ocean. Sometimes, you have to fight your way out of it. Other times, you have to ease your way out of it. Of course, I'm speaking as a person who doesn't even know how to swim!

"You asked if I've ever suffered from 'artist envy.' I have, indeed. Back when I first started writing, I envied writers whose work got accepted by the small-press magazines that were sending me rejection slips. Later, I envied writers who were published, acclaimed, and rich. I envied those whose publishers stayed with them, while mine kept dropping me. I also envied writers whose books sold in the millions, enabling them to make a living off their work.

"I'm still envious of those things. Who wouldn't want to be Stephen King, who writes best-sellers that receive critical acclaim? But I put things into perspective now. I started a whole new sub-genre within the field of fantasy fiction. I did something no one else has done, or at the time, even thought of doing. I'm happy with that. It makes me feel that my life has been worthwhile. So that's where things are right now. By the time this letter reaches you, the situation may have changed.—Love, Charles."

19

CLAIMED

As my quest to find Charles R. Saunders reached the end, I felt like a failure. I'd found his body, but no one to claim him. I sensed that a piercing memory, a searing emotion, had marked Charles early in his life and propelled the rest of his days. With Imaro, we know that "unrequited vengeance burned like a torch in his eyes, yet beneath the lamina of that emotion lay a core of grief so bitter it threatened to consume him entirely." What blazed in Charles's eyes? What was at his core? I think he planted it deep in his books, liberating himself. Readers purify their own emotions and memories in the refining fire of his words. For Imaro, that marking moment comes when he's five rains old and abandoned by father and mother. At times of crisis, when the mighty warrior feels helpless, or bound, or weak, the old memory scalds him. He boils over and erupts. Much of the violence in the saga is Imaro showing how strong he is to hide what he fears is a fundamental weakness. What was Charles hiding?

I had learned more about my old colleague than I ever would have dreamed possible. I'd read more than 250 letters Charles wrote over fifty years to a range of friends. Each letter was about three pages, adding up to more than seven hundred pages of Charles writing about his life. They were an autobiography composed for close friends. Yet his origin story eluded me. He occasionally mentions aunts and uncles, his mother, cousins, and different generations of his seemingly large family, but rarely uses anyone's name or location. And in all 180,000 or so words of personal correspondence that I read, he mentioned his father just once, when comparing accents, and said the man was from Mount Pleasant, Ohio. I read pages of Charles's interviews over the years, introductions to his books, and his columns. I spoke to more than a dozen of his friends. Nobody ever asked him about his father, or his birth family. It was an astonishing accomplishment: Nobody seemed to even notice the absence. For fifty years, he'd written and talked about Imaro, the son-of-no-father, but even Imaro meets his father in the end.

The powerful scene comes late in the saga, when Imaro is in his mid-twenties. He's been rampaging down Nyumbani and stops at the stone ruins of something like what's called Great Zimbabwe in our world. As Imaro's name grows in Nyumbani, people begin to see his importance. One witness can only remark, "You are something new." Kings and queens seek his counsel. And one day he finds himself face to face with a ruler like no other—a ruler who looks like him. Seeing himself in his father's features shocks Imaro to his core. His father is in his forties; his dark hair is threaded white. "His umber skin stretched tightly across a frame that supported a giant's thews. On his broad-featured face was the mien of a man in full control of himself—and his world. Although their faces were discernibly different, their bodies could have been carved by the same sculptor, from the same stone."

The two men square up. "A sudden tension snapped through the courtyard like lightning flashing in a clear sky. The two giants faced each other like bulls about to do battle over the leadership of a herd. 'Let us see, warrior, if you can truly call yourself strong.'"

It is a test of strength, but when Imaro, whose name means "strong," is poised to win, he halts. He does not want to defeat this other man. He does not, at that moment, want to be stronger than his father. The ruler is stunned to realize this young man could overpower him and turns to his wife to ask, "Is this our son?" Imaro is offered his rightful place as heir. His father, we learn, was captured and enslaved as a young man. He proved he was a warrior in gladiatorial combat. He fought his way to freedom and conquered the throne that had once enslaved him. He knows he has a son but knows not his name—Katisa has told him only that one day their son will come to him. That day has arrived. In these last pages, Imaro is where Conan began: powerful, with the world bending to his will. Imaro is offered succession to the throne and with it power and all the things this world can give. The name Imaro lifted above all others. "He had listened to his father's words, as well as his mother's. He nodded and murmured when necessary. And he departed as soon as he could. He did not tell them all the thrones in Nyumbani could not fill the emptiness that was now inside him."

The people chant his name: *Imaro! Imaro! Imaro!* The adulation washes over him "like a wave breaking against a lone crag of stone. Like a stone, he remained unaffected. The fervor of the crowd meant nothing to him." Imaro rejects the throne and leaves the palace.

"The warrior was clad only in a plain loincloth of the type worn by the Abama of Naama. A long sword was belted to his waist. He could have been any of the newly freed Abama who wandered the streets of the Low City, still uncertain of what they would do with their liberty."

Imaro has completed his destiny and no longer wants to do what he is destined to do. He doesn't want to fulfill the dreams of other people, or be someone designed to amaze his father, or win his mother's love. He doesn't want the empire. He wants nothing; he takes it and leaves the kingdom to search for peace.

A year after Charles's lonely death, his family found me. They claimed Charles. The public trustee of Nova Scotia never stopped searching, and deep research led them to discover he had a half-sister, a teacher in Lansing, Michigan. And she wanted to talk to me. We exchanged messages to make arrangements. Our video call connected and I smiled at the two faces that greeted my own. They were also smiling. Ann introduced herself and turned to the older woman beside her. "This is my mother. And this is Jon," she says. Patricia[126] had suffered a bad fall recently, but was determined to talk to me.

"Nice to meet you, too," the older woman says. "I'm pleased to hear you're doing this writing. That's very good for the memory of him. That's excellent. How did you know him, Jon?"

I tell them about the Halifax *Daily News* and Charles's unexpected posthumous arrival in my life.

"You do know him very well then. That's precious," Patricia says. "I don't know if I can be of much help to you, but whatever I can tell you about Elizabeth, I will. When I was at university, I stayed there with my mother and stepfather. I went to Ohio after that. Elizabeth will be things that happened a good while back."

I take a shot: Charles always said he was from Elizabeth. Did she know anything about Charles's father?

Yes, she knew him: She was married to him for half a century.

I try to hide my astonishment. Charles's father had become a semi-mythical figure for me, more part of Nyumbani lore than our world. But suddenly I was speaking to the man's wife and daughter. "I can tell you plenty about his father's side of the family," Ann says. "I'd be happy to share with you. Our father was Robert Brian Saunders."

His name has been hiding in plain sight the entire time. Charles R. Saunders. The *R* stood for Robert. Patricia says Bob's bright

126 Pseudonym used by request.

intellect set him apart from a young age. Teachers noticed it and he did well in school. He was a diligent, straitlaced student.

I take another shot. Did Patrica ever meet Charles, or did she only know about him through his father? "I saw him when he was little. I would say four or five. He was an awful cute youngster," she says. "He was precious. My brother was a paper boy. We carried papers to his home, and his grandparents. They were a lovely family and they had a nice, large-frame home and a nice big yard. I'm sure his days were pleasant."

Patricia has clear memories of delivering the newspaper to the distinguished family and the charming grandson in the 1950s. "Well you know, Elizabeth is a very small place. It was along the Monongahela River and many swam in that river years back. You couldn't do it today. In the summertime, it was done frequently. They learned to dive and everything else. It was fun," she says, smiling. About 1,900 people lived in Elizabeth in those days, and it was almost a suburb of Pittsburgh. Patricia's father was the deputy sheriff at the Pittsburgh courthouse. Most of the men in Elizabeth worked in steel mills.

"I don't know if Chuckie ever talked to you about his schooling, but I don't think he went to grade school in Elizabeth. I wasn't acquainted with his mother, Charlene, because she was in an older group, much older than myself. And she had moved to Philly or Harrisburg, I'm not certain, to work. Did Chuck talk about Philadelphia?"

I bite back a laugh. It's hard to imagine my distinguished friend, the celebrated author Charles R. Saunders, as a Chuckie. Or Chuck. I tell her I've heard him connected to Norristown around that time. Patricia nods. That was near Philly and makes sense to her.

Young Charles loved to read and, even in elementary school, his writing stood out. Teachers told him he had a flair for it, and he earned a string of A's. "Hey, you want alienation?" he said later.[127] "I'm Black, and I don't sing, dance, or play basketball! Imagine living in a Black neighbourhood and not singing, dancing, or playing basketball. Yes, I was very alienated from my surroundings throughout childhood and adolescence." He rarely mentions childhood friends but does note two were identical twins. One had vitiligo. In later years, he wondered if that twin left it as it was, or dyed his skin lighter or darker to cover the spots. He knew people who'd done both. His mother, Charlene, had a twin, too. His name was Charles. Another meaty ingredient to stir in the gumbo.

Years after meeting Chuckie, Patricia met Bob Saunders in another town. He wasn't from Elizabeth, but he told her he'd been with someone from the town before, and had a child with her. A son. "He didn't talk about Chuckie or Charlene. It seems like in the beginning, he felt that Chuckie had nothing to do with him. He just didn't talk, and it bothered me. I think it bothered him. All the time. I think he did not give the time to our son, because I think he felt guilty about Chuckie," she says. "I don't know enough because I didn't ask questions, Jon. I should know more. He was a good guy. There are so many things to be sad about, but I'm so glad that Charles was able to do this literature . . . I'm just sorry that we didn't have more time with him." She trails off.

I clear my throat. "Can you tell me more about his family?"

Patricia didn't know Charlene, though they would exchange hellos if they saw each other out shopping. "She was very attractive. Tall, dark hair. Medium complexion. Nice features. And I would say very pretty," Patricia says. She knew Charlene's twin brother better. Charlene worked. She always worked. "I'm pretty sure she was already working, I think before he was born. I'm not certain. I can't

127 Elliot interview.

tell that." She recalls Charlene working in Pittsburgh at the time of Charles's birth.

Patricia tells me Charles's maternal grandparents were good people. She knew his grandmother's sister fairly well. They came from strong people who built the church on the far side of the river. But they'd moved to the other side of the water by the time Charles was with them. "His family, his grandparents, I think they were more loners. They didn't go out a lot. I don't even know what church they attended," she says. "They were tall. Both, the grandfather and grandmother. He had family."

Ann turns the camera to herself and asks me if I see a resemblance between her and Charles. "Well, I've got Charles right here," I say, lifting up the photo of him that sits on my writing desk. I show them. They laugh, delighted.

"He looks just like a Saunders," Ann declares. Patricia agrees. "Everything about his shape. High cheek bones. His face. Tall. He looks so much like me," Ann says. Charles shared a complexion with his mother's family, she says, but had the high cheekbones and build of their father's people. She asks about his build. I tell her he stood like a heavyweight boxer and she nods. That would have made him more massive than most of his slender family. I ask if they have any photos of Bob, and soon Ann finds a few. She shows me a black-and-white photo of her father in his twenties, standing with his feet planted, hands together behind his back. He's the spitting image of skinny Charles at that age, bobbing across the Lincoln campus. Bob, too, is clean-shaven with short hair and he stares directly at the camera, head cocked inquisitively. Tall and thin.

Charles was born in 1946. Patricia and Bob had a son in 1954 and named him Robert. Ann followed in 1965. Charles and Charlene were never spoken of, but once, when Chuckie was in high school, Charlene called. Bob was out of town, so the two mothers talked. Charlene had married by then, though Patricia doesn't think the stepfather adopted Chuckie, as his name was never changed from Saunders. "So that's good," Patricia says quietly. "The reason I remember Chuckie is because he would visit my husband's Aunt Marg, and we would hear about Chuckie. Or I heard about him. Most of the family call him Chuckie."

Bob's family had an old farmhouse in Mount Pleasant, Ohio, where the elder generation lived, grew crops, and kept cows and horses. As a boy, Charles spent time with his father's family, but not, it seems, with his father. His father's father was a coal miner who rose to the rank of foreman. He was highly intelligent and passed that down to Bob, who gifted it to his own children. Ann later spent time on the same farm. She'd heard the crick built up so much that when she finally saw it, she was disappointed to discover it was just a creek, and to learn the holler was only the hollow. The older generation still hand-agitated and rolled clothes to clean them. Charles spent many summers at "Granny Saunders's farm." His father's parents grew their own food and made jam. The visiting kids would sled in the winter, or swim in the crick in the summer. The family farm still relied on an outhouse and used a coal stove for cooking. They always had a good store of homemade whiskey, which could bring problems, Patricia says.

"Can you tell me about Bob?"

"Now that's a good question," she says, preparing to share the story of her late husband. He had a brother, Jim, and two sisters, Ruth and Virginia. Jim introduced Patricia to Bob. Born in 1921, he was eleven years older than her, and she was in her third year of college.

"It doesn't surprise me that Charles was as intelligent as he was because my dad was very smart," Ann says. Daughter and mother tell me you only had to show Bob something once and he knew how to do it. He worked with engines and mechanical things professionally, but later in life developed a private passion for crafting jewelry. "I'm sure he could have written if he wanted to," Patricia says. "I think he gave Chuckie a lot of his genes."

But Bob only read how-to guides and manuals. How to build a house. How to install a toilet. He read them for pleasure and stored the knowledge. And occasionally, he'd dazzle his family by fixing something thanks to a book he'd read years ago. Bob moved his young family to Michigan, just a few hours from the Canadian border. Patricia had a cousin who moved to Canada to avoid the Vietnam War draft, and they often visited him on cross-border excursions. "We love Canada!" the women say in unison, recalling pleasant family drives over the Ambassador Bridge to shop and eat in Canada for the day. Charles was at that point living just a few hours down the road in Hamilton, but his name was never spoken. Ann never once heard her father say his firstborn son's name or acknowledge him in any way. It was comparable to Charles's situation, where he never once spoke his father's name to a friend or his wedded family, or acknowledged him in any way.

"Bob was about six foot two, six foot three," his widow says. "He was thin, but he wasn't skinny. He was extremely handsome. He was determined. He didn't put up with anything from anyone. He had his own ideas about politics, and if people didn't agree with them, he really didn't have much to do with them. He was a Democrat. I look like a person who has many mixtures. He was very fair, but identified as African American. But he could pass as a white person. He told me stories about how he went to places that would not allow his African American friends to get in—he would really be upset by that. It left an impact on him."

A wizard with wires, he found work at a department store, then for the U.S. government, maintaining the telephone "red line" between the U.S. and USSR. The family lived and worked in Turkey and Portugal when Ann was young. After retirement, they went to Arizona, where he got into jewelry making. He surprised his family with his love for the fine, decorative work. Before that, he'd mostly preferred practical things.

I ask about Robert, Patricia and Bob's son. Robert was a sensitive, quiet person, she tells me, and he loved to read. "Who was his favourite? I can't think of it," his mother says. "I was always buying it for him. I'm blanking ... Oh! Burroughs. He read Burroughs."

Incredible. Edgar Rice Burroughs. The creator of Tarzan, Charles's arch-nemesis. Evidently both brothers loved the scope of the author's imagination in creating a dreamable Africa. I wonder if the racism was a stone in Robert's shoe, too? They didn't get those first Tarzan books from their father. But the family farm in Mount Pleasant offered a wider range of books. The classics, the Bible. And perhaps Edgar Rice Burroughs. It's possible the brothers discovered the same copies as kids, years apart, each unknown to the other.

It may have been there that Charles discovered and devoured comics and novels about Tarzan of the Apes. "I was hooked. They offered just the relief I needed from the rigours of a rotten adolescence," he once said.[128] "When I got to the racist parts, I cringed a little, but then it was 1961, and I was just as brainwashed as everyone else about Africa, so I swallowed all that stuff about witch doctors and cannibal cuisine and all the rest of the stereotype. Later, when I began to discover the truth about Africa, I reread some of the Tarzan books and got mad as hell at myself for having been so naive. It was not until much later, though, that I thought about trying to write something better."

Robert tore through books. When he started kindergarten, teachers asked him to teach the other kids how to read. His bright light dimmed under his father's gloom. Patricia says Bob kept a painful distance with his second-born son. Bob drank and smoked

---

128 Elliot interview.

heavily during Robert's childhood, as if something was chewing him up inside. Robert looked exactly like Charles, Ann says. The brother she grew up with was tall, too, but lighter as an adult, at 170 to 180 pounds. Ann says her brother loved fantasy and often escaped into its worlds. When I tell her some of Charles's favourites, she nods to many of the titles and authors. Robert read the same books. He loved to write, but never tried to publish anything. He was very smart and talented, but undone by the pain that he tried to balm with alcohol. The memories haunt his mother and sister.

Did Charles ever meet his father? I ask. Yes, they answer, at least once. In 1969.

Before Charles went to Canada, he went to his father. Patricia peers back over more than five decades, struggling to remember the extraordinary day that was never spoken of again. "You said I was in the car," Ann prompts. "Probably about the time he was drafted."

Patricia agrees. "It would have to be then. That's what I understand he went to Canada for. I'm not as good at ninety-two as she was at four," Patricia says, smiling at her daughter. "She's a little smarter than me anyway."

Ann smiles back. "My mother remembers the last time she saw him. They were taking him to the airport, and I was in the car with them."

Charles met his father, his wife, and their four-year-old daughter. His half-brother, Robert, was not invited, or declined to attend. The four family members piled into the car. His father was in his late forties and Charles was twenty-three. The same ages as Imaro and his father at their titanic meeting, a scene Charles would first write fifteen years later. Neither woman recalls how it came to be, but Bob Saunders agreed to see his son and drive him to the airport to fly to Canada. "My father didn't approve of him leaving the country and not joining the war. It was never spoken of. I don't think it was viewed very well," Ann says. "I'm starting to read *Imaro*, but I've got to tell you it's really a hard thing for me to read, because throughout the book he's referred to as the 'son-of-no-father.' You can see where that had an impact on Charles, and it's really apparent in his books. I just started part two of the book. It's hard for me to read. Every time I hear that, it just strikes some chords in me because it shows how that really impacted him. How he felt about maybe not having a father to play a role in his life."

Ann had forgotten all about that day—and her half-brother—by the time she was a teenager. Then her mother took her aside one day and told her that her father had another son. She shared his name, but little else. They never spoke about Charles after that brief conversation, and I think the letter from the public trustee prompted Patricia to tell Ann about the trip to the airport. Robert and Charles never met. The impact of Charles's exile seems to have hit their father hard, and reverberated in the way he treated Robert. The fifteen-year-old boy started drinking the year his brother left, and he couldn't stop. The pain driving the drinking did not depart. By forty-nine, he was dying. He moved in with Ann. She was with him when he passed. "I just wish I had been there for Charles. That makes me sad, when I think about that. It's a whirlwind time for me, first getting this letter that I have this brother . . . I wish I would have been there," she says. Ann pauses to gather her thoughts. "My father was an alcoholic, too, but he stopped drinking. He was a very different person. One day he just decided to stop drinking and he never drank again." She was eleven when it happened. She says that was him: strong-willed and unstoppable once he made a decision. "He didn't really have an understanding of other people that couldn't really do that. 'Well, I did it, why can't you? You should stop.'"

Charles's name was never spoken in her house, and neither was Robert's in the end. "I don't want to talk poorly about my father, but my brother, Robert, and my father didn't have a relationship. They didn't talk for the last ten or fifteen years of their life. Something about my father, I don't know. It's not surprising to me that Charles left. It's not surprising that Charles was never discussed. My dad, he never mentioned him to me, which is just sad. I don't know what the reason for that was." Patricia also feels guilty that Charles didn't know her family. Her brother, the one with the newspaper route, went on to become head of a university library and had a personal collection of five thousand books. "He would have loved to have known that Charles was an author," Ann says. "He would have loved Chuckie," Patricia adds.

Bob Saunders got stomach cancer in 2001. He endured the disease, the chemotherapy, and the failing health without a word of complaint. He was a strong-willed person who seemed determined to muscle death out of his way. But he couldn't, and six months after hearing his death sentence, he died. His wife's heart broke, for her lost husband, and for the lost chance at a reparation with his sons. Ann and her mother moved in together.

Now they have questions for me. What was Charles like? Was he loud or quiet? He was quiet, I tell them. Tall, quiet, and brilliant. Three words that nearly everyone used to describe him. Patricia is surprised to learn he was fascinated by boxing. "Chuckie was? Oh, that's interesting." She's curious if he went to church. He didn't. She finds that interesting, too. She always imagined he was a Catholic.

"What were his favourite foods?" Ann asks. I tell her about the fish and radishes.

Ann grew up with no memories of Charles but with a yearning to live in Canada. "I should have followed my instincts thirty years ago and become a citizen. Now that I think my brother was in Canada . . . it's strange to me. If I would have known all that time that I had a brother there, I definitely would have," Ann says.

After Charles left America in 1969, the next update they got came in May 2021: the letter from the public trustee of Nova Scotia telling them he was dead. "It's funny, because in May 2020, I started to think, 'I wonder where my other brother is. I'd like to get some more information of that. It's so strange, because that's the time he passed away and I was thinking, *I wonder how I'd go about finding you.*"

She'd tried Ancestry.com but found nothing. She hadn't heard anything about him in decades and had no idea if he was dead or alive, in Canada or the U.S., or even what name he used as an adult. "I have no memory of him, and that makes me very sad. When I see him, I see, *Oh my gosh he looks just like my father and my brother and me,* so I feel a connection. But I don't have any memory of him."

Patricia carries grief, too. "I'm sorry mostly because my son and my daughter didn't get to spend time with him. I really wasn't surprised to find out that he was into science fiction, because my son loved it. They would have gotten along so well," she says. "I was so sorry, because I really didn't get to see him until he was leaving for Canada. We had a good trip and visit together that day."

"This makes us feel closer to Chuckie," she adds as we come to the end of the call. "I sort of feel him by talking with you. It's been excellent."

I agree.

Before we sign off, Patricia tells me one last thing about Bob's life that stuns me silent: Before Charles's father was a father, he was a warrior. And he fought in an all-Black world.

20

A SHIP OF BLACK WARRIORS

Bob Saunders rarely spoke about his war, but in September 1994, he was watching TV with his wife when the U.S. president, Bill Clinton, came on. Clinton said he wanted to recognize the Black men who had fought in the Second World War. With him was the head of a group called the USS *Mason* Association. Bob knew him. The *Mason* man stood at a podium in a congressional committee room on Capitol Hill to receive an award from the president of the United States.

"For decades, African Americans were missing in our memories of World War II," Clinton said. He promised they would be "forgotten no more" because their service helped beat the Nazis and racism in the U.S. "In helping to show the world what America was against, you helped to show America what America is for ... You helped liberate us all from segregation."

Bob bitterly told his wife he'd served on the *Mason*, but nobody had called him to meet the president. He felt left out. Again. "My husband was not invited—I think because, and this is awful to say, my husband didn't look like he had any Black blood. I'm sorry to—no, I'm not sorry to say. I think because of jealousy or whatever, he never did get the award. We only found out after," his wife told me. Patricia shared that story at the end of our interview but knew little else about his service. Just that name—the USS *Mason*. I tracked down a book titled *Proudly We Served: The Men of the USS Mason*, by Mary Pat Kelly. I read it, but Bob Saunders was not mentioned. However, in appendix C, I found a complete crew list. There he is, on page 191: SAUNDERS, Robert B., MOMM2C—V6. I learned that means Motor Machinist's Mate 2nd Class. As such, he spent most of his time in the bowels of the ship, in the engine room, operating, maintaining, and repairing the ship's propulsion mechanisms, steering engine, and all the machines behind the food, laundry, elevators, marine boilers, and pumps.

At the start of U.S. involvement in the Second World War, racist white Americans prohibited Black people from serving the U.S. Navy. Even in the army, Black warriors would be steered into becoming cooks, serving white soldiers from a segregated supply unit. The U.S. Navy was essentially entirely white. Nobody could figure out how to have a segregated unit on a ship, and they couldn't imagine a world where white and Black people shared a living space, so they kept Black Americans out of the navy and out of nearly all combat. The racist white people claimed Black people had a "fear of water," or of combat in general, and couldn't be relied on. Many Black people knew the truth was that white people were afraid of seeing how well Black Americans could fight abroad. What if they brought that fight home? It was comparable to how white boxers had refused to fight Black challengers for decades, hiding their cowardice behind prejudice.

On June 1, 1942, the U.S. Navy opened ranks to general Black enlistment, and by February 1943, thirty thousand Black sailors were serving—usually forced to accept steward roles. Only 6,662 were accepted for general service. Bob Saunders signed up with his brother Jim. Both wanted to join the army, but Bob got deployed to the navy; Jim went into the army. The U.S. Navy took the extraordinary step of declaring that Saunders's ship, the USS *Mason*, would have an all-Black crew of 160 sailors, overseen by a white officer corps. The plan was to raise the Black sailors quickly through the ranks so that eventually it could be an all-Black ship—officers as well as crew—and the navy could avoid having Black and white men serve together. Saunders and his crewmates would be the first Black U.S. sailors to take a warship into battle.

The USS *Mason* patrolled the North Atlantic to protect convoys carrying critical war supplies from the U.S. to the U.K. It was one of five hundred maneuverable ships guarding the convoys, attacking U-boats, and willing to take a torpedo to protect their ships. The sailors reflected on their warrior years in *Proudly We Served.* "I had a young son and I felt if I could get into the service and do good, it would be an opening for him and others like him," explained sailor Lorenzo DeFau. He knew about the Nazis' persecution of Jews and wanted to stop it. "I can kill two birds with one stone. I could take part in trying to stop this action and also open doors here at home."

Some of the men boasted they suffered from a Black "superiority complex," perhaps as a defence against the constant racism they faced from Nazis and from white Americans. Like DeFau, a lot of the men were fathers and fought to break the colour barrier in the hopes that their sons could follow them and flourish in the armed forces. Free Europe from the Nazis and free American from the racists. DeFau, like many of the crew, knew that plenty of people thought he was a fool to fight for a racist America. "But it was my home being violated, threatened," he said. "A man will go forth and defend his home. You defend your family, you defend your country, because there's no other place that's home."

Black servicemen on shore patrol were told to never discipline white people and that if they had to break up a fight, they could only stop the person of colour from fighting—not the white guy. Black people were denied promotions, lest it led to a Black person commanding white people.

Saunders and his *Mason* crew were prepared to die in the war. It was a "bonus" about serving at sea: Nobody came home wounded from the navy, they said. It was sink or swim. "The *Mason* was an experiment. They wanted to see if we could take to the sea. They wanted to see if we were capable of becoming regular sailors and fitting in with the white guys," one sailor remarked.

When the *Mason* joined the fight in the first half of 1944, France had fallen and Canada and the U.S. were providing critical support to the U.K.'s fight against the Nazi onslaught. More than one thousand merchant ships had been sunk, and the Germans had killed forty thousand people on the ocean. The *Mason* would be part of the effort to stop that. It was smaller than a destroyer but quick and heavily armed with depth charges, 55-calibre guns, and anti-aircraft weapons. It also had a state-of-the-art radar to hunt Nazi U-boats. The engine room was the beating heart of the ship, driving the 1,500-horsepower motors. Everything on the three-hundred-foot-long ship was painted battleship grey, but the engine room was constantly smeared with black oil. The engineers doubled their efforts to keep it pristine as the *Mason* took to the water in the spring of 1944 for a shakedown cruise to prepare for a transatlantic voyage to escort the ships supplying the D-Day invasion. The *New York Times* covered the launch. Thomas W. Young became the first American Black war correspondent aboard a U.S. Navy ship. "The USS *Mason* Goes to War—History is Made," read one headline. Many Black newspapers held it up as a source of pride. Many white Americans believed their racist views were correct: Black people couldn't—or wouldn't—fight, they thought, and sat back for proof. On the *Mason*, the crew escaped into the world of all-Black warriors.

On July 1, 1944, the *Mason* sailed into the Atlantic with its first convoy. The men marvelled at the vastness of the ocean. They travelled dark, so the bright stars filled the universe above and sparkled on the water below. As they approached Europe, the *Mason* crew could hear the guns booming in France. A Nazi airplane spotted them. The alarm rang and men raced to their battle stations. One sailor reached his position and puked on his typewriter. Others loved the thrilling rush of combat and were eager to get their first kill. But they weren't attacked that day.

The *Mason* guided the convoy to Plymouth, England, and then sailed onward to Belfast. The crew got shore leave in Northern Ireland. After facing so much racism from white Americans at home, Saunders and his crewmates wondered what type of reception they'd get from white people here. Their worries soon vanished as the locals apologized for the bad weather and thanked them for their service. The Irish treated them like human beings, better than many white Americans did, and better than the United Service Organizations, which barred Black servicemen from white facilities even in Europe. One *Mason* sailor said he felt like *he* was being liberated. "The Irish people didn't look on us as our skin colour. They looked on us as Americans—as American fighting men," he said. There was a tense moment at a dance when a sailor heard a local girl ask him about "blackit" and he wondered what the hell she was talking about. But she repeated it slower, and this time he heard "blackout." Nothing to do with his skin tone. She just wanted to know if they had blackouts in the U.S.

The *Mason* escorted multiple convoys across the Atlantic Ocean, protecting them all. Bob would often say that he "went into the navy Black and came out white," suggesting his fairer skin was a problem for some of the other sailors. He left the navy a changed man—bitter from his service, and increasingly bitter from a sense that his service had been written out of the history books. His ship was decommissioned in October 1946, the same month Charles was conceived.

Charlene was in Pittsburgh, working. Charles always said he was from Elizabeth, "a small town near Pittsburgh," but once, in a private letter, he admitted he'd actually been born in Pittsburgh. Bob Saunders likely moved to Pittsburgh after the war and met Charlene.

They became pregnant. Charles was born in July 1946, nine months after the USS *Mason* was decommissioned on the east coast. I don't know what happened to the little family, but during Charles's toddler years, Charlene returned to her kin in Elizabeth. Intriguingly, when Katisa returns to her Ilyassai people carrying a young Imaro in her arms, "she consistently refuses to name" his father. Did Charlene cause a similar scandal when she returned from Pittsburgh with a son with no father?

I read the *Mason* book a couple of times and learn more about the ship online. I can't find any clues as to why Bob Saunders's name was not honoured in the book, so I track down the author, Mary Pat Kelly. It takes a while, but I find her in Belfast, and we schedule a video call. She is American, and white, and in Belfast researching another project. She starts by telling me she knows she's an unlikely author for such an important book about Black history. She hadn't intended to write about the *Mason*, but while researching U.S. servicemen in Ireland during the Second World War, she came across a newspaper report from Thomas W. Young about the Black crew of the USS *Mason*. She found a few of the surviving crew and interviewed them for her Irish documentary. A few days later, some of those men contacted her and asked if she could write a book about the *Mason*. "They were offering me an opportunity to join their circle and write down the tale," she says. The men were old, and many of their one-time crewmates had died. The story was in danger of being lost. She found one sailor, then another, then another. They connected her to the people they'd stayed connected to; none of them had stayed connected to Bob Saunders. The author knew him only as a name on the crew list.

Mary is upset when I tell her he felt spurned. She wanted to speak to everyone, she says, but had no way to reach Bob Saunders.

I offer to connect her to Bob's surviving family. They speak, and the family sends her photos of Bob in uniform. Mary is part of a group working on an exhibit about the USS *Mason* at the National Museum of African American History in Washington, DC. She will see that the warrior Bob Saunders's name and image get their rightful place in history.

21

SWORD AND SOUL

Charles left a grieving world. Ron Fortier suffered a double blow. Less than a year after Charles died, Derrick Ferguson died, leaving unfinished his dream of writing a new Damballa novel. Ron turned his suffering into a story about Charles and Derrick. "The swift-moving current threatened to drag Derrick Ferguson under just as he was about to break free from its grasp. His head rose up out of the flowing river's surface and he gulped air; his arms flailed outward in some semblance of actual strokes. That was where the desperation lay, as he knew how to swim, if only the damn current would give him a break and let him use that skill," he begins in a story called "Fort Champion."

It's a classic fantasy beginning: the hero in danger, forced into action to save himself. Derrick gets to the far shore and emerges dripping wet in a blue hospital gown; no shoes, no pants. A voice calls him onward. Derrick looks, amazed, and realizes it's Doc Savage, a pulp hero from the 1930s—and he's with Lester Dent, the writer who created him. Doc pulls Derrick into an army jeep. The jeep judders along a dirt road directly into the woods and pulls up at a wild west fort that looks like it was dragged out of an old John Ford cowboy movie. The place bustles with military people of all ages and outfits, preparing to battle invaders. Derrick is told the General wants to see him.

He walks by warriors swinging swords and battle axes, or loading munitions onto army trucks. Lester Dent leaves him in the care of a "small, balding man, with a clipboard in his hands and a pipe in his mouth. He introduces himself with a grin: 'Edgar Rice Burroughs; welcome to Fort Champion, Mr. Ferguson. Come on inside and we'll get you fitted out proper.'" Charles's old foe, Tarzan, is there too. Derrick steps forward, but someone yells a warning as a heavy broadsword slices the air just over his head. He follows the reverse trajectory to its source and sees two men arguing. One is a mountain in a man's body, the other tall but rangy. He soon meets Conan and Robert E. Howard. They urge him to see the General. Howard points the path to him. Two hundred yards away, he sees two big men, one with skin the colour of umber, the other of mocha. The umber-skinned man stands six foot three and wears only a tan loin cloth and holds a huge, oval shield and a long, deadly spear. The second man is older, slightly taller, and wearing slacks and a knit sweater beneath a light blue Inverness cape. His grey hair erupts from his head and chin. Over his lively brown eyes, the man they call the General wears large, plastic-framed glasses. Derrick draws within thirty feet before the taller gentleman detects him.

"'Well, look who's here at long last,' beams Charles Saunders. 'The one and only Derrick Ferguson.'"

Derrick is stunned to finally meet his writing hero, and he recognizes Imaro instantly. Charles sends Imaro on a mission and takes Derrick for a walk alongside the river from which he had just been rescued.

"'Am I dead, Charles?' was his first question.

'Yes, Derrick. You are. There's no way to sugar-coat that.'

'Then what is this place? Is it heaven?'

'Yes, it is,' Charles actually chuckled when replying. 'Not exactly the puffy white clouds and the singing baby angels you envisioned, heh?'

'I don't know. I never really thought of it all that much while I was living.'

'Most of us don't. But you need to understand it is not simply heaven. Derrick, this is your heaven.'"

Derrick stops walking. Charles explains that Derrick's soul has created all of it: the fort, Burroughs and Tarzan, Howard and Conan, even Charles and Imaro. But it's also all real. Each character takes turns telling a story, and they all bring it to life. Fantasy is reality in heaven. It's not one or the other; it's both, fused. And when Dent or Burroughs or Howard has an idea for a story that involves Derrick, he'll play his part, too. The river is the River of Life. Love is the one thing death can't wash away, Charles tells him. What and who you loved in life, you bring with you into death; nothing else can cross the river.

Imaro rumbles back to them in a jeep, on which is mounted a .50-calibre machine gun. Next to the warrior is a young Black man with short hair and a lean, powerful physique. Derrick is amazed. It's Dillon, his own creation, in the vehicle with Imaro. Derrick leaps into the jeep, grabs a pair of shades, and slips them over his eyes. The jeep shoots forward, spins a doughnut and heads back up toward the horizon as Derrick lets out a loud "WAHOOOO!" The end, we learn, is only the beginning of the story.

⟶

My mind races. Everything falls together. Imaro is the son-of-no-father thrown out of his clan on a false accusation of cowardice. Fatherless Charles was exiled from America with the bogus claim that he was afraid to fight in Vietnam. Imaro is five as the saga begins; by chance, or fate, the first glimpse I have found of Charles comes at five years old. When Patricia delivered newspapers to his home in the summer of 1951, Charles, too, was the son of an absent father, and his mother had just left him alone with her people. Was this the origin moment for Imaro? For sword and soul? "Full disclosure: I started the genre forty years ago; and, much later, I coined its name," Charles wrote in 2011.[129]

Charles described himself as a voice howling in the wilderness—and at first, only Tarzan howled back. After the DAW death, he thought he'd failed. But with his rebirth in 2000's *Dark Matter*, he discovered that the seeds he'd planted had grown new forests. He started to see that it wasn't just about him and his writing. There were entire worlds at stake. One night in the 2000s, he and Uraeus spoke at length about the meaning of his work. "Yes, I'm writing sword-and-sorcery fiction. But considering the African-based setting, I ought to call it 'sword, sorcery and soul,'" Charles wrote.

But the phrase sounded awkward.

"Then it hit me. It should be called sword and soul. Those three words sparked great enthusiasm in Uraeus, and I gave him permission to use it as the designator of his nascent publishing company, Sword & Soul Media."

Those three words took Charles a lifetime to write. "When you add that soul to it, when the name hits the ear of a Black person, it's very intriguing," Uraeus told me. "What is that? It's very provocative. So grand, so far-reaching, concentrated into three words: sword and soul. It just captures everything. Our experiences, our culture, historical ups and downs that he wove into it. Man, it's just magical. It's a magical phrase. The perfect moniker for his legacy."

In coming up with that phrase, Charles clearly drew on the title of his 1990 boxing book, *Sweat and Soul*. I flipped through it, feeling that something was just out of my grasp. I'd tracked down a rare copy in an ancient and famous second-hand bookstore in Dartmouth. I paid extra for the signed edition: "To Bridge—A

129 Introduction to *Griots: A Sword and Soul Anthology*, 2011.

thousand thanks for giving me this opportunity!—Charles, 2 August 1990." That would be Dr. Bridglal Pachai, who in 1990 was the director of the Black Cultural Centre. I had not seen him for a few years and realized he must have died. He loved books, and only death could have parted him from this one. I thumbed to the end, where I found what I sought in the short author biography: "Although he never put on the gloves, he has been a boxing fan since the day his grandfather plunked him in front of a round-screen TV set to watch Jersey Joe Walcott win the heavyweight title by flattening Ezzard Charles in 1951."

Our one glimpse inside Charles's childhood home comes on a warm, dry evening on July 18, 1951. Chuckie had celebrated his fifth birthday six days earlier and, perhaps as a treat, his grandfather let him stay up late. We know that his father was by then absent, and his mother had left him. It was a huge night for his birth town, Pittsburgh: Forbes Field, home of baseball's Pittsburgh Pirates, was hosting a bout to determine boxing's heavyweight champion of the world. It was Pittsburgh's first heavyweight title fight. The reigning champion, Ezzard Charles, would defend his title against old Jersey Joe Walcott. Chuckie surely delighted in hearing the commentators say his name over and over again as the champion Charles looked to beat Walcott for a third time. Perhaps it was on that night that the boy decided he would one day be Charles.

Ezzard Charles would go down in history as one of boxing's all-time greats, a timeless pound-for-pound king. I find the video online of the two Black men competing for one of the world's most prestigious titles: the baddest man on the planet. Ezzard Charles had won a decision over Walcott in 1949. Walcott lost another decision to Charles in March 1951. But Jersey Joe got another title shot that July. Ezzard Charles was making his ninth defence and needed opponents. On that warm night in Pittsburgh, Walcott was thirty-seven years old and had come off the docks for his second stint as a pro fighter. The commenters joked he'd first turned thirty-seven quite a few years ago and was well into his forties. He looked old. There was no doubt the champion was thirty.

But Jersey Joe gained confidence as the rounds progressed. It became clear that he might lose, but he wouldn't quit. Blood trickled out of the champion's mouth as they met in the middle of the ring for round seven. Jersey Joe Walcott strolled forward and flashed a brutal left hook that bolted to the champ's jaw, twisting Charles's head around to face the camera. The champion plunged nose-first into the canvas like a felled tree. The shocked crowd leapt to its feet, roaring at the incredible sight. So did I. Walcott was swarmed. He was at the time the oldest man to ever win the crown. It turned our Charles into a lifelong boxing fanatic. And then I glimpse something in the moments after the victory. Amid a sea of faces showing extreme emotions, a different visage emerges. I freeze the film, back it up. Walcott's corner swarms him and obscures our view of the new world champ. But for an instant, we see him. I pause it. His stony face glares across the ring at his fallen foe; he looks furious that Charles fell so easily. The hair, the skin colour, the muscles, the facial features. The menace. The baddest man on the planet. It's the face of Imaro.

I believe Imaro was born that night, as if the Cloud Striders themselves reached into Charles's soul and touched him, and made him different. He was afraid and alone, and then he wasn't. Someone burst out of his soul to rescue him: the one who was forsaken, the greatest of all warriors. When Imaro finally meets the ruler of Cush and can ask her anything, this is what he says: "Who am I? Who is my father? Where is my mother? Why does death follow me wherever I go?" These were the questions that followed Charles throughout his life. Imaro finds no answers in Cush. "Why should I care who my father is? Why should I care where my mother went after she left me in the manyattas of the Ilyassai?

I am the son-of-no-father. That is who I will always be. And I will always be a warrior."

When Charles read Tarzan for the first time, a few years after the title fight, he fell in love with the African setting. When he read about Tarzan lynching Black people, his soul revolted. He saw a Black warrior leap out of the jungle and destroy Tarzan, much as Imaro would wipe out three Mizungus in the first story Charles ever told about him. And when he read Conan for the first time, a decade later, he discovered Imaro's home—inside of himself. It wasn't Africa, but Africa through the lens of sword and sorcery. It was Home; Nyumbani.

Before Charles wrote Imaro stories, he wrote fantasy fiction pitting legendary boxers against each other. He took the name for the genre he founded from his boxing book, turning the sweat into a sword. I think the kindling for Imaro was created in a Pittsburgh boxing ring on July 18, 1951. More wood was gathered at Lincoln University against the backdrop of the war in Vietnam. I think the spark that brought these elements into a creative fire was the shocking killing spree of Donald Lambright, son of Stepin Fetchit. I flip through *Stepin Fetchit: The Life and Times of Lincoln Perry* by Mel Watkins until I find the passage. By 1941, Perry had abandoned his wife and son. He refused to pay child support. And then he uttered these cruel words: "Winnie and I were never married. It was all a publicity stunt. I also want you and everybody else to know that that is not my baby." Donald was a toddler. A son-of-no-father. Charles's former classmate erupted into horrific violence and killed people before ending his own life in 1969. The year Charles met his father. The year of exile. The year Imaro was conceived.

I suddenly remember a weird scrap of paper in the box Charles de Lint sent to me. I dig it out. It's a slightly bigger than a postcard and consists of five paragraphs written by Charles R. Saunders "in a moment of madness" in 1977, during the creation of Imaro.

Imaro's sword flashed like lightning in the sullen darkness, ripping hungrily into the overhanging gut of the Alabama highway patrolman.

"You Black son-of-a-bitch!" the patrolman gurgled as he sank in a morass of his own spilled intestines. Imaro looked down on him silently as he wiped his blade on his leopardskin loincloth.

Imaro grunted dispassionately. He stared down the asphalt road with the dotted white line fading into the distance. Once again, he looked quizzically at the wheeled metal monster he had overturned in one gigantic surge of strength.

At that moment, a small Black man in outlandish garb crawled from the wreckage of the police car.

"Whoo-ee, you one bad mothafucka," he marvelled.

No doubt it's Pomphis. Charles perhaps wondered if he could work his warrior into our world, but then found sword and sorcery, and Nyumbani. Pomphis shares Charles's outrageous intelligence, and Chuckie would grow to be a man surpassing the stature of Imaro. Charles first thought of Imaro when he was a small boy, in a vision where the warrior's strength rescued him. He would credit Imaro with saving his life once again, on the dark day Charles tried to end his life. And Charles would save Imaro's life when DAW and Night Shade tried to end it.

As Charles wrote and rewrote the Imaro saga, he diminished Pomphis's role. When he crafted the first novel, he towed their meeting in "The City of Madness" all the way to the end. And in modern editions, Pomphis doesn't appear in the first book at all. We meet him at the start of the second book, long after we know Imaro on his own, and Imaro with Tanisha. Modern readers lose that frantic first impression of man-child and child-man who rescue each other and bond instantly, and for the rest of their lives. "At the time Imaro first began taking shape in my imagination, Pomphis was there too,"

Charles once revealed.[130] In the first story, in the city of madness, we see the founding image of Imaro: a powerful hero rescuing a helpless child. Later, Charles would make the superior artistic and psychological decision to begin Imaro's story not with him rescuing a childlike man but with him as a child in need of rescue.

Imaro is a warrior out of ancient African legend. He is Beowulf, Gilgamesh, or King David, and greater than Tarzan or Conan. Reading Charles R. Saunders turns every other novel into a first draft. That prologue scene of the child Imaro standing in the rain, on the cusp of orphanhood, stands out as one of the greatest openings in literary history. Everything is packed into that singularity, and the series explodes from that timeless point.

During Charles's last years, many other writers were hard at work in sword and soul. One reviewer of Charles's late work reflected on his wider impact. "History buffs will readily embrace sword and soul as writers present historically correct fantasies using real places and actual people that reveal the richness of our African past," author Stafford L. Battle wrote. "This is more than brown or black-skinned Conans stomping through the dense jungle killing monsters. You will find no white Tarzan characters dominating the local natives. Sword and soul—at least in one aspect—is the retelling of our African heritage as kings and queens, conquerors, explorers, warriors and dreamers who influence the evolution of world civilization. Here is where we really expand into the universe of thought."

Charles was thrilled with the response. "Can't beat this, eh? My writing has not made me rich or famous, but it has, at least, earned me respect, and recognition, and I'll accept that any day."

In *Griots: A Sword and Soul Anthology*, Charles and his collaborator Milton Davis edited a collection of sword and soul stories

---

130 Introduction to "The Blacksmith and the Bambuti" in *Nyumbani Tales*, 2017.

written by a new generation of writers. In it, Charles calls sword and soul "a horizon, not a box. A frontier, not a niche."

"Sword and soul is a broad term, not a confining one. Essentially, it is fantasy fiction with an African connection in either the characters or the setting . . . or both. The setting can be the historical Africa of the world we know, or the Africa of an alternate world, dimension or universe. But that's not a restriction, because a sword and soul story can feature a Black character in a non-Black setting, or a non-Black character in a Black setting. *Caveat: Tarzan of the Apes need not apply.*

"A sword and soul story may also be set in a future in which science and magic have become interchangeable, or one in which modern technology has long since been lost. Regardless of the setting, magic and heroism form the underpinnings of sword and soul.

"Just as soul music can include everything from blues to hip hop, sword and soul encompasses everything from Imaro to . . . well, go ahead and read the stories in this book and you'll see."

22

HE LEAVES WARRIORS BEHIND

Jua the sun poured heat from a cloudless sky. Imaro hesitated between forest and savanna—two entirely different worlds. He had appeared in many guises on earth. First, as an Afro-sporting muscleman holding the severed head of an enemy in the 1977 *Dark Fantasy*. Then as Tarzan with a tan on the DAW novel. He took other shapes on the subsequent books, but none were his true form. But now, etched into granite, his face is revealed for the first time at the Dartmouth Memorial Gardens. Beside him are carved the words "I go, but I leave a warrior behind." Imaro, head angled slightly down, sword clutched loosely in his right hand, looks back across the grass to a tablet of bronze and granite, bearing the image of a wizard of a man, and a fist raised in the Black Power salute, next to the words "Charles R. Saunders, 1946–2020. Black Journalist and Author."

"He hesitated, uncertain where his next footsteps should take him," Charles writes in "The Afua." Imaro is at the northern extent of the Tamburure. He's been alone for six moons. He's spoken to no one as he wandered far beyond any Ilyassai. He lives off the land. He wonders if he can live in this northern forest before him. Behind him is his past. Does his future lie there, or in the new world ahead of him? "For a moment longer, Imaro stood, shifting his spear from one hand to the other as he looked from the forest to the plain," we read. "Then he decided. The forest was a place of trees, not a Place of Stones. It was a living place, not a dead place. He did not think he would find the Naama or the Mashataan in its depths. But he might well find something that would fill the emptiness that gaped like an abyss inside him."

People flowed over the hill. The drummers first, sliding hands on smooth leather wrapped tight over tall, cylindrical instruments. They were from the African Nova Scotian drum collective called Home. Or, to give their name in Swahili, Nyumbani. Friends eased down the slope to the solemn gathering at the edge of the forest. At eleven a.m. on Saturday, August 28, 2021, the music began. Two drummers sat facing each other. Lower notes, followed by higher ones. Two voices, talking. Calling. Bells, jangling from a drummer's leg, splashed new sounds. More people poured over the hilltop. They were given an order of service featuring a strong photo of Charles, gazing out from his extraordinary inner worlds. Under his face were the words of Maya Angelou: "There is no greater agony than bearing an untold story inside you." It was perhaps the one agony Charles was spared.

The drums increased the energy, drove a reflective pace. Calling, calling, calling. Echoing off the hill, the trees, and into the blue sky. A breeze blew across the late August day, waving the grass like a passing hand and stirring dance in the tall, slender trees. People looked in awe at the mighty Imaro, gazing protectively over Charles's grave. The drums clattered with an urgency. The wind sounded like snakes rattling through the tree leaves. A mighty spirit seemed to be forming itself, calling us together. Things fall apart. But sometimes, things fall together. The drums slowed their mystic conversation, talking of quieter things in the summer sun. An urgency lifted the drums as Rev. Rhonda Britton approached the grave. An American by birth and Nova Scotian by choice, she understood something of Charles's life. As the minister of New Horizons Baptist Church, the biggest Black church in the province, she understood more. Dale

Farmer-Saunders, Charles's late wife, had attended the church. The reverend had presided at her funeral, too. The drums fell silent.

"We gather here today on this beautiful day to bear witness to the life of our brother, Charles R. Saunders. Charles passed away in 2020, and we're coming together today to say our farewells and to remember his life," she said.

She prayed, offering gratitude for the glorious day, and the extraordinary human. "We thank you for this prolific author and journalist, this hero who believed so strongly that we are warriors, here to defeat the evils of this world," she said, her words streamed live to grieving friends and family in Canada and the United States. The bells sounded in response to her prayer, and then the drums spoke up in a fast chatter, repeating each other, reinforcing both voices, making one song. Someone in the gathering chirped and yipped back. A smooth red car pulled up, disgorging more drummers. The drums quieted. The wind whirled.

Dr. Afua Cooper approached the grave, a professor and poet from Jamaica who, like Charles, had long ago found a home in Africadia. "It's wonderful to commemorate this son of the African diaspora with rhythms from his tradition, from the African tradition," Afua said. She spoke about funerals in Ghana, where you can tell the dead person's age by the colours of the clothing on the mourners. Red and black for the young dead, black and white for those who have lived full years. She spoke about the lost knowledge, lost wisdom, lost in the Middle Passage. But the drums stayed with the people.

"I want to honour Charles with a poem, and the poem is called 'Negro Cemeteries,'" she said. The poem was published in Cooper's fifth book of poetry, *Copper Woman and Other Poems*, but it sounded like it was written on this day.

"The poem is a bit surreal, and because Mr. Saunders wrote futuristic literature, I felt that this poem is appropriate because it deals with the past, present, and future in this material world and also in the spiritual world. It's based on a real-life situation that happened in Priceville, Ontario, about two decades ago, in which the Black cemetery was discovered. One day it rained and after the rain, these headstones started to pop up. And I said to myself, *What's going on? What are the ancestors trying to tell us?*" She spoke their answer, telling us of a man walking his farm after a thunderstorm and rubbing the mud off the emerging tombs to read their words:

Like Osiris, they rise from the Earth in a green resurrection.
African skeletons shake the dust from their bones.
Skulls with rattling teeth recite litanies of ancient woes
tongues spouting where none existed before
speaking in funereal language
Griots rising from the graves
and recount stories of their journeys
hafiz tongues uncleaving
reciting surahs of the dawn.

(The drums woke up, started talking.) Afua spoke:

babalawos emerge from the storm
divining with their shells and stones
I see the drummers advancing—them a run, them a come,
playing the talking drums
the bata crumb
the djembe
the kete and the funde
sending messages across this land

(The drums stopped.)

They say, Give us strength! Give us strength!

(The drums trilled.)

And we say rise up! Rise up! Rise . . . up!
Fallen fighters, rise up, up, up, up!

Dr. Cooper left the grave. The drums shouted. Rev. Britton spoke to them, saying that in African culture, the drums talk, the drums call people together and they spread news. "The drummers are there, pounding out the rhythm of the people, calling us, giving us messages. We have drums that accompany us when we speak. Drums that mourn when we lament. We have drums," she said. "Charles would love this, to have the drums speaking when he is not here with us. He still speaks."

Judy Kavanaugh approached the grave to speak about her longtime colleague and friend. "Charles started working at the *Daily News* in 1989, a few years after he moved to Halifax from Ottawa. He stayed at the paper the next nineteen years, until it was shut down. I worked with him for most of that time," she began.

For two decades, they sat ten feet apart, night after night. She spoke about his column, and his editorials, and his work as an editor. "Writing and editing are two very different skills, and Charles was one of the few journalists who excelled in both. At a paper the size of the *Daily News*, we had about six copy editors working at computers around a big table every night. More than anything, it always reminded me of a large family of brothers and sisters doing homework together around the dining room table," she said.

Huh, I thought. I had remembered it as friends. But no. We were family.

"There was bickering. There was laughter. We all helped each other get the job done. There were serious conversations in all those years editing news stories, but there was always a fair bit of goofing around," she continued.

She named the newspaper's copy editors and other journalists who stood at the grave. We probably had enough of us there to put out another edition. She remembered when Charles was diagnosed with diabetes and how he handled it as he handled so many things: Quietly, he went to work. She noticed the bag of chips on his desk morph into a bag of radishes. "And he ate a lot of fish, much to the annoyance of those of us who shared a microwave with him," she said to laughter. "And he walked. A lot. And he kept it up and he got healthier. He probably added years to his life through those efforts, and I want to give him credit for that."

She spoke of his switch from a column to the unsigned editorials. "It was a promotion, but also a bit of a sacrifice on his part because he lost the celebrity of having a column with his name and photo on it. And it seemed that readers had lost the chance to read one of our best African Nova Scotian writers," she said. "But in fact they were reading his perspective every day. They just didn't know it."

She spoke of his gift for understanding all sides of an issue and then arguing clearly and persuasively in favour of the side he found to be true. And she spoke about the day the suits decided the paper was worth more dead than alive. "After the first shock, many of us—myself included—moved away to newspaper jobs in other provinces because there wasn't anything happening in Halifax. Before I left, I asked Charles what he was going to do. He said, 'I'll just retire.' He had continued to write fiction on the side and was looking forward to getting back to that full time."

They exchanged birthday wishes on social media, but little more. She regretted that now, she said, and learned that the friends you don't hear from may be the ones you most need to check in on.

A blue car pulled up. More drummers emerged. Judy left the grave.

Andre Fenton stepped up to the grave, the last speaker. A few words in, the microphone cut out. No one watching from afar could hear him, and those in attendance struggled to catch to his words. They fell only on the grave.[131]

He started by quoting Charles: "'I go, but I leave a warrior behind.'

"Folks have always told me about Charles. Charles Saunders was a family friend and was married to my aunt for many years. His boldness played a role in my career, and other Black writers who chose to be different," Andre said.

"For Black writers, we usually get put into boxes and are told what we should, and shouldn't, write about. There's an expectation to put our traumas on plates, to feed the hunger of those who could never walk a block in our shoes.

"But Charles aimed further than the blocks. He was a trailblazer who aimed to move mountains, found truth among the stars, translated it to page, and illuminated bookshelves, breaking free from the four walls by simply lifting the ceiling. Charles was ahead of his time, but lit a flame that will never die. He lit a flame that gives us hope, that sparks creativity, and gives us permission to raise the roofs of these expectations. I'm forever thankful.

"Charles Saunders showed us that Black writers are allowed to dream and tell stories that they don't want us to. I released my first fantasy novel little over a year ago, and in the acknowledgments of that novel I wrote that it's not every day we see an African Nova Scotian fantasy story. But it's not every day we get to celebrate the work, commitment, and boldness that Charles introduced to the genre of fantasy, and I wouldn't have been able to do this work if he hadn't made a path for Black writers to follow.

131 Andre Fenton's speaking notes, shared with the author.

"He goes, but he leaves warriors behind. Charles left a piece of himself in all of us, in our bookshelves, in our creativity, in our memories, in our minds and in our hearts. He taught us all that we are allowed to be brave enough to dream, explore the worlds in our imaginations, and not to blend into the spots where society says we're supposed to be. Because Charles gave us the strength to dream freely."

Andre left the grave. More drummers arrived.

A soloist approached the grave and sang "Great is Thy Faithfulness."

I cried. My wife Giselle squeezed my hand as I struggled to compose myself. My family had visited his grave after the stones had been installed in the spring. Our children, Roslyn and Xavier, had marvelled at how jacked Imaro was, and to see the final resting place of the man their daddy couldn't stop talking about. I had spent so much time exploring Charles's inner world that I had forgotten about the impact he'd made on the outer world, the love he had created and embedded in his books for us to find. I had invited Andre to speak because he's an amazing author whose work and stature reminded me of Charles. I didn't know they were kin until Andre spoke those words at his grave. I didn't know Rev. Britton had buried his wife, either, until she told me. And I only realized the Imaro stone captured the moment told in the story "The Afua" as Dr. Afua Cooper spoke her poem.

Standing with the remnant band of brothers and sisters who had worked with Charles on the Halifax *Daily News*, I felt the powerful presence of our friend. I nodded to an older woman I had met before the service. She had been sent by the one who sent me. The author of the email that began my quest was watching the livestream from her distant home, and had asked her dear friend to represent her bodily at the funeral. We had embraced and shed tears for the man who brought us all together. I thought of the old woman/young woman illusion, where you stare at an unmoving image and your mind switches it from a portrait of a person of great age, to a person of youth. I had come to see Charles as an otherworldly author made of paper and ink. But standing at his grave, the image switched, and I saw the man I knew in flesh and blood. The gentle man I came to admire on those quiet, unforgettable nights sitting around the copy desk like family. Charles made Africville my home. He made Africa my home. He will make it your home, too. The words carved into the Imaro stone reveal the ultimate legacy of the sons with no fathers. "I go, but I leave a warrior behind—*Imaro*. Created by Charles R. Saunders, Father of Sword and Soul. Rest in Power."

Rev. Britton returned to the grave for a last tribute to the "powerhouse" writer. "I couldn't help but exclaim, what a tremendous legacy. Not everyone leaves behind such indelible footprints that mark their journey on this earth, that say, 'I was here,'" she said, pointing to the ground. She surprised the grievers with her next remark. It wasn't from scripture but from *Rent*: How do you measure a year in a life?

Rev. Britton spoke about the Creator's love, and how no one can separate us from the Creator. "Some of you may be concerned that Charles passed from this life too soon. He was seventy-three. We generally think of that as a pretty full life. The song from *Rent* says that a year consists of 525,600 minutes. But in asking the question how do you measure, it reminds us that we should not focus on counting our years, but on making our years count. Charles Saunders made his years count. He touched lives he never knew. He spoke into our existence as human beings on how we can better do this thing called life. We've heard Charles described as a recluse in recent years. From our various perches, it may appear that Charles's reclusiveness robbed him of some of the quality of life he should have been able to enjoy," she said, sharing another laugh with the wind. "But we really do not know. Because human beings all march to the sound of a different drum, Charles may have been in perfect step with his beat."

She paused, then spoke again. "How do you measure a life? Remember the love."

She spoke about Charles's first burial, alone, a year ago. But this morning, with his friends and family here and afar, she gathered brown, fragrant dust in her hand and knelt to seal the tomb. I felt a burden lifted, a heart strengthened. "Earth to earth, ashes to ashes, dust to dust," she said. "He's gone, but he's left a warrior behind."

ACKNOWLEDGEMENTS

I heard Charles's voice today, for the second time since he died. "When I started writing, it was for a specific purpose, which was to counteract the distorted picture of Africa that has existed in most fantasy literature," he said. "I went to primary sources, mythology collections, African history books, and from those sources I constructed an alternate Africa." He was talking to CBC Radio on August 11, 1980.[132] They spoke to him as he was writing "an enormous novel," as the host said in the introduction to the third interview they'd aired that summer about the Ottawa Fantasists. Charles explained why he chose to work in fantasy. "I think it and science fiction are the only forms of literature remaining that really give free rein to the imagination." The other recording I've found of his voice was posted to the "Black Introvert's" YouTube channel and was first recorded on August 10, 2008. Exactly twenty-eight years passed between the interviews, but Charles's mission had not changed.

I wrote this book as an illuminated manuscript to the collected works of Charles R. Saunders. You have completed your first quest by reading it. Now, I send you on your second, greater quest: to read the books themselves. As I write this in 2025, that may be the tougher task. It took me more than a year, and a considerable amount of money, to assemble my own CRS collection. I've read

132 John Bell's personal recording, lent to the author.

all of his books twice, and some many more times than that. Find his books and buy them. Your efforts will be rewarded. There is good news, too. We all owe Charles's estate a debt of gratitude. For years, they have been working to bring Charles's books back into print. And in February 2025, they celebrated a milestone: The U.K. publisher Gollancz printed a beautiful new edition of *Imaro.* And guess what? They want to publish the entire saga. You know what has happened before, and you know one of the key reasons why: Not enough people bought the books to sustain a full run. You can change that today. Make Imaro the smash hit he was always meant to be. Put your money where your heart is and show publishers we want sword and soul books—we want Imaro and Dossouye and Damballa and Abengoni. We want all of the books Charles inspired, too. And we'll pay for them.

Another way you can support Charles's legacy is through the Writers' Federation of Nova Scotia. You read how Taaq Kirksey travelled all the way to Charles's front door to deliver him a big cheque for the movie project, which is still inching forward. Well, Charles cashed the cheque, but he didn't spend it. When his estate received those funds after his death, they worked with the team that marked Charles's grave to mark his name permanently on the literary scene of his home province. With the WFNS, we used that money to found the Charles R. Saunders Prize for Emerging Writers. It gives the winner a cash prize and a mentorship to help them bring their own writing dreams to life—just like Charles did with so many people in his days on earth. If you can put some of your own money next to Charles's last gift, we can strengthen and grow the prize. We've already awarded two winners: Theo Feehan-Peters and Nailah Tataa. If you are an emerging writer lucky enough to live in Nova Scotia, you can put your name in contention for the next prize. You can do all of that at Writers.ns.ca.

Working with Charles in life, and after life, has changed my life. He lived all my literary dreams and nightmares, and now the dreams don't seem so far-fetched, and the nightmares aren't as scary. In the end, Charles wrote for the love of writing and for the love of readers. There is no higher calling for us writers, and no greater reward for our readers.

Charles once said, "Bare is the back without a brother behind it," and that has been true for me, too. I did not write this book alone; many sisters and brothers had my back at critical moments. Thank you, Sheree R. Thomas, for your wonderful opening essay on our mutual friend. I was delighted you lead with Dossouye; some of us think that in time, she will prove to be the mightiest warrior of them all. Taaq Kirksey felt like a literary brother to me, as both of us processed the loss of Charles and went about our own ways to establish the lasting legacy of CRS. Taaq first opened my eyes to the depth and importance of Charles's work and answered my endless questions. Milton Davis and Troy Wiggins gave me their first-person accounts of how Charles changes lives. Thank you both. You saw some of the work Paul Bacon did for Charles in these pages. Paul helped me understand Charles's place in the fantasy world and pointed me toward many helpful books to better see what he was doing. Paul also read this manuscript and couldn't help himself from editing it into better shape. It felt like the three of us were together again for a night on the news rim. Charles's friends Morris Fried, Joe Williams, Joseph Bernard Ellois, Charles de Lint, David C. Smith and Janet LeRoy gave me the gift of Charles's letters and remembered words, which in turn allowed you to know the human heart behind these great works of literature.

My agent, Ron Eckel, was not my agent when I sent a rather desperate email to CookeMcDermid. He wrote back to me, and that led to a phone conversation, which led to many other conversations.

I first told the story to him, which helped greatly when it came time to put it on the page. He has been a champion for Charles and played a crucial role in bringing this book to life. He also connected me to Joe Lee, who became my editor at McClelland & Stewart. You read in this book that Charles "had the ability to see through what I was trying to do and give me advice on how to rework it to better serve my story, which is something that great editors do." That's exactly what Joe did, with patience and passion, over several years. It took me so long to get it right that Joe became a father in between drafts! Congratulations, Joe, and thank you for always knowing what I meant to write, and helping me figure out how to write it. By the end, the entire team at McClelland & Stewart came to love Charles—and Imaro, and Dossouye—and did everything they could to make my book a success. Thank you!

I can't imagine how I would have written this book without my wife, Giselle. She has been with me for every book, and this one was no different. In fact, she was there before this was a book, when I was just stumbling around in a fog looking for any good step forward. We actually met at one of the post–*Daily News* wakes (Paul Bacon introduced us!), and so she understood many parts of this book. She helped with the fundraiser, she went to the funeral, and she's been my number one fan. But not in an Annie Wilkes way. My children were seven and four when I started writing this book, and twelve and nine when I finished. The best way to see a superhero is through a child's eyes, and Xavier and Roslyn helped me understand what Imaro first meant to Charles when he himself was a child in need of strength. I bounced many ideas off them, and was constantly surprised by their responses. Thanks, kids!

And finally, thank you Charles R. Saunders, for your extraordinary dedication to your craft, and for your heroic perseverance in getting it all down on the page, word by word, and for getting it published, again and again, so we could explore your worlds.

Throughout the writing of this book, I felt your presence encouraging me and guiding me. I don't know what you found on the other side, but I suspect it was fantastical beyond our imaginations. And I hope one day, we meet on the far shore of the river and I can finally ask you all those questions. And give you a big hug.

Jon Tattrie, Halifax, Nova Scotia, May 5, 2025